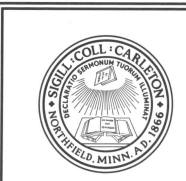

"The World Must Be Peopled"

Shakespeare's Comedies of Forgiveness

Michael D. Friedman

Madison • Teaneck
Fairleigh Dickinson University Press
London: Associated University Presses

Associated University Presses
440 Forsgate Drive
Cranbury, NJ 08512

Associated University Presses
16 Barter Street
London WC1A 2AH, England

Associated University Presses
P.O. Box 338, Port Credit
Mississauga, Ontario
Canada L5G 4L8

The paper used in this publication meets the requirements of the American National Standard for Permanence of Paper for Printed Library Materials Z39.48-1984.

Library of Congress Cataloging-in-Publication Data

Friedman, Michael D., 1960–
    The world must be peopled : Shakespeare's comedies of forgiveness / Michael D. Friedman.
        p. cm.
    Includes bibliographical references and index.
    ISBN 0-8386-3941-0 (alk. paper)
    1. Shakespeare, William, 1564–1616—Comedies.   2. Forgiveness in literature.   3. Comedy.   I. Title.
PR2981 .F66   2002
822.3'3—dc21   2001054835

PRINTED IN THE UNITED STATES OF AMERICA

For Cheryl,
who taught me everything I know
about peopling the world

Contents

Illustrations

Acknowledgments

WRITING A BOOK ABOUT PERFORMANCE CAN BE AS COLLABORATIVE as the process of performance itself. This study could not have come into being without the assistance, cooperation, and support of far more people than I can mention by name in this short space. However, the contributions of certain individuals and institutions have been so crucial to this venture that I must take the time to thank them specifically.

First, I express my appreciation to the University of Scranton, which supported this project financially with internal research grants, a sabbatical leave, and annual release time. I also owe a great deal to my colleagues in the English Department, particularly Jones DeRitter and Stephen Whittaker, who frequently allowed me to engage them in debates about theoretical issues or the meanings of specific passages. Joan Robbins deserves a huge amount of credit for agreeing to collaborate with me on productions of *Two Gentlemen* and *Measure for Measure*. I could not possibly have come to the insights I eventually achieved without the endless hours we spent struggling to explain these plays to each other and exploring the ways in which they might be staged. And for their bibliographical help, I am indebted to a long line of student research assistants, most of whom I worked with through the University of Scranton's Faculty/Student Research Program: Ben Nicholson, Christina Elvidge, Terry Bayne, Renée L'Eplattenier, Michael Bowie, Rebecca Steinberger, Donnie Minnick, Tricia Reddington, Joanne Festa, Cecelia Mecca, and Elizabeth Aldridge.

Next, I wish to thank my colleagues at other institutions who contributed in various ways to the composition of this book. I am especially grateful to my own Shakespeare professors: Marvin Morillo at Tulane University, who first aroused my passion for the plays; Brian Gibbons, then at the University of York, who gave me my first chance to direct Shakespeare, as well as my initial instruction in examining the plays through production; and most of all, Bill Carroll and Jim Siemon at Boston Univer-

11

sity, who directed my dissertation on *Much Ado* in performance with incredible rigor, patience, and generosity. Several other people read sections of this work at various stages and offered emotional support along with valuable suggestions for revision, including Alan Dessen, Heather Dubrow, Daryl Palmer, and Megan Lloyd. Herb Coursen and Debbie Barrett-Graves also deserve special thanks for helping me to locate materials that I could never have found on my own.

I also learned a great deal as a result of the efforts of the casts and crews of the productions of the comedies of forgiveness in which I have participated: *Two Gentlemen* at both the University of York and the University of Scranton, *Much Ado* at Boston University, and *Measure for Measure* at the University of Scranton. I also extend my gratitude to the students who took my course on *All's Well* in performance at St. John's University, particularly Jen Maggs, who entirely changed my way of thinking about the play by stuffing her winter coat up under her shirt and asking me, "Hey Dr. Friedman, how pregnant *is* Helena anyway?"

Portions of chapters 3 and 4 have appeared previously in *Comparative Drama*, *Studies in Philology*, and *Studies in English Literature* and are reprinted here in revised form with the permission of those journals. Passages derived from promptbooks in special collections are quoted by permission of the Folger Shakespeare Library and the Shakespeare Centre Library, Stratford-upon-Avon.

Finally, I owe the biggest thanks to Cheryl, Rachael, and Casey, who sacrificed more than anyone else to bring this project to fruition.

"The World Must Be Peopled"

Chapter 1
Performance Criticism and the Model Narrative

> The need for theatrically conscious reading is widely acknowledged, but what exactly is this and by what means can it be achieved? Live performance before a live audience during a consecutive period of time is not easily re-created in the mind of a reader or critic, and yet this is the very element in which Shakespeare's plays were intended to exist and to reveal their distinctive natures. In other circumstances, their words are bound to be misunderstood and their dialogue, structure, spectacle, characters, argument or theme distorted. None of these features should be considered except as part of a complicated, uncertain, idiosyncratic, and ever-changing theatre performance.
>
> (Brown 1996, vii)

THE PASSAGE ABOVE ASKS ONE OF THE CENTRAL QUESTIONS WITH which this book will engage: what exactly is performance criticism (or "theatrically conscious reading") and how might one practice it? John Russell Brown posits that, since Shakespeare conceived of his dramas as "Live performance[s] before a live audience," performance criticism is scholarship that attempts to re-create the experience of such an event in the reader's mind. Brown admits, however, that this goal is not easily accomplished. For one thing, the mediums of theatrical performance and performance criticism are so different that a printed analysis of a performance can present, at best, a pale shadow of the theatrical spectacle. In addition, as Laurie Osborne points out, a written account "can invoke the absent performance only by subjecting it to a narrative structure necessarily distanced from its material occurrence" (1996b, 124). In other words, while many of the myriad elements of a stage production, like lights, costumes, set design, and stage business, are experienced by spectators simultaneously, performance criticism necessarily

15

renders a deformed vision of these elements by narrating their employment in a sequential fashion. Despite these difficulties, Brown asserts that any critical approach to performance that does not endeavor to replicate the spectator's theatrical experience will unavoidably distort the significance of all aspects of Shakespeare's plays.

Brown's conception of performance criticism represents what I will call the *diachronic* approach, which limits itself to discussing a single production as it occurs "during a consecutive period of time." Ideally, by such a method, the critic examines all facets of a production as part of a complex interaction between various theatrical elements. The critic does not consider any aspect of the performance in isolation, for to do so would be to misrepresent that element's function within the entire theatrical event. Since characters and their relationships change and develop over the course of a play, a particular stage moment, described in such a way that it is removed from the context of preceding and subsequent scenes, may appear to signify something completely different to a reader of this description than it does to an audience member who views this sequence in light of the whole performance. Like a snapshot that appears to grant a dancer the ability to remain suspended in midair, an account of a performance that detaches single elements from their context gives them a prominence and a static quality absent from the theatrical presentation of those elements. Therefore, the critic who employs the diachronic approach locates every facet of the staging of a play within the framework of the same specific production, attempting to capture in written form, as fully and as accurately as possible, the theatrical impact of that particular performance.

An alternative attitude toward the practice of performance criticism, which I will label the *synchronic* approach, does not share with the diachronic method the goal of re-creating in the mind of a reader an audience's experience of a specific production of a play. Instead, the synchronic approach aims to produce critical insights through a three-part process: exploring the range of potential performance choices circumscribed by the printed text, describing the varying effects of such choices, and examining the cultural and historical reasons that one effect rather than another might be considered desirable. In contrast to the holistic nature of the diachronic method, the synchronic approach welcomes the isolation of specific elements from the rest of a production and their comparison to similar aspects of performances from different locations and historical periods. To express this distinction another way: if one imagines the performance of a play as an event that occurs along a segment of a time line from the beginning of act 1 to the end of act 5, the diachronic approach is concerned with the horizontal progression along that single line from start to finish. The synchronic approach, however, envisions numerous parallel segments, all representing individual productions, and it focuses on the imaginary vertical line that might be drawn between the corresponding points along the horizontal lines. For example, a critic using a synchronic approach might identify a crucial passage in a play, such as Beatrice's notorious command "Kill Claudio" in *Much Ado about Nothing* (4.1.288), and document the various ways in which the scene containing this passage has been played in differing eras and locales.[1] Such a process provides an essentially analytical, rather than quasi-theatrical, experience for the reader.

In counterbalance to the risk of distorting isolated moments out of context, the synchronic approach provides a historical perspective absent from the diachronic approach. Since no theatrical element in a Shakespearean performance is developed or perceived in a vacuum, it must be acknowledged that all performance choices are conditioned by the decisions made in previous productions, and the impact of such choices is influenced by earlier versions of the play that spectators may or may not have seen. Thus, the diachronic approach suffers its own potential for distortion by isolating particular productions from the context of the play's theatrical history. Given that both methods of performance criticism pursue distinct goals and exhibit complementary strengths and weaknesses, it may be best to avoid declaring one approach superior to the other in an absolute sense. Instead, it seems wise to assert that one method may produce more insightful results depending upon the material that the critic wishes to study. The diachronic approach, because of its dependence on copious detail about a particular production, appears best suited to the examination of modern productions, especially those that the critic has seen personally (more than once, if possible), so that the critic's own assessment of the theatrical experience may be incorporated into the study. The critic may also interview other audience members, actors, designers, and the director to gather further information, and if the critic is fortunate enough to be associated with the production in some capacity, perhaps in the role of dramaturg, he or she may be allowed to observe design meetings and rehearsals and participate in the decision-making process.[2] If the critic can maintain objectivity about the production despite such close involvement with it, the resulting analysis may feature telling observations about the resemblance between the experience of the play envisioned by the theatrical personnel and that which is actually delivered by the stage embodiment.

On the other hand, the diachronic approach becomes more challenging when applied to a production from the distant past. If the critic could not have attended the performance and does not have direct access to anyone who did, he or she must rely on existing sources of information: eyewitness accounts, reviews, illustrations, promptbooks, or performance editions. The amount of available data and its breadth of coverage will vary from production to production, but in general, the older the production, the less likely it is that the critic will be able to re-create a spectator's theatrical experience from these sources. Due to the nature of the evidence, certain details, like the completeness of the playscript or the quality of the actors' individual performances, tend to be more easily recoverable, while other aspects of the production that affect its reception, such as lighting and scenery, are frequently overlooked. Reviews in particular tend to be selective rather than exhaustive, and they are therefore prone to touch upon the same high points for every production of the same play: How did Silvia respond to Valentine's offer to turn her over to Proteus at the end of *The Two Gentlemen of Verona*? How did Bertram react to Helena's return from the dead at the close of *All's Well that Ends Well*? Since these productions are usually available to the critic only through a sparse collection of disjointed details, the synchronic approach, which operates by assembling descriptions of isolated sequences from various performances, seems better suited to the examination of historical productions.

Because I am interested in selected aspects of the complete production histories of the plays under discussion in this book, I will investigate them using the synchronic approach moderated by a cognizance of the danger of misrepresenting the import of any particular facet of a production detached from its context. At this point, then, I would like to return to and elaborate upon the tripartite process of the synchronic approach. The first part, the exploration of the range of potential performance choices, starts with the critic's recognition of some problematic aspect of the text (or texts) under scrutiny. The present study began with the observation that the character Claudio in *Much Ado* has long been considered an impediment to a successful production of the play, and that stage performances have therefore employed various strategies, at identical points in the comedy, in order to remedy the perceived problem. By focusing on the particular theatrical techniques utilized at these points, I have developed a sense of the spectrum of choices offered by the text, as well as an awareness of the many ways in which productions have manipulated the text in order to achieve their objectives. Furthermore, as Anne Barton remarks, the problem of Claudio is analogous to the complications generated by three other male figures in Shakespearean comedy, whom I call the Forgiven Comic Heroes:

> Like Proteus in *The Two Gentlemen of Verona*, Angelo in *Measure for Measure*, and Bertram in *All's Well that Ends Well*, Claudio is one of Shakespeare's cads: a young man who behaves abominably to a loving and generous woman, causes her great suffering, and then, after a perfunctory repentance, is dismissed with her into a happiness he scarcely seems to deserve. (1993, 11)[3]

My awareness of the similarities between these characters and the difficulties associated with their unmerited forgiveness has enabled me to detect comparable theatrical strategies in the stage performances of all four plays. Thus, in this example of the synchronic approach, the vertical lines of analysis drawn between corresponding moments in the plot intersect with parallel horizontal lines representing productions of more than one play.

The second phase of the synchronic approach, the description of the varying effects of performance choices, involves a great deal more speculation than the process of identifying what those choices were in the first place. With many historical performances, there is no surviving evidence of audience reaction to a particular facet of a production. In such cases, I will hypothesize about the intentions of theatrical personnel and contemporary spectators' most likely responses to their efforts, but I concede that my assertions are colored by my own late twentieth-century point of view and must be judged accordingly. In other instances, the contemporary reaction of one or more viewers does survive, and these comments provide confirmation that such a response was experienced by at least one viewer, possibly more. If no trace of an alternative reaction exists, I will tentatively consider the surviving response to be representative. In rarer cases, reviews and eyewitness accounts clash in their assessment of the effect of a specific performance choice. Such contradictions often lead to the most interesting insights because they locate sites in a production where competing aesthetic or ideological positions come into conflict. When such contradictory descriptions appear, the critic should not attempt to resolve the discrepancy in pursuit of a monolithic audience response, but should instead try to account for the disparity with reference to the opposing value systems that shape the reactions of various spectators.

Ideology also plays a prominent role in the final step of the synchronic approach, the examination of the cultural and historical reasons that stage productions seek particular effects at particular times and places. Historical trends in the theatrical treatment of a play's problem areas may reveal to the critic the ways in which performance choices are often based on ideological assumptions about "natural" behavior or "normal" relationships between classes of people rather than the evidence of the text itself.[4] Throughout the stage histories of the four plays taken up in this book, the portrayals of Claudio and his counterparts have been determined to a significant degree by certain premises about how young men "naturally" behave toward their elders, their male friends, and the women whom they supposedly love. When the play itself runs contrary to these assumptions, theater practitioners have frequently elected to alter the text or use other elements of staging to counteract the effect that the text, in its original state, seems bound to produce. Repeated examples of substantial theatrical intervention at the same place in the text signals the presumed existence of ideological discord between the play and those viewers for whom it is being prepared for consumption. By comparing the effects of these interventions with probable responses to the unaltered text, the critic may discover the cultural and historical motives operating behind such changes.

Through an emphasis on both the theatrical histories of these plays and the ideological aspects of their reproduction on the stage, I hope to combine two points of view that, according to James C. Bulman, tend to separate performance critics into discrete camps:

> Some claim to be disinterestedly historical in their approach; others are avowedly ideological. Historicists attempt to recreate authentic

contexts for performances of a given play and thereby to gauge what
the play has signified for its audiences at different times and in different cultures: in other words, they use performance history to discover what, and how, meanings are produced. Ideological critics, on
the other hand, tend to delineate interpretive options independent
of performance history: their "reading" of performance is thus less
empirical and more politically invested than that of historicists.
(1996, 4)

Although, as Bulman notes, these attitudes toward performance
rarely overlap, they are not mutually exclusive; nothing prevents historicists who have discovered "what, and how, meanings are produced" from also asking *why*. In addition, critics
utilizing the synchronic approach may easily propose "less
empirical and more politically invested" stagings alongside the
performance choices they have derived from historical productions.[5] After beginning with a set of stage enactments and working toward the ideological motives behind them, synchronic
critics may also reverse this process by consciously affirming a
particular ideology, then proposing alternatives to traditional
performance choices that may serve to convey such a stance in
the theater. This complementary method presumes that, since
all decisions about how a scene from a Shakespearean play
"should" be enacted are based on ideological assumptions anyway, it is more honest and clear-sighted to recognize and to
examine one's assumptions than to imagine that one can derive
a staging from the printed text without ideological mediation.

Therefore, I must acknowledge that the ideology of feminism
serves as a mediating device between the texts of the plays in
this study and my conception of their performance. I understand feminism as the belief that women deserve rights and
opportunities equal to those of men, and thus a feminist production of a Shakespeare play would be one that calls for changes
in the patriarchal structure of society that might allow for the
attainment of such equality. This call for change may take either
a positive or a negative form. In other words, a feminist production may strive to encourage the reevaluation of women's place
in the social order through the presentation of strong female
characters who enlist audience sympathy for their resistance to
the limitations imposed upon them by patriarchy. Or, a feminist
production may attempt to portray these restrictions and their
deleterious effects upon women as clearly and as forcefully as
possible in order to provoke spectators to deplore their linger-

ing presence in our own time. In most cases, feminist productions employ some combination of these two approaches, but in this study, I prefer the second technique because of my primary focus on the Forgiven Comic Heroes and the ways in which their appalling treatment of the women who love them goes largely unpunished. Feminist criticism of Shakespeare displays a particular concern with the formation of gender roles, both male and female, and their repercussions for the behavior of men and women in the arenas of courtship, marriage, procreation, and childrearing. Although my emphasis rests primarily on four male figures in the plays under discussion, my impression of how these plays might be staged is largely determined by my sense of how certain performance choices will affect a production's orientation toward the status of women.

My imagined stagings of various key sequences in the plays will also be shaped by generic considerations. Much of the modern critical displeasure with *Two Gentlemen*, *Much Ado*, *All's Well*, and *Measure for Measure* arises from a tendency to assume that the four plays are romantic comedies that simply fail to live up to the expectations of their comedic subgenre. For example, Robert Y. Turner writes of *All's Well* that

> there is a discrepancy between what we feel and what we should feel. We know we should sympathize with the hero and heroine of a romantic comedy or at least rejoice at their reunion in Act Five. Yet our moral sensibility flinches at the aggressive Helena who traps the hero into marriage and at the same time is repelled by Bertram who snobbishly rejects Helena and lies ruthlessly in the trial scene. Consequently, *All's Well* is a failure in the opinion of most scholars who have discussed the play. (1960, 502)

Such an assessment, I would argue, misjudges the plays by applying to them generic standards that Shakespeare is not trying to meet. Instead of assuming that Shakespeare stumbled four times in precisely the same fashion, it may be time to hypothesize that the conclusions of these plays are designed, not to elicit joy at the reunions of heroes and heroines, but to draw attention to the contrived nature of the pardons that bring about these matches. Therefore, I propose that the four plays in question may be more fruitfully assessed with reference to a different comic subgenre I will call *the comedy of forgiveness*.

Critics now commonly treat Shakespeare's late comedies under the separate heading of romances because they share certain elements of plot, theme, and characterization. Similarly, the comedies of forgiveness merit their own designation because they conform more or less to the same *model narrative*, a single story involving various conventional literary figures, whom Shakespeare fleshes out and distinguishes, without obliterating the similarities between them (see Figure 1). I do not mean to argue here the reductive claim that *Two Gentlemen*, *Much Ado*, *All's Well*, and *Measure for Measure* are four versions of the same play. Rather, I contend that these plays all utilize the same underlying structure involving identical character types, but that Shakespeare splits, combines, and redistributes the features of these types among various characters, creating dramatic works that, despite their similarities, achieve vastly different effects. As would be the case for any subgenre, no play adheres to the model narrative absolutely, but at least three of the plays exhibit any individual aspect of the story, and the fourth usually suggests it in some fashion. Moreover, each of the four plays deviates from the model to a differing degree, and the deviations themselves are distinct in each case, as if each play represents a singular variation upon the same theme.

The model narrative proceeds as follows: the young Comic Hero begins the play in the companionship of another male character, the Friend, who exhibits traits associated with the *miles gloriosus*, the swaggering braggart soldier of Roman comedy, coupled with a distinctly antiromantic and antimatrimonial attitude toward females. These two comrades inhabit a world epitomized by male friendship until the Comic Hero, by falling in love, getting engaged, and/or marrying, forms an alliance with a particular type of woman, the Griselda. This ingenue, like Chaucer's patient heroine, is a virtuous, obedient, and reticent woman whose devotion to her role as the mate of the Comic Hero knows no bounds. However, the relationship between the

	Forgiven Comic Hero	Vice	Friend	Authority	Griselda	Shrew
Two Gentlemen	Proteus		Valentine	Duke of Milan	Julia	Silvia
Much Ado	Claudio	Don John	Benedick	Don Pedro / Leonato	Hero	Beatrice
All's Well	Bertram	Parolles		King of France	Helena	Diana
Measure	Angelo / Claudio	Lucio		Duke of Vienna	Mariana	Isabella

Figure 1—Table identifying the model narrative roles of characters in all four comedies of forgiveness.

Comic Hero and the Griselda is threatened by the Vice figure, derived from the morality play tradition, who draws the Comic Hero away from the Griselda through temptation or slander. Shamefully abandoned, the Griselda "dies," and the Comic Hero typically fixes his affections upon another woman, the Shrew, whose primary distinguishing characteristic is that she speaks freely in a way that both arouses and antagonizes men.[6] The most familiar embodiment of the difference between these two female figures occurs in *The Taming of the Shrew*, where Shakespeare plays the scolding Katherine off against her modest sister Bianca, but a similar contrast may be drawn between Silvia and Julia, Beatrice and Hero, Diana and Helena, and Isabella and Mariana.

The Comic Hero's suit to the Shrew is unsuccessful, however, and society, represented by the Authority figure, a matchmaking ruler with paternalistic ties to the Griselda, endeavors to reunite the juvenile lead with his former partner. In order for this reunion to take place, the Vice figure must first be exposed and scapegoated for the crimes of the Comic Hero so that the young man may be accepted back into the social fold, later to produce legitimate heirs, who may begin the narrative once again. The term "scapegoated" is appropriate here because, although the Vice figure may bear some guilt for influencing the juvenile lead, Shakespeare clearly shows that the contemptible deeds of the Comic Hero go well beyond what can be imputed to the Vice figure alone, yet the members of society appear perfectly content to heap *all* of the blame upon the Vice figure and to exonerate the Comic Hero. Faced with the revelation of his wrongdoing, the Comic Hero generally expresses some amount of contrition, but his speeches of repentance are so hollow and brief that they seldom satisfy readers and audiences. However, they do seem to appease both the Griselda, who miraculously returns from the dead and receives the Comic Hero with open arms, and the Authority figure, to whom the Comic Hero allies himself through marriage to the Griselda. The Friend, despite his earlier antimatrimonial position, also marries at the end of the play, joining the Comic Hero and the Authority figure in a reconstituted version of the world of male camaraderie in which the play began.[7]

Much of the critical displeasure with the four plays noted above stems from the disparity between the Comic Hero's degree of culpability in his bad treatment of the Griselda (as well as the Shrew) and the degree of punishment he receives for those acts.[8] On the page, it appears as if the Comic Hero offends mightily, apologizes weakly, and is forgiven too quickly and generously for his sins. Therefore, it is not surprising to discover that, historically, stage productions have attempted to narrow the gap between what the Comic Hero deserves and what he gets by using elements of performance either to reduce the Comic Hero's blameworthiness or to increase the sincerity of his repentance and the severity of his punishment. Most directors seem to agree with Robert Grams Hunter that viewers cannot simply observe the Comic Hero's forgiveness within the play; they must also be persuaded to exonerate him in their own hearts:

> An on-stage happy ending in these plays is dangerously easy to attain. The forgiveness of the offenders by the offended is all that is needed. But if we in the audience are to participate in that felicity, we must also participate vicariously in the means to it. We must pardon the offenders. If we cannot, the play does not, for us, end happily, and we are denied the comic experience. (1965, 102–3)

For Hunter, "the comic experience" depends upon the audience's vicarious participation in the play's joyful conclusion uncomplicated by any residual doubts about the fitness of the Forgiven Comic Hero to share in that felicity. Because each of the four comedies of forgiveness departs from the model narrative in a unique way, the strategies utilized by theatrical personnel to attempt to achieve this happy ending vary from play to play, but overall, they share with the plays' critical histories an attempt to reshape the work to make it conform more closely to the conventions of romantic comedy.

In Shakespeare, the model narrative for romantic comedy differs from that of the comedy of forgiveness in several ways.[9] A romantic comedy also features both a juvenile lead and an ingenue, but in contrast to the corresponding characters in a comedy of forgiveness, the young boy and girl exhibit a mutual erotic desire and an intention to marry before the sexual culmination of that desire. Their union, however, is blocked by the Senex, a parental figure who opposes the marriage on the basis of class hierarchies or other social factors that have no bearing on the erotic attraction between the young boy and girl. The action of the play then largely concerns the successful efforts of the boy and girl to circumvent the Senex and achieve their ultimate desire in marriage. However, while both romantic comedies and comedies of forgiveness end in promised weddings, the routes they take to that destination diverge considerably. In a comedy of forgiveness, although the Griselda's affection for her mate is seldom in doubt, the Forgiven Comic Hero either wavers in his affection, like Proteus and Claudio, or exhibits no erotic desire for his wife at all, as do Bertram and Angelo. Rather, his passions are commonly directed at the Shrew, whom he does not wish to marry, but merely to use for sexual purposes. Furthermore, the parental Authority figure, instead of opposing the marriage, often actively promotes the match, sometimes to the point of forcing it on the Comic Hero for his own good. At the end of a romantic comedy, the younger generation triumphs over the elder; at the conclusion to a comedy of forgiveness, the elder generation triumphs over the Comic Hero, whose desires are subordinated to the wishes of the larger social order.

Considering the four plays chronologically, Shakespeare moves further and further away from the model narrative of romantic comedy in his presentation of the relationship between the Comic Hero and the Griselda. *The Two Gentlemen of Verona* does feature the textbook romantic comedy plotline of Valentine's love for Silvia opposed by her father, the Duke of Milan, and it appears as if, at some point in the composition process, Shakespeare contemplated putting Proteus and Julia in the same dramatic situation. As Arden editor Clifford Leech notes (1969, xviii–xix), the text refers inconsistently to the existence of Julia's father, who "stays" for his daughter at 1.2.131. Later in act 1, Proteus laments, "O that our fathers would applaud our loves / To seal our happiness with their consents!" (1.3.48–49). This statement implies that Julia's father (and Proteus's) will play the role of the Senex, but by the next act, Julia's father seems to have vanished, for when she elects to leave Verona to seek Proteus, she leaves her goods, lands, and reputation to her maid Lucetta (2.7.86–87). The parental obstruction Proteus fears does not materialize, and Julia's father is never mentioned again. In *Much Ado*, Shakespeare endows Claudio with an unmistakable romantic desire for Hero, but in the church scene (4.1), convinced of Hero's disloyalty, Claudio exhibits a violent disgust at female sexuality foreign to the typical hero of romantic comedy. And Hero, while she certainly endures a great deal for the sake of her marriage to Claudio, is nevertheless notoriously silent on the subject of her feelings for her future husband, and the possibility remains that she accepts

Claudio to obey her father, who eagerly promotes the match, rather than to fulfill her own erotic affection.

Bertram of *All's Well* departs even further from the stereotype of the hero of romantic comedy in that he displays open antipathy toward the woman he eventually marries. Chosen by Helena to be her husband, Bertram replies to the King of France, who imposes the match upon him, "I cannot love her nor will strive to do't" (2.3.145). Nevertheless, the King pressures Bertram into taking Helena's hand, but having wed her, he deserts her for the Italian wars. Later in the play, thinking that Helena is dead, Bertram claims to have come to love her (5.3.52–55), but this unconvincing declaration occurs within an apology to the King filled with dubious assertions designed to excuse Bertram's proud behavior.[10] Finally, when Helena reappears not only alive but pregnant with Bertram's child, he agrees to "love her dearly, ever, ever dearly," but only *if* she can prove that the child is his (5.3.310). The fourth play, *Measure for Measure*, strays most distantly from the model narrative of romantic comedy in that Angelo never expresses any strong feelings about Mariana whatsoever; for him, their union is a purely financial arrangement, and when her dowry disappears, so does his willingness to marry her. After their betrothal *de futuro* is converted into an espousal *de praesenti* through the bed trick,[11] Angelo is forced by the Duke of Vienna to follow through on his duty to wed Mariana in a religious ceremony, but unlike Bertram, Angelo withholds any offer to return his wife's affections and begs instead for an immediate sentence of death. The "quickening" (5.1.493) that the Duke perceives in Angelo's eye when Isabella's brother Claudio is revealed could conceivably indicate a revival of Angelo's spirits that he owes to Mariana, but this interpretation of Angelo's emotional state is by no means certain. When the Duke orders his deputy, "Look that you love your wife, her worth, worth yours" (5.1.495), we receive no spoken confirmation that he ever will.

Shakespeare's significant departures from the conventions of romantic comedy in the comedies of forgiveness imply that, in those four works, the playwright is not primarily concerned with an idealized true love whose course merely does not run smooth; rather, he seeks to explore a common and imperfect love whose course is fraught with detours, roadblocks, and potential dead ends represented by male tendencies toward fickleness, suspicion, lust, and sexual irresponsibility. In the face of these imperfections, the young heroine of the comedy of forgiveness, if she wishes to gain a husband, must pardon the sins of her lover in a way that her counterpart in romantic comedy is seldom forced to do. Moreover, the Authority figure of the comedy of forgiveness, if he wishes to preserve the institution of marriage, must impose wedlock rather than oppose it, for without his intervention, the Comic Hero may simply pursue sexual conquests outside the bonds of matrimony. Thus, the model narrative of the comedy of forgiveness illustrates both the unruliness of male sexual desire and the lengths to which individuals and society feel that they must go to channel this dangerous appetite toward socially approved objectives, such as marriage and legitimate procreation, in order to perpetuate the male-dominated status quo.

Examined in order of composition, the four comedies of forgiveness focus on progressively later stages of this channeling process and the specific aspects of male sexual desire that threaten to disrupt accepted patterns of monogamy, matrimony, reproduction, and childrearing. *Two Gentlemen*, which dramatizes the period of courtship leading up to marriage, investigates the instability of male sexual attraction through the character Proteus, who vacillates between two objects of his passion, Julia and Silvia, before settling down with Julia in act 5. *Much Ado*, by comparison, concentrates less intensely on courtship and more fully on marriage, reaching an attempted wedding by act 4. These nuptials are disrupted by Claudio's suspicion of Hero's infidelity, which derives from the fear that marriage exposes a man to the threat of cuckoldry. Hero's "death" and "rebirth" as a maid at the end of the play allays this fear sufficiently for Claudio to enter the state of matrimony. Although allusions to the issue of procreation exist in *Much Ado*, neither pregnancy nor childrearing is ever dramatized.

The third play, *All's Well*, features no courtship at all, and it forcibly marries off the Comic Hero in the middle of act 2. Bertram's reluctance to marry stems partly from his disdain for Helena's low birth, but also from a desire to sow his wild oats abroad, so he abandons his marriage unconsummated and pursues the sexual conquest of the Florentine virgin Diana. Helena's bed trick converts Bertram's intended act of lustful copulation with Diana into legitimate conjugal relations leading to procreation, manifested in her appearance, pregnant, at the end of the play. *Measure for Measure*, as I will argue in chapter 5, is a much more complicated case because Shakespeare uncharacteristically splits crucial aspects of the Comic Hero between Angelo and Claudio, Isabella's brother, who displays the unruliness associated with childrearing, the final stage of the channeling process. Before the play begins, Claudio has already courted and betrothed himself to Juliet, whom he calls "fast my wife" (1.2.136). After their espousal but before a religious ceremony, they engage in sexual relations and conceive a child, which evidences their guilt in the crime of fornication. Angelo resolves to put Claudio to death for this infraction, which would create another fatherless child for the state to support, but the Duke, when he "returns" to Vienna, pardons Claudio for his crime and mandates that he marry Juliet, thereby compelling him to take financial responsibility for his offspring. Thus, taken as a group, the comedies of forgiveness illustrate the manner in which the social order constrains men to funnel their lust into marriage to an appropriate partner, despite the inherent risk of cuckoldry, so that they may father legitimate heirs and accept the costs of raising them. As Benedick declares when he accepts his duty to love and marry Beatrice, "the world must be peopled" (2.3.233–34).[12]

By my assessment, the operation of this social and biological imperative toward self-perpetuation characterizes the comedies of forgiveness far more accurately than does a drive toward the culmination of romantic desire. And yet, the vicarious pleasures to be derived from witnessing the victory of true love over parental interference are undoubtedly intense, while the delights of beholding society's triumph over the recalcitrant impulses of the individual may be decidedly less potent. So it is not surprising that, historically, when theatrical personnel have performed these comedies, they have habitually cut troublesome passages, transposed scenes, added stage business, and interpolated non-Shakespearean dialogue into the production text in a partially successful attempt to recast the comedies of forgiveness in the mold of romantic comedy. However, since the late 1960s, coinciding with the birth of the women's movement in the United States and in Europe, there has been a significant shift in the theatrical tendency toward effacing those aspects of the comedies of forgiveness that resist assimilation into the genre of romantic comedy. The behavior of Shakespeare's Forgiven Comic Heroes has always provoked the ire of readers and spectators,[13] but it is only since the rise of feminism that some stage productions have dared to raise such anger in performance and allow it to continue unabated through the final scenes of the plays. With considerably less recourse to the omission of crucial lines, the relocation of scenes, or the insertion of new dialogue, these contemporary productions have managed to concretize the indeterminate details of the written text in such a way that the Forgiven Comic Hero's treatment of women is not smoothed over, but rather brought to the forefront of the audience's attention. Occasionally, however, in their effort to express a feminist point of view, such productions have also found it necessary to violate essential aspects of the subgenre of the comedy of forgiveness.

To illustrate this potential conflict, the following four chapters will examine the comedies of forgiveness individually in far greater detail. First, an analysis of the manner in which the specific play coincides with or diverges from the model narrative will reveal both the distinct attributes of that play and the ways in which it meets the challenges posed by a particular aspect of male sexual desire. Next, a selective exploration of the play's stage history will expose certain crucial segments in the text where productions have tended to make performance choices that soften the audience's response to the Forgiven Comic Hero. A review of more recent productions, dating from the early days of feminism, then supplies alternative performance choices that demonstrate a willingness to resist the automatic reconfiguration of the play as a romantic comedy. Yet since the concern with gender roles and expectations exhibited by these productions usually focuses on the female characters, the corresponding social pressures that force men into gendered social positions are frequently slighted, and in extreme cases, fundamental aspects of the comedy of forgiveness, like marriage, are effaced because they are oppressive to women. So, at the end of each chapter, I propose new stagings of pivotal segments designed to take a feminist stance that coincides with the preoccupation of the comedy of forgiveness with the redirection of male sexuality toward the legitimate peopling of the world. Instead of soliciting an audience's pardon of the Forgiven Comic Hero, I hope to cause spectators to question why the on-stage characters are so quick to forgive him, and thereby to heighten awareness of the collective forces that mandate his recuperation at the expense of women.

My final chapter returns for a more thorough examination of the parts played by Silvia, Beatrice, Diana, and Isabella, the Shrews of their respective plays. In a manner that parallels the channeling of the Forgiven Comic Hero's sexual desire, all four of these talkative female characters undergo a gradual process of verbal suppression that I name "the taming pattern," alluding to the similar retraining of Katherine's speech habits in *The Taming of the Shrew*. At some point in each of the four comedies, the Shrew swears to refrain forever from participation in courtship and matrimony, to live and die a maid, but the play's drive toward society's self-perpetuation overcomes this resistance and pushes her, with questionable willingness, into marriage and legitimate reproduction. This match coincides with a period of silence on the Shrew's part that has always been understood, until recent decades, to indicate her speechless consent to her new condition. With the arrival of feminism, stage productions of the comedies of forgiveness have recently become willing to interpret the Shrew's silence as opposition to her proposed nuptials. I find in these plays, however, little evidence to back up such an interpretation; rather, the texts tend to support a reading of female silence as submission to the will of a man, specifically the woman's father or husband. Therefore, I put forward stagings of the conclusions of these plays that suggest that the Shrew does enter matrimony (in accordance with the thrust of the comedies of forgiveness), yet these enactments also encourage an audience, in the interests of a feminist perspective, to regret the sacrifice of the Shrew's independence that such an alliance demands. The chapter concludes the work with a glance ahead toward *The Winter's Tale*, which employs and adapts the taming pattern to accord with the reconciliatory agenda of romance. In the later play, Shakespeare employs the Shrew Paulina to turn her bitter tongue against the Forgiven Comic Hero, Leontes, and thereby to close the gap between what he deserves for his cruel treatment of the Griselda Hermione and the punishment that he receives. Paulina's extended role as a verbal scourge for the crimes of Leontes removes the necessity for theatrical intervention to achieve his forgiveness by the audience, but her ultimate fate is the same as that of her sister Shrews, the silencing of marriage. Although Paulina may not produce heirs for her own husband, Camillo, through the younger generation, Perdita and Florizel, the peopling of the world goes on.

While carrying out this investigation in the chapters that follow, it may appear as if I have made three assumptions of my own that grossly oversimplify the dramatic enterprise. Staging a play before live spectators is an uncertain and complicated process, but performance critics, searching for coherent ways to express the operation of a complex dynamic, often resort to language that makes the function of directors, actors, and audience members seem to be more straightforward and transparent than it genuinely is. Although I will speak of directors as if they are solely responsible for all aspects of a production, and of spectators as if they all respond identically to every stage sequence, and of actors as if their performances do not vary from one evening to the next, I acknowledge that none of these assumptions resembles the truth without extensive qualification, which I hope to provide here.

In spite of the common verbal construct whereby we refer to a production as "belonging" to its director (as in "Trevor Nunn's *Macbeth*"), it is also widely acknowledged that a theatrical event owes its genesis to an entire team of collaborators whose individual shares in the final results cannot be easily distinguished. W. B. Worthen, for instance, recalls to our attention that "while the director may be responsible for orchestrating the production's many languages, it is often difficult to say just where the director's hand has been at work, and where responsibility lies elsewhere, in the specific contribution of playwright, actors, designers, audience, or in the felicitous synergy of their efforts" (1997, 48). Performance choices generally are not handed down dictatorially by directors to their underlings, but emerge from a give-and-take struggle between the interests of various participants, whose contributions are shaped by practical limits of space, ability, and financial resources. Moreover, during the course of an extended theatrical run, the director typically distances him- or herself from a production's day-to-day operations, and the nature of the performance may change considerably as the actors, freed from the director's ever-present authority, begin to take fuller control of the staging. For these reasons, credit for the production belongs to everyone involved, but *responsibility* for it falls ultimately on the director's shoulders. Everything that happens in a production carries with it the director's implied approval, so the buck stops there. In this book, I will habitually attribute all choices to a production's director (or the equivalent authority figure for productions before the twentieth century), but I do so with the understanding that these decisions rightly belong to an unidentifiable person or group of people among the entire company.

Even when a director is personally and solely responsible for a performance choice, and the actors, designers, and/or technicians charged with carrying out this choice perform their duties bravely, like Ariel, bating nothing of Prospero's instruction, what the director intends may not be communicated to viewers exactly as he or she wishes. Akin to the intentions of the playwright, the director's purposes may only be guessed at, and in any case, the meaning of a performed segment cannot be restricted to a solitary significance that the director might have contemplated. As David McCandless points out,

> The director's job is not to orchestrate a single performed meaning—clearly an impossibility—but to structure a meaningful experience, to control a performance's chain of signifiers, to compose a kind of aural/visual poem through manipulation of the *mise-en-scène* in order to elicit a spectator response provisionally congruent with his vision, so that, on some (possibly subconscious) level and to an extent necessarily limited by the vagaries of audience response, the spectator grasps something of the director's concept. (1997, 33)

No matter how successfully directors govern a production's "chain of signifiers," they cannot guarantee that every spectator will interpret dramatic signs as expected. Bulman maintains that the unavoidable multiplicity of audience response should discourage performance critics from making universal statements about how stagings affect viewers:

> [A]ny attempt to generalize about audience response to a given performance is suspect; for just as an author may envisage a community of readers but have no control over their individual responses, so, at a performance of a play, the cultural pressures that have helped to shape the production cannot guarantee that each member of the audience will experience the play in the same way. Critics who rely on traditional research tools to reconstruct a performance—theatre reviews and programs, eye-witness accounts (their own and others'), promptbooks and directors' notes—frequently succumb to the temptation to generalize about its meaning for an audience. (1996, 4)

While one must admit that all viewers do not react in exactly the same fashion to every aspect of a production, it is equally necessary to acknowledge that some degree of shared audience response is evident at any competent performance of a Shakespeare play.[14] Theatrical spectatorship is a communal experience, and part of the satisfaction of the event is the chance to participate in a collective reaction to the dramatization. In succeeding chapters, I will often "succumb to the temptation to generalize" about how audiences may have interpreted various

enactments based on the recollections of one or more viewers. I
do not advance these claims as dependable accounts of the identical responses of all audience members at each and every performance, but as speculations about the most likely reaction of
the majority of spectators most of the time.

The fact that an audience on a given night may respond
uniquely to a performance should remind us that one of the distinguishing features of theatrical production, as opposed to the
literary experience of a play, is its contingency. For two pivotal
reasons, every performance, even within the same production,
is substantially different from all other performances of that
play by the same ensemble. In the first place, actors, despite
arduous rehearsal, do not offer exactly the same portrayals of
their characters in every performance, nor do they attempt to
do so. Performers on stage continually test out new ways to
move, speak, and interact with each other; some of these experi-
ments succeed and are incorporated into subsequent performances, while others are immediately discarded. Therefore, any
production exists in a constant state of evolution, and the final
performance of a theatrical run may deviate in significant ways
from the show on opening night. Second, actors play their parts
in front of a different group of people at every performance, so
the interactive dynamic that arises from that confrontation
changes each time the actors set foot on the stage. Particular
aspects of the meaning of a production stem primarily from this
actor/audience interchange, which does not remain constant
from performance to performance.

For these reasons, I find it helpful to consider Clare-Marie
Wall's distinction between the printed text of a play and two
types of theatrical texts, which she calls "the *production text*"
and "the *performance text*":

> The *production text* I would define as the framework of set, costume,
> lighting, sound, music, and the broad generalized outline of charac-
> terization, movement, motivation, intonation, etc. reached in
> rehearsals by actors and encouraged and confirmed by (usually) a
> director. A different entity altogether is the *performance text*, the
> actual encounter, unique in each matinee or evening event, in
> which actors face audience members, and combustion occurs. The
> *production text* is the catalyst: the *performance text* is the explosion.
> The *production text* is the road system: the *performance text* is the
> two hours' traffic. The *production text* is the frame: the *performance
> text* is the living picture. (1997, 1)

In contrast to a production's numerous *performance texts*, which are revised for each audience, there is only one *production text*, composed during the weeks preceding opening night, which remains relatively stable for the length of the production's run. For instance, an actor's delivery of a particular line may vary tremendously from night to night within the same production, but that same actor's costume or stage business (in its broad outlines) probably will not. The qualitative differences between these two kinds of theatrical texts render them suitable objects for distinct schools of performance criticism. Since the notion of a *performance text* assumes a multiplicity of performed versions of the same *production text*, the comparative study of *performance texts* matches the diachronic approach, which limits itself to the consideration of a single production. Various elements of a *production text*, however, take only one incarnation, and therefore they may be easily contrasted with the corresponding aspects of another director's *production text*, as is characteristic of the synchronic approach. Therefore, in my synchronic examination of various enactments of the four comedies of forgiveness, I will generally confine myself to aspects of their *production texts*, which do not exhibit the radical contingency of their *performance texts*.

This procedural accommodation also provides an answer to scholars who object to the examination of Shakespeare films alongside stage productions as examples of "performances" of the plays. These critics reasonably protest that the viewing of a film features no interplay between actors and audience, so the nature of the moviegoer's experience does not duplicate that of the theatergoer. Furthermore, as Bulman warns, the widespread study of film may mislead critics into thinking of "performance" as a fixed entity: "Because film and video allow us repeated viewings of a single performance, they encourage us to assimilate that performance to the condition of a literary text—a stable artifact rather than a contingent, ephemeral experience" (1996, 2). While it is certain that the transient characteristics of theater separate it from the more static quality of cinema, some elements of a stage production (the components of the *production text*) are less contingent and ephemeral than others. The script, say, of a theater performance, aside from minor accidental variations, may remain constant from night to night, so its cuts, interpolations, and rearrangements may legitimately be compared to the similar features of a screenplay. Since I intend to incorporate evidence from both film and television versions

of the plays in this study as instances of performances, I will
limit my scope to those aspects of such enactments that can,
with validity, be contrasted to the stable elements of the production text of a theater performance.

Film and television productions of Shakespeare's plays contribute to the overall quality of performance criticism because
their continuing existence on videotape provides substantially
more reliable evidence of performance choices than do traditional sources of information about stage performances. Due to
the ephemerality of theatrical productions, scholars possess a
narrow window of opportunity to experience them directly, and
when they miss such a chance, they must depend upon custom-
ary archival and printed sources of data: eyewitness accounts,
reviews, promptbooks, performance editions, photographs, and
the memoirs of actors or directors, in an attempt to reconstruct
the details of those enactments.[15] All of these sources are dubious in their own ways, and the information they yield must be
handled skeptically. Unless conflicting accounts of the particu-
lars of a production exist, however, I will tentatively treat all
documentary evidence as dependable with the following reser-
vations.[16]

Eyewitness accounts and reviews of productions can be unintentionally deceptive. Both are written by people with first-
hand experience of a performance, but while eyewitness
accounts may originally occur in private writings (like letters or
diaries), reviews are composed specifically for public consumption. Therefore reviews, especially those that appear in
newspapers soon after opening night, may display the many
shortcomings inherent to such publications, summarized here
by Leonore Leiblein:

> We know the limitations of theatre reviews: they tend to be hastily
> written, often contain errors of fact, are frequently edited into inco-
> herence, and occasionally have axes to grind. Reviewers seem to be
> more comfortable writing about things like acting (and hence char-
> acter) and often ignore things like lighting, sound design, and use of
> space. At their worst theatre reviews may be written by people who
> know little, and couldn't care less, about theatre, and who work for
> people whose prime interest is to sell newspapers. (1996, 168)

All observers, no matter how hard they try to be unbiased, also
have ideological preferences that color their readings of a performance; thus "reviewers—sources of supposedly reliable evi-

dence—in fact construct narratives which foreground their own cultural perspectives, thereby creating fictions that pass, or once passed, for objective reporting" (Bulman 1996, 3). Finally, not all observers are intimately familiar with the plays they review or their production histories, so they are not equally skilled at the identification of radical divergences from the text or striking new approaches to the performance of a particular sequence. These factors combine to make a performance critic's dependence on both eyewitness accounts and reviews a perilous practice.

To counteract the potential for error and bias in a review, the performance critic should consult as many reviews and other sources of information as possible in order to corroborate the facts of any account. Discrepancies between accounts may stem from changes to a production made after the show has opened (the replacement of an actor or the removal of a segment that did not work as expected in front of audiences), so the critic needs to be aware of the point or points in the run at which the reviewer attended the performance. For scholarly purposes, the most helpful reviews are those written by observers who saw the production multiple times and can therefore reveal which aspects of the staging (and audience reaction) remained stable and which varied from performance to performance. Academic reviewers who not only view a production repeatedly but also arrive at the theater armed with a thorough knowledge of Shakespeare's works and their stage histories often furnish the most valuable evidence for performance criticism, but even such accounts must be treated gingerly. Shakespeare scholars tend to "read" productions of his plays with the tools of literary criticism, and as Alan C. Dessen remarks, extensive theatrical experience may render scholars atypical spectators:

> Seeing *Cymbeline* for the eighth time can be an asset (a seasoned playgoer is aware in advance of especially problematic moments or choices) but seeing *Dream, Twelfth Night,* or *Macbeth* for the fiftieth time can be a distinct liability. What is fresh and meaningful for a normal playgoer may (unfairly) elicit a jaundiced reaction from a jaded palate. Miranda's "brave new world" can easily be overshadowed by Prospero's "'Tis new to thee." (1997b, 4)

Although my analysis of twentieth-century productions relies heavily on reviews from scholarly journals, I have attempted to balance my sense of the response to such performances by con-

sulting accounts in non-academic periodicals as well. Each type
of review has its drawbacks, but the survey of a variety of reactions can help guard against overreliance on any single reviewer's idiosyncratic perspective.

For productions from the nineteenth century and earlier, I
depend less upon reviews and more upon information gleaned
from promptbooks and performance editions of the plays. But
again, such documents have the potential to mislead or misin-
form the unwary critic. The warning of Charles H. Shattuck,
compiler of the most complete catalogue of Shakespeare
promptbooks, bears repeating:

> Promptbooks are tricky, secretive, stubborn informants. They chat-
> ter and exclaim about what we hardly need to know: that certain
> characters are being readied by the callboy to make their entrances;
> that the scene is about to change or the curtain to drop; that the
> orchestra is about to play at the act-end. They fall blackly silent just
> when we most hope to be told where the actor stood or how he
> looked or what he did. Rarely do they give us a hint of voice or tem-
> per or histrionic manner. They tell lies, as anybody knows who ever
> produced a play and failed to write into the book his own last-min-
> ute revisions or the happy inspirations that come to the actors mid-
> way in a run of performances. (1965, 3)

Plainly, promptbooks do not tell the whole truth, and what they
do tell may not bear any resemblance to what actually occurred
on stage. Yet even though promptbooks cannot offer definitive
proof that a particular performance choice was employed in a
production, a notation in a promptbook does indicate that such
a choice was at one time seriously considered, and in the
absence of conflicting information, it constitutes a provocative
piece of evidence concerning the most probable staging of that
scene. Likewise, despite lengthy titles proclaiming that their
text and stage directions reproduce the play "as it was performed by" some prominent actor-manager at a certain theater,
performance editions of the plays cannot prove beyond a
shadow of a doubt that any specific cut or interpolation was ever
put into effect.[17] The published screenplay of a modern film
bears a similarly problematic relationship to the cinematic
product, since the printing schedule may require the manu-
script to be sent to the publisher before the film is complete
(Campbell 1977, 6). A screenplay, however, may be checked
against a copy of the film for discrepancies, but the details from

other kinds of performance editions cannot be verified so easily and should only be trusted with caution.

The use of photographic evidence of stage productions requires similar discretion, for the camera, in spite of its ostensible ability to record the truth without mediation, does not necessarily permit straightforward access to the specifics of a performance. As Thomas Postlewait recognizes, "photographs may provide unreliable testimony because both their final cause or aim (publicity shot) and their formal cause (aesthetic principles of portrait) subvert their documentary potential" (169). Dennis Kennedy elaborates on the problems for the theater historian generated by these two factors:

> Unless a photographer has set out to document a production carefully and precisely, his or her pictures can present the same difficulty as set designs or scene drawings, despite the compelling power of their apparent veracity. Most theatre pictures have been made not for archives but for publicity, and the mission of the historian rarely coincides with the press agent's, at least in theory. Sometimes photographs show poses and blocking arrangements that differ markedly from the performance, even, in the name of convenience, introducing into a scene actors who have no legitimate business there. (1993, 20)[18]

If, at a photo call, the photographer alters the lighting, the groupings of the characters, or other aspects of the mise-en-scène in order to create more arresting publicity stills, the resulting photos falsify the significance of the stage picture. Even when the photographer simply takes unposed snapshots at a dress rehearsal, he or she may record details of costuming or stage business that are later changed or updated. To guard against the misconceptions that reliance on photographs may introduce, Kennedy advocates correlating them against photos taken by other photographers at different times, as well as other forms of documentary evidence (23). When such corroboration is unavailable, I take the evidence presented by such photographs as suggestive but not definitive proof of specific performance choices.

Finally, the memoirs of actors and directors recalling their contributions to particular productions can throw beneficial light on the intentions of theatrical professionals and the means by which their designs achieve dramatic embodiment. Although such recollections provide glimpses of the theatrical decision-making process unavailable through any other source, those who are directly involved in a stage production are not always the best people to offer accurate information about it. Over time, the memories of the most sincere autobiographical writers suffer from gaps, lapses into error, and the inclination to embellish a good story. Thus, the most trustworthy accounts tend to be those composed by actors and directors during the run of a production or very soon after it closes. Even when the details of a performance are fresh and clear in a reporter's mind, however, these memories do not offer evidence that the intentions of the dramatic company were successfully communicated to the audience in performance. While actors on stage for a particular scene may be entirely correct in their descriptions of an audience's response, they cannot necessarily judge with precision the reasons for it. The memoirs of theatrical personnel, by themselves, clearly do not constitute infallible testimony regarding the staged event, but this unique evidence derived from a point of view from within the performance itself also cannot be disregarded.

The contingency of dramatic performances and the unreliability of all forms of theatrical evidence compound with one another to render the practice of performance criticism an admittedly insecure pursuit. If what we seek is the incontrovertible truth about the nature of Shakespeare's plays on the stage, performance criticism cannot produce for us what we desire. Poststructuralist theory has provided necessary correctives to overconfident essentialist notions of performance, but in its emphasis on the destabilization of fixed authority, postmodern scholarship has also shaken the foundations upon which any form of criticism might stand. For if any degree of uncertainty at all about performance and audience response to it leaves us unable to proceed in the analysis of the theatrical event, then as critics we are paralyzed. I believe that valuable performance criticism of Shakespeare is possible, but it requires a respect for dramatic inventiveness, a cognizance of ideological assumptions (including one's own), and a reasonable standard for the consideration of both textual and theatrical evidence. Performance criticism will never generate discoveries of unquestioned veracity, but when practiced with healthy skepticism, it may lead to very useful generalizations about the ranges of meaning of Shakespeare's plays in the theater and on the screen.

Chapter 2

"Were man but constant, he were perfect": *The Two Gentlemen of Verona*

All the people are, in spite of everything, likable: If Proteus is to be allowed to live by the audience, you must find your most likable actor and cast him there. In the end, I think you come out with a joyous—I hope—feeling from the audience. Not a complex one, yet the[re] are complexities underneath the surface.

(Waleson 1987, 14)

THE PRECEDING RECOMMENDATION, OFFERED BY STUART VAUGHN, the director of the 1987 New York Shakespeare Festival production of *The Two Gentlemen of Verona*, typifies the orthodox theatrical treatment of the play and its Forgiven Comic Hero. In spite of everything he does, Vaughan tells us, Proteus *must* be portrayed as a likable character, or else spectators will not be able to pardon him for his misdeeds. The director suggests that a sympathetic Proteus will allow the play's final scene to inspire viewers with a joyous feeling, but his tentative interjection "—I hope—" betrays a lurking suspicion that even this strategy may not be sufficient to achieve an uncomplicated happy ending. Tellingly, Vaughan also feels obliged to apologize for the lack of depth in the type of conclusion he seeks, for there are "complexities underneath the surface" of the play to which a simple, two-dimensional treatment does not do justice. Nevertheless, Vaughan seems to fear that, if he permits Proteus's unattractive traits to balance out his characterization, the director will risk turning the wrath of his audience against the Forgiven Comic Hero, and the production will not close with the exuberance of a conventional comedy. Throughout the stage history of *Two Gentlemen*, directors and performers, like Vaughan, have repeatedly chosen to seek traditional comic closure at the expense of Proteus's depth of characterization. Yet the choice, I would

41

argue, is illusory; a production need not sacrifice the complexity of the text's depiction of Proteus simply to evoke a single, designated reaction proper to comedy, for unmitigated joy is not the only appropriate response to a comedy of forgiveness.

Two Gentlemen, unique among the plays examined here, represents a hybrid between the comedy of forgiveness, focusing on the troubled alliance between Proteus and Julia, and romantic comedy, as exemplified by the forbidden love of Valentine and Silvia. Within this blended structure, Shakespeare employs the Duke as the obstacle between his daughter and her lover rather than as the Authority figure who unites the Griselda and the Forgiven Comic Hero in matrimony. This deviation from the model narrative of the comedy of forgiveness increases the tendency for theatrical personnel to view the entire work as a romantic comedy and to strive for the kind of effects thought desirable within that genre. Shakespeare diverges from his typical pattern in the comedy of forgiveness in another way by splitting the traits of the Vice figure between two characters, Launce and his master Proteus, who also serves as the play's Forgiven Comic Hero. This unique redistribution of qualities motivates performance choices that tone down the offenses of Proteus and increase his fitness for inclusion within the marital unions that conclude the play. Yet recently, several productions have enacted alternative stagings of 5.4 that illuminate, rather than occlude, the reconsolidation of male bonds through the bodies of women that makes the forgiveness of Proteus essential to the ending of this comedy. Such stagings, however, sometimes suggest that no marriages at all take place after the final scene. A historical review of performance choices made at crucial points in the text will reveal the ideological contrast between these two common theatrical treatments of the play's conclusion and suggest new choices for a production of *Two Gentlemen* as a comedy of forgiveness.

The play begins with a farewell scene between Proteus and his lifelong companion Valentine, whose witty jibes against Proteus's love for Julia (1.1.3–8, 29–35) establish Valentine's function, within the model narrative, as the Comic Hero's Friend. Valentine's antiromantic stance emerges as a protest against Proteus's affection for the Griselda, which threatens to supplant male friendship as the primary emotional bond in Proteus's life. Yet when Valentine falls in love with Silvia, the daughter of the Duke of Milan, he abandons his contempt for amorous sentiment and indulges in the stereotypical behavior of the Petrarchan lover, particularly the elevation of his celestial goddess above all other women. Valentine's hyperbolic praise of Silvia (and his consequent devaluation of his friend's mistress by comparison) leads Proteus to exclaim, "Why, Valentine, what braggardism is this?" (2.4.159). Valentine's braggardism, though it lacks the military flavor evident in the swaggering of Benedick, Parolles, and Lucio, aligns Valentine with the boastfulness of the *miles gloriosus*, from whom the Friend of the Comic Hero derives his dramatic lineage.

Valentine's exaltation of his lady unintentionally drives a wedge between the two comrades, for it leads Proteus to become Valentine's rival for Silvia's love. While Valentine prepares his elopement with Silvia, Proteus delivers a soliloquy that encapsulates the fickleness of male sexual desire and the dangers it poses to traditional social relationships. In this speech, Proteus relinquishes his passion for Julia in favor of a "newer object" (2.4.191), his best friend's mistress. This inconstancy represents a serious threat to the social institutions regulating courtship, for it violates the spirit of the handfasting ceremony that Proteus and Julia have recently conducted. Before parting, the two lovers clasp hands, exchange rings, and "seal the bargain with a holy kiss" (2.2.7). As Margaret Loftus Ranald notes, "This scene possesses the outward signs of a sixteenth-century betrothal in words of the future tense. This contract, though unwitnessed, would give the couple a quasi-legal claim on each other, and thus the actions of Proteus are even more inexcusable" (1987, 54). Furthermore, the instability of Proteus's affections also rebounds against the institution of male friendship itself, for Proteus's ardor for Silvia cools the "zeal" he once felt toward his companion Valentine (2.4.199). Near the end of the play, Valentine observes Proteus's attempt to force his passion on Silvia and berates him as a "common friend, that's without faith or love, / For such is a friend now" (5.4.62–68). In order to repair the damage that the treacherous inconstancy of Proteus does to the social conventions of courtship and friendship, the play must resolve a contradiction within the notion of friendship itself that impels Proteus to violate Valentine's trust.

René Girard pinpoints this contradiction through his application of the concept of *mimetic desire* to explain Proteus's immediate transferal of his affection from Julia to Silvia. According to Girard, mimetic desire describes the spontaneous tendency of friends to copy each others' likes and dislikes:

> When two young men grow up together, they learn the same les-
> sons, they read the same books, they play the same games, and they
> agree on just about everything. They also tend to desire the same
> objects. This perpetual convergence is not incidental but essential
> to the friendship; . . . it really depends on a mutual *imitation* so spon-
> taneous and constant that it remains unconscious. (1988, 233)

Proteus exhibits the operation of this imitative process during
his soliloquy when he asks himself, "Is it mine eye, or Valenti-
nus' praise, / . . . / That makes me reasonless to reason thus?"
(4.4.192–94). Since Silvia and Julia are equally fair, as Proteus
admits, it is not his eye but Valentine's praise of Silvia that
unconsciously prompts Proteus suddenly to adore the object of
his friend's passion. As Girard puts it, "Proteus desires Silvia
not because their brief encounter made a decisive impression
on him but because he is predisposed in favor of whatever Valentine desires" (232). The contradiction inherent to a friendship
contingent upon mimetic desire is that, although some desirable
objects, like music or literature, can be shared equally without
conflict, a particular woman, within a society that demands
monogamy, cannot be possessed mutually by two men. Therefore, the two friends become caught in what Girard calls "the
mimetic double bind, the simultaneous discovery by Valentine
and Proteus that, in addition to the usual imperative of friendship: *imitate me*, another imperative has mysteriously appeared:
do not imitate me" (240). Proteus lacks the constancy in love that
would allow him to resist the pull of mimetic desire, and by giving in to the temptation to imitate his friend, Proteus paradoxically violates the conventions of both courtship and friendship.

In order to achieve his illicit desire for Silvia, Proteus, in a
second soliloquy (2.6.1–43), concocts a scheme to foil Valentine's
intended elopement. By announcing to the audience his intention to use treachery to accomplish his purposes, Proteus associates himself with the morality play Vice, one of whose
essential functions is to plot evil intrigues against the virtuous
characters.[1] Like the Vice, Proteus informs the audience in
advance of his plan to employ deceit against Valentine and his
rival Thurio so that spectators may enjoy dramatic irony as they
witness his manipulation of his gullible victims. Yet unlike the
other comedies of forgiveness, this play does not exploit the Vice
figure to seduce the Forgiven Comic Hero; in fact, *Two Gentlemen* deviates from the model narrative in its unusual assignment of some of the qualities of the Vice figure to the Forgiven

Comic Hero himself. This overlap has severe consequences for the conclusion of the play because the scheming Vice figure cannot serve as a scapegoat for the sins of the Forgiven Comic Hero if they are one and the same person. No one else can be blamed for the transgressions of Proteus but Proteus himself, and therefore his swift pardon by Valentine and Julia in act 5 strikes readers and viewers even more acutely as too lenient to be believed.

Furthermore, Shakespeare assigns other qualities associated with the Vice figure to Launce, Proteus's servant, so that together, master and man display most of the features commonly exhibited by the morality play character. While Proteus manifests little of the Vice's sharp sense of humor, Launce seems to exist in the play almost entirely to make up for this lack, for he has no functional role at all to perform in the plot. When Speed, Valentine's boy, comments on Launce's "old vice" to "mistake the word" (3.1.280), he associates Launce with one of the Vice's most prominent traits, "his addiction to word play" (Spivack 1958, 202). Soon after, Launce comically delays Speed's departure to meet the banished Valentine and anticipates his own delight at the whipping Speed will receive from his master for his late arrival: "I'll after, to rejoice in the boy's correction" (3.1.372–74). Launce's mischievous prank, along with his wicked enjoyment of the consequences that befall his gull, closely resemble the motiveless malignity of the Vice, whose immoral acts proceed, not from any clear psychological motivation (as is the case with Proteus), but from his function as the allegorical representation of the root of all evil.

In addition, Launce does fulfill the Vice's role as the scapegoat in the model narrative, but he does so only on a metaphorical level by suffering for the crimes of his dog, Crab, whom the play associates with Proteus. Launce's master admits that his love for Silvia is "spaniel-like" (4.2.14), which links him with the play's literal canine, whose inappropriate exploits continually bring punishments upon his innocent master. For instance, Launce relates how he has not only taken the blame for his dog's urinary indiscretions under the Duke's table, but also how he has "sat in the stocks, for puddings he hath stolen" and "stood on the pillory for geese he hath killed" (4.4.30–33). Since Proteus has also become a dog, Launce's tale represents a parodic account of the Vice figure's function as a scapegoat for the Forgiven Comic Hero. Thus Launce, according to the model narrative, should assume the guilt that ought to fall on his mas-

ter, Proteus, but Launce does not even appear in the final act of
Two Gentlemen, when Proteus is caught in the midst of his most
heinous crime, his attempted rape of Silvia.[2] Launce prefigures
this attack in his admonition of Crab for the dog's recent offense
against the Duke's daughter: heaving up his leg and making
water against the gentlewoman's farthingale (4.4.34–38). Crab's
desecration of Silvia's skirts parallels Proteus's affront to her
chastity,[3] but unlike Crab, Proteus has no literal scapegoat on
whose head the offender's sins can be placed. In this play, the
secondary Vice figure, Launce, performs the part of the Forgiven Comic Hero's scapegoat only metaphorically, and this
function has therefore been insufficient to deflect indignation
away from Proteus, who must take all the blame for his own
Vice-like evil.

Proteus triumphs in his treacherous intrigue against Valentine, but he enjoys no such success deceiving Silvia. In response
to his advances, Silvia rails against him as a "subtle, perjur'd,
false, disloyal man" (4.2.92) whom she despises for his faithlessness in love and friendship. Silvia's caustic verbal eloquence
identifies her as the Shrew of the model narrative, whose chid-
ing voice irritates yet provokes the desire of the Comic Hero.
Recognized as a fraud, Proteus compounds his falsehood by
lying about the current state of his relationship with Julia. To
Silvia's accusations, he replies, "I grant, sweet love, that I did
love a lady, / But she is dead" (4.2.102–3). Although Proteus
invents Julia's demise as an excuse for his disloyal acts, her
"death" resembles the typical pattern of the comedy of forgiveness, wherein the Griselda's betrayal by the Comic Hero
prompts her to counterfeit her own mortality. One might expect
that Julia, disguised as a page, directly witnessing her lover's
perjury, would find her own adoration of Proteus begin to wane,
but the commitment of the Griselda to her partner is so strong
that she will endure any hardship or indignity to preserve the
relationship. She therefore agrees, as a demonstration of her
unselfish love, to help Proteus win Silvia's affection.

Silvia escapes Milan to seek Valentine in the forests of Mantua, where he has become the captain of a band of outlaws, who
eventually capture Silvia. Proteus liberates Silvia from these
ruffians, but she offers him no gratitude: "Had I been seized by
a hungry lion, / I would have been a breakfast to the beast, /
Rather than have false Proteus rescue me" (5.4.33–35). During
this segment, Silvia reverts to her shrewish mode, and her voice
rises to its highest pitch of contempt for "false perjur'd Proteus"

(5.4.39). Her disdainful tone, along with her refusal to requite his loving service, pushes Proteus beyond the bounds of mere disloyalty into an abhorrent, felonious assault:

> Nay, if the gentle spirit of moving words
> Can no way change you to a milder form,
> I'll woo you like a soldier, at arm's end,
> And love you 'gainst the nature of love: force ye.
>
> (5.4.55–58)

Until this point, Proteus has wooed Silvia as Valentine did, according to the rules of Petrarchan love, whereby the suitor places his mistress on a pedestal far above his own lowly station. He has serenaded her with flattering songs and even risked his life to save her from distress, yet his efforts have not succeeded in changing Silvia from a cruel, shrewish lady to a "milder form." Since she refuses to conform to his expectations, Proteus abandons the rules of Petrarchan love and adopts the laws of war, which reverse the power dynamic between men and women in traditional courtship. Instead of placing himself in a position of servitude to his mistress, Proteus will exercise power over her by wooing her "like a soldier," as if she were part of the sexual spoils of a rampaging army. This attempted rape, which runs " 'gainst the nature of love," therefore represents Proteus's most odious crime against courtship practices.

Valentine prevents Proteus from carrying out his violent attack, and even though Proteus never speaks any words of repentance to Silvia, he does offer a succinct apology to his companion for his breach of the code of friendship:

> My shame and guilt confounds me.
> Forgive me, Valentine: if hearty sorrow
> Be a sufficient ransom for offence,
> I tender't here; I do as truly suffer,
> As e'er I did commit.
>
> (5.4.73–77)

Like the expressions of contrition provided by the other Forgiven Comic Heroes, Proteus's speech of "shame and guilt" is brief, but apparently sincere. Thus, the objections of readers and audiences to this sequence usually stem from the ease and hastiness with which Valentine accepts this apology: "Then I am paid; / And once again I do receive thee honest" (5.4.77–78). As Linda Anderson notes, "it is largely the lack of even a consideration of revenge against Proteus that makes the play's ending difficult for a modern audience to accept" (1987, 23). Indeed, the only "penance" that Proteus must ever endure is to "hear / The story of [his] loves discovered" at the end of the play (5.4.168–69).

Even more troublesome for critics and spectators of all periods has been Valentine's magnanimous offer, "And that my love may appear plain and free, / All that was mine in Silvia I give thee" (5.4.82–83). For centuries, editors have labored to rewrite or reinterpret this couplet so that it does *not* signify that Valentine offers to surrender Silvia to her attempted rapist, but close parallels in Shakespeare's sources suggest that Valentine intends to prove his forgiveness by giving up his rights as the lover of Silvia to Proteus.[4] Placing friendship above love abruptly reverses Valentine's previous priorities, for earlier, when Valentine first confesses to Proteus the depth of his passion for Silvia, he begs his friend, "Forgive me that I do not dream on thee, / Because thou seest me dote upon my love" (2.4.168–69). Valentine's proposal to sever his ties with Silvia for his friend's sake represents an overcompensation for his earlier neglect of Proteus and a well-meaning but insufficient solution to the mimetic double bind.[5] Glorifying friendship at the expense of love is no more satisfactory than exalting love over friendship; indeed, Valentine and Proteus must ultimately discover a way to accommodate both friendship and love while avoiding the conflicts inherent to mimetic desire.

The answer for the two young men lies in Proteus's eventual acceptance of the need for constancy in love. When Julia, still disguised as Sebastian, reprimands Proteus for breaking his solemn vows of love to her, she claims that it is a "lesser blot" for "Women to change their shape than men their minds" (5.4.107–8). Proteus readily assents to Julia's assessment of his past behavior and vows to love more steadfastly in the future:

> 'Tis true: O heaven, were man
> But constant, he were perfect. That one error
> Fills him with faults; makes him run through all th' sins;
> Inconstancy falls off, ere it begins.
> What is in Silvia's face but I may spy
> More fresh in Julia's, with a constant eye?
>
> (5.4.109–14)

Although Proteus would still likely fall short of perfection even if he *were* constant, his acceptance of inconstancy as the root of all his failings is a step in the right direction, for he thereby acknowledges that male fickleness represents a serious threat to the social institution of courtship. Moreover, by embracing constancy, Proteus learns how to resolve the mimetic double bind. Seen through "a constant eye," which resists the distracting pull of mimetic desire, Julia's face exhibits all the beauties of Silvia's visage in an even fresher embodiment. Therefore, if Proteus possesses Julia, he also possesses the perfections of Silvia, to whom he is mimetically drawn yet must not attempt to compass for the sake of his friendship with Valentine.

Constancy in his choice of a partner allows Proteus to accommodate both love and friendship, a reconciliation emphasized by the stage picture indicated in the dialogue immediately following Proteus's discovery. Valentine, in a reconstitution of the betrothal ceremony performed earlier by Proteus and Julia, rejoins the hands of the two lovers: "Come, come; a hand from either; / Let me be blest to make this happy close: / 'Twere pity two such friends should be long foes" (5.4.115–17). This reenactment of Proteus and Julia's handfasting reinscribes the value of the courtship ritual damaged by Proteus's infidelity. The tableau also features Proteus simultaneously hand in hand with his lover and his friend in perfect harmony. Some critics argue that, in response to this reunion, we should "do as Shakespeare bids: accept Proteus's repentance as well as Julia's forgiveness of him" (Thompson 1971, 66); nevertheless, a long line of scholars have refused to condone the facility with which Julia pardons the wayward Proteus. Memorably, E. E. Kellett complains,

> Julia forgives him as easily as he had forgotten her; and all . . . comes right in the end. There are many sudden and worthless repentances in the plays; over and over again . . . a man who has committed the worst of offenses has only to confess in order to make all straight; but . . . no more shameful view of marriage was ever exhibited to the world than is shown here. (1923, 95)

Kellett's indignation arises from the expectation, common to romantic comedy, that the play endeavors to bring Proteus and Julia together in an ideal union; however, given the obvious shortcomings of the groom, this marriage fails to appear ideal. Alternatively, if we view *Two Gentlemen* as a comedy of forgiveness, striving primarily to heal ruptures in the world of male camaraderie sustained during the transition from bachelorhood to husbandry, it becomes clear that Julia's swift forgiveness of

Proteus, though neither laudable nor psychologically plausible, is necessary to the generic framework.

Modern feminist critics are less likely to object to the play's view of marriage than to the way in which the end of *Two Gentlemen* forfeits the independence of speech and action accorded to Silvia and Julia during the rest of the play. Janet Adelman, for example, asserts that, in order to achieve the fantasy of reconciliation between male friendship and heterosexual bonds, the play must abandon its three-dimensional portraits of the female characters:

> [T]he autonomy of both Silvia and Julia as fully realized figures has to be sacrificed: Silvia stands by silently as she is swapped from Valentine to Proteus, who has just tried to rape her (indeed, she never speaks after the rape attempt); and Julia is not permitted to notice, or to care, that her man is a would-be rapist. The sacrifice of the autonomy of these hitherto sensible characters suggests the extent to which the deepest concern of the play is with the male bond. (1985, 79)

This essential preoccupation with male bonds is also evident in the behavior of the Duke, who, in response to Valentine defending his right to Silvia against Thurio, suddenly applauds the banished man's spirit and deems him "worthy of an empress' love" (5.4.135–36). Within the frame of romantic comedy, these lines constitute the routine capitulation by the Senex to the mutual desire of the young boy and girl. Within the context of the comedy of forgiveness, however, the crucial aspect of this turnaround is the way in which Valentine's vitality abruptly raises him in the Duke's eyes from an "overweening slave" (3.1.157) to "a gentleman, and well deriv'd" (5.4.144). Valentine's meteoric rise in status, simply for intimidating the craven Thurio, reveals how intently the play wishes to reintegrate Valentine into the upper echelons of the male-dominated social order. His marriage to Silvia cements his alliance with the Duke, so Valentine recaptures his place among the other gentlemen at court.

Valentine's reentry into the male hierarchy is important to the play as a comedy of forgiveness in that Valentine's marriage to the Duke's daughter and his reestablishment of his friendship with Proteus create the otherwise absent bond between the Forgiven Comic Hero and the Authority figure. In addition to the play's division of the characteristics of the Vice between Proteus and Launce, the play's next major deviation from the model narrative involves the Duke's role as a Senex in the romantic comedy plot rather than as a matchmaker in the comedy of forgiveness story. Shakespeare, in contrast to his practice in *Much Ado*, *All's Well*, and *Measure for Measure*, brings the Griselda and the Forgiven Comic Hero together in *Two Gentlemen* without employing a manipulative paternal figure. The Duke has absolutely no connection to Julia, and therefore Proteus's marriage to her at the end of the play, by itself, cannot create a tie between the two men. Instead, Valentine must serve as the link between the Duke and Proteus, drawing Proteus into the Duke's circle of gentlemen through Valentine's friendship with Proteus and his marriage to the Duke's daughter.

As Camille Wells Slights observes, it is possible to view the entire play as "a comic exploration of the nature and function of a gentleman" (1983, 15). When Proteus first arrives in Milan, Valentine assures the Duke that Proteus exhibits "all good grace to grace a gentleman" (2.4.69). Yet once Proteus falls in love with Silvia, he abandons the virtues that stamp him as a gentleman and embraces the treachery toward Valentine that labels him a Vice-like villain. When Proteus slyly maneuvers the Duke into encouraging him to poison Silvia's affection for Valentine through slander, Proteus truthfully observes, " 'Tis an ill office for a gentleman, / Especially against his very friend" (3.2.40–41). Proteus renders himself unfit for inclusion at the Duke's court through this violation of gentlemanly behavior in the same way that Crab, thrusting himself "into the company of three or four gentleman-like dogs, under the Duke's table" (4.4.17–18) reveals his own unsuitability for fellowship with courteous canines by pissing on his comrades. When Valentine forgives Proteus for his offenses against friendship and once again receives him "honest," he readmits Proteus to the camp of those who demonstrate loyalty to the code of gentlemanliness.

The final lines of the play cement the several ties that join Proteus and Valentine to each other and to the Duke in a rehabilitated version of the world of male fraternity in which the action began. As Valentine proclaims to Proteus, "our day of marriage shall be yours, / One feast, one house, one mutual happiness" (5.4.170–71). Now gentlemen again, and friends again, Valentine and Proteus will further solidify their alliance by entering the wedded state on the same day and by living together in the same house for the rest of their lives. Significantly, they achieve this aspect of their relationship through Silvia and Julia, whose agreement to marry their lovers allows

Proteus and Valentine to experience husbandry together. Silvia acts as the crucial link in this chain, for she represents the conduit between the two gentlemen of her household and her father the Duke. Therefore, the play cannot permit Silvia to express any reluctance to marry Valentine or cohabitate with Proteus, her would-be rapist, because these actions facilitate the main goal of the comedy of forgiveness, to bring the Forgiven Comic Hero into the state of matrimony as a means of assuming his position within the male hierarchy. This conclusion, while it appears to satisfy the two gentlemen, Julia, and the Duke, has not fared so well with readers, who complain either that the play disregards traditional comic conventions or that it silences and degrades women by, among other things, refusing to punish Proteus. Therefore, stage productions have historically endeavored to refashion the play as a romantic comedy, which involves redrawing Proteus as a more likable, forgivable character. Within the past few decades, however, some productions have elected instead to draw attention to the play world's exploitation of women to unite men. As the following selective examination of the stage history of *Two Gentlemen* will show, the generic and ideological orientation of any specific production is evident in its performance choices at key moments of the play, especially in the final scene.

*   *   *

In 1762, the first recorded production of *Two Gentlemen*, Garrick's at Drury Lane, used a performance text prepared by Benjamin Victor, who heavily revised Shakespeare's scenic arrangement and dialogue and removed the play's most notorious incident, Valentine's offer of Silvia to Proteus. This revised text was revived for three performances at the same theater in 1790 after John Philip Kemble had become manager, and Kemble himself produced a new version of Victor's adaptation in 1808 (Leech 1969, xlvii–xlix). Because these early performance texts take considerable liberties with Shakespeare's play, an examination of Victor's and Kemble's frequent cuts, interpolations, and redistributions of speeches in act 5 reveals some of the ways in which eighteenth- and nineteenth-century producers felt that the original work defeated generic expectations for comedy, particularly in its portrayal of Proteus. During the twentieth century, many productions have continued the trend toward the rehabilitation of Proteus, although they generally eschew the insertion of new dialogue in favor of significant stage business as a method for reshaping the meaning of the text. In the closing decades of this century, however, other productions have offered stagings of the conclusion of the play that render Proteus less easily forgivable by the female characters as well as by the audience. Such performances also tend to problematize the play's final moments by refusing to portray the reunions of the couples as the triumphant victories of true love commonly found in romantic comedies. My own projected staging of the end of *Two Gentlemen* aims to achieve this distinction between romantic comedy and the comedy of forgiveness without sacrificing the play's comic treatment of marriage.

Shakespeare's 5.4 begins with Valentine's apostrophe to his absent lover Silvia. When he hears the shouts of his cohorts, the outlaws, he withdraws to observe his mates pursue Proteus, Silvia, and Julia. Victor, in his version, transfers Valentine's opening speech to his own 5.2 and begins his 5.4 with a mimed sequence in which Proteus rushes on the scene with his sword drawn to save Silvia from her captors (1763, 50). Kemble then elaborates on Victor's addition by interpolating dialogue into the mimed rescue segment: his 5.5 opens with a brief paraphrase of Shakespeare's 5.3 (Silvia in the hands of the outlaws, whom Kemble names Carlos and Stefano), which concludes with the following passage:

> *Sil.*   I'll go no further;—kill me even here.
> *Ste.*   Nay, no resistance.
> *Car.*   Follow patiently.
> *Sil.*   Help, help, for mercy! help, some rescuing arm!
>
> *Enter* Proteus
>
> *Pro.*   Ha! Silvia's voice!—Love, guide my weapon sure!
>   Unhand the lady, slaves;—or meet your death.
>   [*Proteus strikes the sword out of Carlos's hand,
>   who flies;—he then engages Stefano, who finds
>   himself overpowered, and escapes.*
>   Prosperous adventure!—and most blest encounter!—
>   (9:64)[6]

Both Victor and Kemble take an offstage action from Shakespeare's text and bring it before the eyes of the audience, impressing spectators more vividly with the courage of Proteus's one chivalrous action. Kemble's version further ennobles Proteus through its dramatization of Silvia's plight and the brave, heroic language that the adapter gives to her rescuer.

This method for raising a spectator's opinion of Proteus was borrowed centuries later by director David Ostwald, whose 1981 production at the Oregon Shakespeare Festival also strove to present a more admirable Proteus. As reviewer Charles Frey recalls, "Silvia's rescue by Proteus, nowhere enacted in the text, was nonetheless staged. Much of the stage business served to elevate Proteus and make Valentine and the servants look silly or irrelevant" (1982, 401). Clearly, the stage embodiment of Silvia's deliverance can help improve an audience's opinion of Proteus; in Ostwald's production, this choice appears to be part of an overall strategy to denigrate the other characters so that Proteus will look better by comparison.

After Proteus overpowers the outlaws, both Victor and Kemble present Shakespeare's dialogue between Proteus and Silvia, overheard by Valentine, essentially unchanged. However, at the point where Proteus resolves to rape Silvia, the two adapters diverge from Shakespeare's text in subtle ways that would likely soften an audience's attitude toward Silvia's attacker. Victor's rendition begins with Valentine still hidden alongside a few of the outlaws:

> Pro. Nay, if the gentle spirit of moving words
>   Can no way change you to a milder form,
>   I'll move you like a soldier, at arms end,
>   And force you. [*He seizes her.*]
> Sil. O Heavens!
> Val. [*comes forward*] Ruffian! let go that rude, uncivil touch!
>   Thou friend of an ill fashion! Seize him.
> Pro. [*starting*] Valentine! [Protheus *retires to the side of the*
>   *scene, guarded, by the* Outlaws, *and attended by* Julia.]
> Val. My dearest Silvia, [*runs and catches her in his arms.*]
>   Kind heav'n has heard my fervent prayer!
>   And brought my faithful Silvia to my arms!
>   There is no rhetorick can express my joy!

(1763, 51)

In Victor's revision, Proteus, noting that the gentle spirit of "moving" words has failed to change Silvia's hardheartedness, threatens to "move" (rather than "woo") her like a soldier. This preference for the F2 reading, coupled with the elimination of most of line 59 ("I'll force thee yield to my desire"), desexualizes Proteus's assault, so that it is not explicit, as it is in Shakespeare's text, that Proteus intends to ravish Silvia. Victor also inserts Valentine's outlaw confederates into the scene at this point so that Valentine can order Proteus apprehended and removed to the side of the stage, where he is united with the disguised Julia. This blocking leaves center stage open for an interpolated reunion between Valentine and Silvia, ostensibly to make up for the fact that, in the original text, Valentine does not speak a single word to Silvia after interrupting Proteus's attack; instead, he berates Proteus for his betrayal of their friendship. Whereas Shakespeare first focuses attention on the two men and the impending collapse of their relationship, Victor, following the conventions of romantic comedy, immediately emphasizes the pairing up of the couples and the joy of Valentine and Silvia at their triumphant reunion.

Kemble's recasting of the attempted rape sequence follows the general outlines of Victor's revision but tones down the sexual violence of the scene even further:

> Pro. Nay, if the gentle spirit of moving words
> Can no way change you to a milder form,
> I'll woo you like a soldier, at arms' end.
> Sil. O heaven!—
> [*As* Proteus *goes to seize* Silvia, Valentine *rushes between them.*]
> Val. Ruffian, forbear that rude, unhallow'd touch!—
> Thou friend of an ill fashion!
> Pro. Valentine!
> Val. Comrades, lay hold on him.—
> [*The Outlaws seize* Proteus:—Julia *runs to him.*]
> My dearest Silvia!—
> Indulgent heav'n at length has heard my prayer,
> And brought again my Silvia to my arms:
> No power on earth shall ever part us more.
>
> (9:64–65)

Although Kemble restores Proteus's vow to "woo" Silvia like a soldier, he also removes the single reference to the use of force remaining in Victor's version of the incident; therefore, in the later revision, the dialogue implies even less plainly a sexual assault. In addition, Kemble inserts a stage direction which makes it clear that Proteus never actually lays a hand on Silvia. Before Proteus can seize her, Valentine interposes his own body and commands Proteus to "forbear" (rather than "let go") his unholy touch. The prevention of any physical contact between Proteus and Silvia would likely cause an audience to blame Proteus less severely for his offense, since it never goes beyond a threat to a bona fide assault. Despite other changes in diction, the rest of Kemble's version also retains Victor's initial stress on the reunions of the two couples in contrast to Shakespeare's focus on the bond between the two men.

By comparison, David Ostwald's staging of this sequence exemplifies the modern preference for added stage business rather than rewritten dialogue as a means to reduce the despicable aspects of Proteus's behavior. In the Ashland production, before carrying out his resolution to force Silvia to yield to his desire, Proteus experiences second thoughts about his furious actions:

> After threatening to rape Silvia but before Valentine intervened, this Proteus of his own volition drew back as if to reconsider. The director said he conceived of Proteus as a youth confused but well-intentioned, and the actor, Barry Kraft, used considerable skills to elicit audience sympathy, even admiration, for Proteus. He never seemed malicious, only driven by his ever-for-the-moment honest passions. Thus he . . . gained an easy pride of place at the ending where most readers and many audiences have felt distinct ill-ease over his swift reintegration into society. (Frey 1982, 401)[7]

Even though Shakespeare's text gives no indication that Proteus interrupts his abuse of Silvia until Valentine steps forward to prevent him, Ostwald's Proteus ceases his rape attempt "of his own volition" and reconsiders the brutality of his attack. This hesitation depicts Proteus, not as a malicious villain, but as "a youth confused but well-intentioned" who simply lets his "ever-for-the-moment honest passions" overwhelm him. Through performance choices that soften Proteus's portrayal in the rape scene and elsewhere, Ostwald overcomes the reluctance of viewers to accept Proteus's "swift reintegration into society."

Another key to the theatrical recuperation of Proteus lies in the stage treatment of Proteus's repentance. Both Victor and Kemble rewrite Valentine's chastisement of Proteus to introduce Valentine's perception that Proteus's crimes deserve harsh punishment; also, both revisers enhance Proteus's penitent response with an acknowledgment that such punishment is appropriate. Kemble's alterations, more extensive than Victor's, begin at Shakespeare's 5.4.67:

> *Val.*   Who should be trusted now, when the right hand
> Is perjur'd to the bosom?—
> To die, but lightly expiates thy offence.

Pro.   My shame and guilt confound me.—
        Thy wrath is just; and I as freely suffer,
        As e'er I did commit: I merit death.
Val.   Go,—bear him from my sight;—and in my cave
        Await my further will.

                                                        (9:65)

Unlike Victor, who allows Valentine to complete his admonition before tacking on the warning, "Prepare for death" (1763, 52), Kemble cuts Valentine's speech off four and a half lines early, but he inserts Valentine's declaration that Proteus's death would barely make amends for the depth of his wrongdoing. Given that, in this rendition, Proteus's misdeeds consist of betraying Valentine by pursuing Silvia and threatening, but not carrying out, an intention to rape her, the death penalty may seem a little severe. The punitive overcompensation evident in both Victor's and Kemble's revision manifests the extent to which Shakespeare's refusal to consider punishing Proteus is viewed as a barrier to an audience's acceptance of his eventual pardon. While Kemble's Proteus alone admits to his enraged friend, "Thy wrath is just," Kemble is following Victor (1763, 52) when he interpolates Proteus's concession "I merit death" to end his apology. Despite the increased brevity of Proteus's speech of repentance, the addition of his assent to the strictness of Valentine's vengeance bolsters the possibility that spectators will ultimately approve his forgiveness. Finally, in Kemble, Valentine explicitly delays a final decision on Proteus's fate by ordering him imprisoned to await Valentine's "further will." This hesitation is clearly designed to remove the objectionable hastiness of Valentine's pardon in the original text and to replace it with a more deliberate contemplation of Proteus's punishment, which may make his later absolution more palatable.

Most nineteenth- and twentieth-century productions of *Two Gentlemen* striving for a forgivable Proteus have relied upon the skills of the performer to render his repentance speech credible to viewers. As Dale G. Priest claims, "a good actor, playing Proteus, could certainly exploit the spatial and temporal parameters of the theater to make his utterance of remorse believable and engaging" (1980, 32). Commonly, the actor also kneels to Valentine at some point during the speech;[8] in the BBC production directed by Don Taylor in 1983, a guilty Proteus weeps with shame at the discovery of his transgressions. A more inventive technique for soliciting an audience's pardon was employed in

director Bill Cain's 1989 Oregon Shakespeare Festival production. Alan C. Dessen remembers that this performance "started
with a four-minute induction that set up what followed . . . as
the retelling of the story (in the vein of the Ancient Mariner) by
an older, repentant Proteus" (1990, 357). Such a strategy tem-
pers a spectator's reaction to the young man's offenses throughout the play with the knowledge that, in his later years, Proteus
still regrets his crimes against Valentine, Julia, and Silvia. By
placing the entire action of *Two Gentlemen* within this frame,
Cain expands Shakespeare's repentance speech of less than five
lines into a lifetime of penitence for Proteus.

Michael Langham's 1957 production in Regency costumes at
the Old Vic hearkened back to Victor's and Kemble's early
adaptations by having Proteus offer to inflict the penalty of
death upon himself during his expression of contrition. Muriel
St. Clare Byrne records that the conclusion to this production
featured "a threat of suicide with a pistol by the repentant Proteus to give a plausible period cue for Valentine's offer to surrender Sylvia" (1957, 471). Even though this gesture may well
enhance an audience's sense of Proteus's remorse, Byrne's
comment suggests that a more influential reason for this choice
may have been to motivate Valentine's offer more believably for
a modern audience. Langham apparently assumes that twentieth-century spectators will accept that a man would give up his
mistress to save his best friend's life, but they will not believe
that he would do so simply to preserve the friendship. In fact,
producers and directors of all eras have sometimes chosen to
eliminate the offer from the play entirely or to allow the actor to
deliver the lines as inconspicuously as possible.[9] When Valentine's couplet is omitted, directors must then manufacture the
motivation for Julia's swoon, which, in the original text,
responds directly to Valentine's offer and leads eventually to the
revelation of her identity. Kemble, for example, makes Julia
react to Valentine's command that Proteus be taken off to await
execution:

> [*The Outlaws are taking* Proteus *away.*]
> Jul.   O me, unhappy! [*She faints*]
> Sil.   Look to the youth.[10]
> Val.   Why, boy, look up:—[*She recovers.*] What is the matter?
>   Speak.
> Jul.   Hold, hold awhile:—[*The Outlaws stop.*]

(9:65)

In this version of the scene, Julia's fainting spell serves to fore-stall the removal of Proteus to his captivity and punishment rather than to prevent him from possibly accepting Valentine's proposal. Such an alteration thereby effaces the need for the director to answer certain crucial staging questions: How does Proteus react to the gift of Silvia? Might he be willing to receive her? And how might an audience respond to him if he is?

Since nothing in the printed text tells us what Proteus thinks about his friend's gesture or how he reacts to it physically, any production that retains the offer must decide how the actor will use nonverbal means to communicate his response. The stan-dard theatrical strategy here is actually to have Proteus do noth-ing; if Julia's swoon follows hard upon Valentine's proposal before Proteus has a chance to react, the audience's attention will be quickly diverted away from the issue of his reply, and the sequence will have little effect upon a spectator's appraisal of Proteus.[11] However, in Ostwald's Oregon production the direc-tor employed stage business designed to convey Proteus's grow-ing maturity. Ostwald, in his own account of the performance, explains, "At this juncture, Shakespeare's stage directions fail us, but I assume that Proteus, having grown beyond his total self-centeredness, refuses Silvia and gives her hand back to Val-entine" (1982, 128). Later, the director provides a more detailed description of his staging: "Valentine then called Silvia to him and, after embracing her, offered her hand to Proteus. Julia, watching in panic, fainted. She, therefore, missed the moment in which Proteus refused Valentine's offer and returned Silvia's hand, placing it firmly into Valentine's" (132–33). Here Ostwald presumes that Proteus has already "grown beyond his self-cen-teredness"; so, the director invents stage business that will indi-cate this assumption to viewers and encourage them to admire Proteus's newfound unselfishness. In truth, it would be equally possible to assume that Proteus has not yet fully progressed beyond the inconsideration that allowed him to betray his friend and his lover, and therefore he might consider accepting Silvia from Valentine.[12] If Proteus were to move toward Silvia as if to take possession of Valentine's gift, only to be halted by Julia, who faints (not as a result of the offer, but as a conse-quence of its imminent acceptance), spectators might ultimately be less likely to endorse the justice of his forgiveness by Julia or by Valentine.

After Julia's swoon, both Victor and Kemble follow Shake-speare's business with the mistaken rings and Julia's revelation of her identity. Kemble, however, intensifies the effect of Julia's admonition by inserting an exchange between Valentine and Silvia as they observe Proteus's guilty response:

> Val. He's touch'd to the very soul.
> Sil. Mine pities them. (9:67)

Kemble presumably interpolates Silvia's expression of pity for Proteus and Julia to prepare for an upcoming change to the original text that occurs in both revisions. At the end of Proteus's speech apologizing for his inconstancy, Silvia, rather than Valentine, reconciles the two lovers, and she then proceeds to reunite the two friends. Victor renders the sequence as follows:

> Sil. Come, come, a hand from either—
>   [*She joins the hands of* Protheus *and* Julia; *and then takes the hand of* Valentine *to give to* Protheus.]
>   Let me be blest to make this happy close:
>   Nor must such friends as you be longer foes.
> Pro. If the poor penitent can be forgiven?
> Val. Forgiven, say'st thou? Ay—thus I am paid [*embracing him*]
>   And once again I do receive thee honest.
>
> (1763, 53)

Silvia's conduct of the ceremonial handfasting implies that she gives her blessing to the reunion of Proteus and Julia, as well as to the rebuilding of the friendship between the two men. Shakespeare's line, " 'Twere pity two such friends should be long foes" (5.4.117), which originally refers to Proteus and Julia, alludes instead, in Victor's edited version, to Proteus and Valentine. If Silvia, the victim of Proteus's assault, can forgive him sufficiently to endorse his reconciliation with his companion and former lover, then surely audiences will not withhold their own approval. By postponing Valentine's pardoning of Proteus until after Silvia endorses the renewal of the friendship and the betrothal, both Victor and Kemble attempt to amend Valentine's overhasty forgiveness in the original text.[13] Also, as Kurt Schlueter points out, "In both versions, the reconciliation between the friends is relegated from the central position in Shakespeare's last scene to a secondary matter, following the reconciliation between Julia and Proteus" (1990, 27). Like romantic comedies, rather than comedies of forgiveness, the adaptations of Victor and Kemble accent the primacy of male-female bonds over male homosocial relationships.

The penultimate lines of the two early revisions also indicate a shift in focus from friendship ties to heterosexual unions. While Shakespeare's play ends with Valentine's speech extolling matrimony as a means to reunite the two male friends in "one house, one mutual happiness," both Victor and Kemble award the final words of the play to Proteus, who reemphasizes his conversion from an inconstant suitor to a loyal, devoted lover. Victor ends the play by inserting the couplet: "A convert to this truth *I* stand confess'd, / That lovers must be faithful, to be bless'd" (1763, 55). Kemble expands this sententious moral into a seven-line appeal for forgiveness addressed in part toward the audience:

> Thanks, generous Valentine:—and I myself
> Will be the trumpet of my Julia's worth,
> Her stedfast faith, her still-enduring love,
> And of my own misdoings.—Pardon me,
> Ye who have ever known what't is to err!—
> And be this truth by all the world confest,
> That lovers must be faithful to be blest.
>
> (9:70)

In both interpolations, the stress falls upon Proteus as a man who has learned a lesson about true love rather than one who has learned to accommodate love to friendship. Moreover, Kemble's expansion explicitly asks for the pardon from viewers that Victor's revision also seeks; Proteus reminds spectators that they themselves have "known what't is to err" and therefore should forgive him his "misdoings."

Although contemporary directors seldom write their own curtain speeches for Shakespeare's characters, they do not hesitate to rearrange dialogue for purposes resembling those of Victor and Kemble. For instance, Gareth Morgan, directing *Two Gentlemen* at Stratford and for the Theatregoround Tour in 1969, transported Shakespeare's 5.4.118–19 to the end of the play so that the final lines the audience heard were

Pro. Bear witness, heaven, I have my wish for ever.
Jul. And I mine.

This relocation of Proteus and Julia's announcement of mutual fulfillment in love grants to their romantic union the special prominence that Shakespeare bestows upon Proteus's friendship bond with Valentine. Like Victor's and Kemble's added speeches, it also appeals to the audience for the forgiveness of Proteus, here based on the eternal happiness that he has brought to Julia. Morgan's production, like other revivals I have examined, displays a tendency toward the type of performance choices that romanticize marriage as opposed to those that illuminate the alliances between men that marriage enables.

However, since the beginning of the 1970s, an alternative trend toward performance choices that complicate the marital unions portrayed at the end of *Two Gentlemen* surfaces in various stage renditions. These productions pointedly concretize 5.4 of the printed text at many of the same places that their predecessors did, but with radically different aims and effects. Overall, they do not use theatrical elements to attempt to rehabilitate Proteus; rather, they make choices that highlight his culpability, render his penitence ambiguous, and throw doubt upon Julia's acceptance of his remorse.[14] These decisions seem calculated to bring the stage presentation of the marriage between Proteus and Julia more closely in line with a feminist reading of the play that emphasizes the problematic nature of their union. Although feminist critics were not the first to observe the troubling aspects of the play's dénouement, they were instrumental in bringing to light the ways in which the play's disconcerting actions occur as a result of a social system that joins men at the expense of women's self-determination. In several recent productions, the concluding moments of the play, particularly the exits of the characters after the final lines, leave a lasting impression of unstable or conflicted marital relationships, often the result of the primacy of the friendship between Valentine and Proteus. Such an ending, I would argue, more closely approaches a rendering of the significance of *Two Gentlemen* as a comedy of forgiveness than does a conclusion that presents both marriages as the ideal unions of romantic comedy.

In contrast to the productions of Victor, Kemble, and Ostwald, which softened the physical and sexual violence of Proteus's assault on Silvia, some late twentieth-century performances have dramatized the attack as violently and as explicitly as possible. Robert Cushman, reviewing Robin Phillips's 1970 RSC revival, writes of Proteus that, "by the end of this production his designs on Silvia amount to a graphically-staged attempted rape" (1970, 107). At Stratford eleven years later, under John Barton's direction, Silvia was forced to endure a "realistically-staged violent attack upon her by Proteus" (Schlueter 1990, 48). The most extreme example I have found of this tendency

toward graphic sexual violence occurred in an all-female production directed by Dolores Ringer at the University of Kansas
in 1989. Ringer's description of her version of the final scene
recalls that Proteus ripped off Silvia's cape, forced her to the
ground, and mounted her before Valentine intervened (1990,
3–4). Later references to this event allude to the incident as a
"rape" rather than merely a rape attempt.[15] If spectators are to
believe that Proteus's sexual crime is indeed committed, then
perhaps this staging goes as far beyond Shakespeare's conception of the brutality of the assault as Kemble's rendition falls
short of it. In any case, all three productions, through explicit
portrayals of this violent outburst, make it much more difficult
for audiences to pardon Proteus or to endorse the forgiveness
he is granted by Valentine and Julia, who witness the attack.

Valentine absolves Proteus of guilt on the basis of his admission of penitence, which, as we have seen, usually depends upon
the actor's ability to express contrition convincingly in order to
persuade spectators to acquiesce to his pardon. This process
has been complicated in a few recent performances, however,
by an actor's ambiguous delivery of Proteus's repentance
speech, which has left viewers in disagreement over the sincerity of his remorse and consequently their own response to his
forgiveness. For example, Paul Nelsen, in his review of the 1991
RSC production at the Swan Theater directed by David
Thacker, claims that actor Barry Lynch's equivocal recitation of
Proteus's lines made his later forgiveness by Julia and Valentine
appear unconscionable:

> Following Valentine's rebuke . . . Proteus stands silent and still in a
> suspended pause before confessing in plain, measured monotone,
> "My shame and guilt confounds me"—more embarrassed than con-
> trite. Is he truly repentant or again manipulating the moment? Hav-
> ing witnessed Proteus' duplicitous machinations . . . we may find
> such instant forgiveness of Proteus and his reunion with Julia as
> ponderously strange. Sympathizing with the women as victims, not
> objects, of desire, we receive the facile pardon and reconciliations
> of the love story as outrageous. (1991, 16)

Since Proteus has already shown a capacity for deceitful exploitation, Nelsen interprets this ambiguous expression of guilt as
another example of Proteus's "duplicitous machinations,"
which leads the reviewer to judge Proteus unworthy of forgiveness. Of course, this account of how audience members receive

Proteus's pardon assumes that other spectators also perceive Silvia and Julia primarily as victims of male desire, which is not necessarily the case. Peter Holland's account of the same sequence in the same production puts more emphasis on Silvia's physical response to Proteus's speech and therefore exhibits a diametrically opposed reading of the segment's effect on spectators:

> Barry Lynch left a colossal pause, showing Proteus considering the possibility of conning Valentine again, before finally resolving on genuine repentance. If the audience hesitated slightly as to the genuineness of the repentance—and Lynch's smirk was so beguiling that one had to have a moment's pause—it was Silvia's silent intercession, a calm gesture of moving towards Proteus, that reassured them. Her judgement that this man was worth forgiveness justified Valentine's generosity, a symbolic act of love and respect for Silvia as much as of friendship for Proteus, an act that re-established the male bonding through the pain of the scene as the earlier scenes had used emotional pain to unite the women. (1992, 128)

Although this account clearly notes both the ambiguity of Proteus's penitence and the "emotional pain" that Silvia and Julia have experienced, Holland's reading of the scene contradicts Nelsen's interpretation by asserting that Silvia's movement toward Proteus after his speech reassures the audience that he is "worth forgiveness." In its employment of Silvia to sanction the pardoning of Proteus, Thacker's staging recalls the strategies of Victor and Kemble, who reassigned to her Valentine's speech reuniting Proteus with Julia and interpolated her encouragement of Valentine's reconciliation with Proteus. But unlike the clear-cut speeches in the early adaptations, the import of Silvia's "calm gesture" of "silent intercession" in Thacker's version is itself ambiguous; for this reason, it may not have carried enough signifying power to outweigh the doubts raised by Proteus's equivocation in the minds of viewers like Nelsen.

A third description of Thacker's staging conflicts with the previous two in its depiction of Proteus's speech as an unambiguous indication of either sincerity or disingenuity depending on the particular performance. Robert Smallwood writes that, during Valentine's lament over his friend's betrayal,

> Proteus rose at " 'Mongst all foes, that a friend should be the worst," fiddled with his coat buttons, bowed his head, knelt. At some per-

formances that little enigmatic flicker of a smile seemed to be discernible before he began to speak. When it was, the repentance was clearly a pure sham, and they were all being duped; when it was not, we had genuine penitence and thus the possibility of a comic ending: extraordinary that a half millimeter flicker of the lip muscles should change a dramatic genre. (1992, 352)

According to Smallwood, who attended several performances of this production, Proteus's speech was unequivocal: on some nights, it was "clearly a pure sham" and on others, "they were all being duped." If Nelsen and Holland witnessed two different performances, their opposing interpretations can perhaps be explained by the fact that the stagings they saw and heard were not absolutely identical. As Smallwood points out, for him, a mere "half millimeter flicker of the lip muscles" changed the dramatic genre of this play in performance from a traditional comedy, with "genuine penitence" and "a comic ending," to something more complex, something closer to a comedy of forgiveness.

The question of the truthfulness of Proteus's repentance also arises in a review by Justin Shaltz of the 1994 Illinois Shakespeare Festival production of *Two Gentlemen* directed by Calvin MacLean:

As Proteus apologizes for his attempted rape of Silvia—perhaps sincerely, perhaps superficially—Silvia shakes her head at him, and she appears confident in Valentine's refusal. When he accepts the apology, she is open-mouthed with shock, and when Valentine offers her to Proteus in marriage, she swoons and faints. Similarly, Julia only grudgingly accepts Proteus' hand. (1994b, 35)

As in Thacker's production, MacLean's Proteus may or may not be sorry for his transgressions, and Silvia's response to his speech potentially directs the audience's response to it, but in this case, MacLean clearly intends to display Silvia's disbelief in the apology, disapproval of its acceptance by her lover, and astonishment at Valentine's proposal to relinquish her to Proteus. If spectators may be swayed to forgive Proteus based on the assent of Silvia, whom he has most seriously affronted, then conversely, her obvious dissatisfaction with Proteus's pardon ought to prompt viewers to resist granting their own approval to Valentine's generous forbearance. Shaltz's review subsequently adds that Julia consents to her own reunion with Proteus "only grudgingly," as if she too has significant doubts about whether or not he deserves her pardon.

The suggestion of Julia's reluctance to concur in the forgiveness of Proteus is another tactic commonly employed in productions mounted since the rise of feminism. In the 1984 revival of *Two Gentlemen* directed by Leon Rubin at Stratford, Ontario, Julia's disinclination to have confidence in Proteus's repentance was set up by performance choices earlier in the play, most prominently at Proteus's departure from Verona. As Roger Warren recollects,

> Julia and Proteus play their farewell scene in bed; their affair has gone so much further than in most productions at this point that even more than usual seems at stake when Proteus betrays her. After that harsh experience, she becomes hard-bitten and resentful, consistent with the society created by the production, less so with the text. (1984, 1056)

Rubin's implication that Proteus and Julia have already engaged in sexual activity leads Warren to consider Proteus's betrayal of Julia a more serious offense than it appears in other productions;[16] it also leads him to understand how such treachery might make Julia "hard-bitten and resentful" towards her lover. Warren finds the consequences of this performance choice internally consistent, but not entirely consonant with Shakespeare's text. Indeed, Warren points out that Rubin displays a willingness, fairly rare in twentieth-century productions of the play, to rewrite the printed text for his own purposes:

> Valentine's notorious speech of forgiveness at the end is altered to make it clear that he is not simply handing Silvia over to Proteus: here he says "all my love to Silvia I also give to thee." The two men embrace, watched in distrust by the girls. It becomes a dark ending, with no easy resolution. (1056)

Rubin's revision appears calculated to remove the notion, distressing to many viewers, that Valentine has the right to surrender Silvia to another man and would actually exercise it. Yet by retaining the line in revised form rather than cutting it, Rubin also suggests that Valentine prizes his friendship with Proteus as highly as his love for Silvia. The embrace between Valentine and Proteus that follows emphasizes the emotional depth of their relationship, which provokes in Julia and Silvia the suspicion that the male bond represents a threat to the primacy of heterosexual ties. Such a staging leads the play to "a dark ending" rather than the "easy resolution" of romantic comedy.

Eight years later, Marti Maraden's directorial effort with the Young Company at the Stratford Festival in Canada also prepared for Julia's hesitation to reconcile with Proteus through the staging of an earlier scene, this time Proteus's unsuccessful serenading of Silvia observed by Julia in disguise. C. E. McGee remembers that, at the end of the play,

> the harmony of Silvia and Valentine was not shared by Proteus and Julia. She reluctantly took the hand of Proteus when Valentine tried to "make this happy close" (l. 117), and the sense that Julia and Proteus's relationship was slightly strained persisted until the very end. That was as it should be, given 4.2, the blocking of which made Julia the center of interest. While Proteus . . . wooed Silvia in a gallery upstage left, Julia—downstage center—spoke with the Host. Shifting the focus to Julia, an effect that I had not seen in any production of this play directed by a man, established forcefully the impact on Julia of Proteus's betrayal, the effects of which still resonated in the finale. (1993, 483)

Because Maraden's blocking in 4.2 highlights the anguish of Julia at Proteus's treachery, McGee certifies that Julia's resistance to being reunited with her unfaithful lover is "as it should be." Therefore, despite the harmony achieved by the couple featured in the romantic comedy plotline, the reviewer can also accept the strain that persists between the Griselda and the Forgiven Comic Hero. Significantly, McGee attributes this unique perspective on 4.2 and its effect on the final scene to the fact that this production was directed by a woman; however, as we have seen, certain modern male directors also manifest in their performance choices a sympathetic approach to Julia's dilemma and an unwillingness to encourage audiences to let Proteus entirely off the hook.

As a final example of this particular tendency, let us consider director Jack Shepherd's handling of the responses to Proteus's repentance speech in his 1996 production during the Prologue Season at Shakespeare's Globe Theatre:

> Valentine . . . notably breaks equanimity on "All that was mine in Silvia I give thee" (5.4.83), shouting ironically as he rebuffs Proteus' supplication and throws him to the floor. And on the floor Proteus remains as Julia shows him the ring and drops her disguise. Julia and Proteus sustain an embrace through the Duke's subsequent

dialogue, but . . . Julia conveyed a sense of ambivalence about her reunion with Proteus and the prospects of "one mutual happiness" in marriage. Their final exit trails the beaming departure of the others as a diminished shadow. (Nelsen 1997, 7)

Like Rubin, who neutralizes the objectionable quality of Valentine's offer by rewriting it, Shepherd transforms the meaning of the line by having his actor deliver it ironically while physically rejecting both Proteus and his apology. Julia then faintly echoes Valentine's harsh rebuff by manifesting "a sense of ambivalence" about her reconciliation with Proteus, which casts doubt upon their future felicity as a married couple. As in Maraden's production, Silvia and Valentine celebrate a harmonious reunion, capped by a "beaming" departure, but Shepherd's Proteus and Julia trail the rest of the characters off the stage "as a diminished shadow," a deflated imitation of their buoyant counterparts.

Shepherd's management of his production's final exit resembles the blocking employed in several late twentieth-century productions in that it attempts to color the audience's ultimate response to the two couples through the manner in which they withdraw from the stage. Since the advent of feminism, directors have commonly orchestrated these exits to imply that the reconstructed bond between the two gentlemen has tarnished or seriously damaged the ties between the two pairs of lovers. Thus, such renditions highlight the friction between homosocial and heterosexual relationships and deny audiences the agreeable visions of impending marital bliss favored by nineteenth- and early twentieth-century performances. For example, in a promptbook based on Charles Kean's 1846 production at New York's Park Theater later annotated by George Becks, there appears, after the final line of the play, the notation "They kiss their ladies & all turn to go" (1890s, 59). Likewise, the promptbook for B. Iden Payne's Stratford revival inserts the final stage direction, "Couples kiss, girls kiss, men shake, exit arm in arm" (1938, 295). In both instances, the kisses between the couples signify the fulfillment of their shared erotic desire in marriage, and their collective exits represent their embarkation on a new life of "mutual happiness." Payne's version of this business also suggests, through the women's embrace and the men's handshake, that the same-sex bonds created or renewed during the play will have no negative impact upon the marital unions solemnized after the conclusion of the action.

On the contrary, performances of *Two Gentlemen* since the beginning of the 1970s generally have not indicated an idyllic future lying ahead for the two sets of lovers. Judith Cook records that, in Robin Phillips's RSC production, "the two couples were left as the curtain fell, staring crossways at each other as if they might change their minds" (1983, 21). Peter Thomson recalls more specifically the way in which Valentine's reading of the concluding line augmented the suspicions aroused by this final stage picture:

> The play ends with a tableau . . . following Valentine's portentous delivery of the final speech. He phrases the last line in such a way as to cast doubt on the prospect it promises: "One feast, one house, one mutual (*pause*) happiness (*with an interrogatory vocal rise*)." Robin Phillips, the director, brought to the play a sense of humour and a dangerous desire to analyse its presentation of adolescent sexual confusion. (1971, 121)

Phillips's "dangerous" treatment of adolescent sexual confusion is manifested primarily in the "unclarified sexual preferences" of Proteus, who demonstrates a propensity to admire the well-developed body of Valentine displayed in modern beachwear (Schlueter 1990, 47). Thus, any doubts about the future happiness of the two couples raised by Valentine's delivery of the final line are rooted in the competing homoerotic component of the friendship between the two gentlemen. Through different means, John Barton's 1981 Stratford production also hinted that the male bond might complicate the married lives of the newlyweds. Schlueter notes that, near the end of the play, "Silvia went off in the company of her father, leaving Valentine alone for his last lines with Proteus" (48). In the visual context of Barton's staging, these final lines celebrate a double wedding that unites the two gentlemen, but does not necessarily bring their future spouses within the sphere of their "one mutual happiness."

Barton's decision to stagger the characters' final exit draws special attention to the bond between Valentine and Proteus, but it does not attempt to create a corresponding sense of solidarity between the two maltreated women. On the other hand, several other recent productions have exploited the indeterminacy of the final stage direction "*Exeunt*" to pair up the four main figures along gender lines rather than by loving couples. Critic and director John Low argues that such an arrangement is in fact consistent with Shakespeare's text:

I feel that the concluding lines call for a grouping of the two men together, separate from the women, before the couples are brought together again for their final exeunts. As an alternative to the exeunts in betrothed couples, however, it would be well in accordance with the tone of the play (within which Valentine's gesture in offering Silvia to Proteus may be seen as part of the design) for the two wronged women to move off together, leaving the men to make their final exeunt together. (1974, 85–86)

In 1978, four years after the publication of Low's remarks, director Daniel Sullivan pursued this alternative staging in his production (featuring a young Tom Hanks as Proteus) at the Great Lakes Shakespeare Festival. Lester Barber recounts one of the "farcical" aspects of the ending to this performance:

As the lovers were properly paired off, Valentine and Proteus started off stage, arm in arm, almost forgetting the ladies entirely. When they remembered and returned, Silvia and Julia turned the tables by suddenly linking arms and marching off together themselves, to the dumbfounded stares of their mates (1979, 213)

By having the two gentlemen start their exit together, "almost forgetting the ladies entirely," Sullivan underlines both the strength of their friendship and its lingering threat to the heterosexual relationships, which reoccur to the men only as an afterthought. Distinct from Barton's staging, Sullivan's version also suggests, through the women's physically unified exit, that Silvia and Julia do not intend to stand idly by if their future spouses continue to place friendship before love. In spite of these separate departures, however, the comic tone of the segment implies that the conflict between same-sex and opposite-sex bonds is not insurmountable.

The significance of this comic treatment becomes more evident when we compare the effects created by MacLean's physically similar but tonally distinct blocking of this sequence in 1994. Shaltz's review of this production, after its account of Julia's grudging acceptance of Proteus's ambiguous repentance, continues with a description of the play's final moments:

When Valentine concludes the play with a blithely vigorous "One mutual happiness!", the men cheer and jubilantly exit the stage, ignorant of the wounded feelings of the ladies. Valentine and Proteus are followed offstage by . . . the Outlaws, Thurio, and the Duke, but Julia and Silvia stay behind. The women appear stunned as they sit together on a tree-log at centerstage. Valentine and Proteus return moments later, smiling and holding their arms out to them as if nothing has happened. Julia and Silvia stand and walk away, then turn and glare fiercely at the men. The lights go out, and the consequences of the romantic escapades are made vividly apparent, thwarting the expected happy ending. (1994b, 35)

While this blocking closely resembles that of Sullivan's production, MacLean's variation sets a more ponderous tone through its contrast between the jubilation of the men and the anger of their betrothed brides. The women are dazed by the lack of concern that Proteus and Valentine display over the emotional wounds they have inflicted, and when the two gentlemen propose an embrace "as if nothing has happened," Julia and Silvia spurn their offer. In place of imminent marriages and "the expected happy ending" of romantic comedy, MacLean substitutes an unhappy conclusion focusing on the plight of women whose lovers actually care more for each other than they do for their prospective spouses.

Somewhere between the lighthearted spirit of Sullivan's ending and the disillusioned mood of MacLean's final sequence falls the tone of the conclusion to Marti Maraden's revival, which also stresses the men's obliviousness to the ways in which their intense camaraderie threatens the survival of their marital bonds. McGee writes of Maraden's production,

> Her interpretation of the play emphasized the tension between the claims of friendship and those of love. This tension resurfaced even at the end of the play, when Valentine and Proteus celebrated the prospect of "One feast, one house, one mutual happiness" (5.4.173) by hugging one another; noticing the surprised looks of Silvia and Julia (which exchange got a big laugh from audiences), the men cut short their embrace in order to pair off with the women. (1993, 483)

Kenneth Steele adds that "the final moments of the production returned to the 'problem' of the women with a vengeance: as Proteus . . . and Valentine . . . reached out their arms lovingly, the ladies stood absolutely motionless and the lights dimmed to blackness" (1992, 15). In this staging, the hug between Valentine and Proteus, interrupted by Julia and Silvia's astonishment at their exclusion from the closing harmony, provokes laughter from the audience, but no less awareness of the "tension between the claims of friendship and those of love" than MacLean's more troubling conclusion. Like MacLean, Maraden directs her two gentlemen to offer a conciliatory embrace to their mistresses to make up for their earlier disregard, but unlike MacLean, Maraden calls upon the women to forego outright rejection in favor of an entirely ambiguous response. While we may suppose that Sullivan's lovers probably work out their differences, and MacLean's couples probably do not, we simply cannot predict the outlook for Maraden's pairs with any assurance based on her production's final tableau.

Recent productions of *Two Gentlemen* that focus on the threat posed by male bonds to marital relationships sometimes darken the tone of the ending of the play to the extent that the performance no longer seems comic at all. If a production, like MacLean's, denies audiences a happy ending by inferring that no wedding takes place, or if another production, like many we have examined, so thoroughly problematizes the marriages that do occur that viewers cannot endorse them, can that performance still be described as a comedy? Certainly, if the definition of comedy depends solely on the culmination of the action in joyous matrimony for all the lovers, then a performance of *Two Gentlemen* as a comedy of forgiveness will never meet that criterion. However, a broader definition might encompass the possibility that some types of comedy, notably satire, accomplish their comic effects through the humorous ridicule of human folly, a strategy that is not incompatible with a performance of *Two Gentlemen* that seeks to illuminate the ways in which male friendship complicates heterosexual love. Maraden's production, which evokes "a big laugh from audiences" when Valentine and Proteus notice the surprised looks of Julia and Silvia, turns good-natured satirical laughter against the men's preoccupation with the formation of male bonds. As a alternative to the dark endings of some recent revivals, I propose a staging of the final moments of *Two Gentlemen* that employs satire as the means to accent the "comedy" in the comedy of forgiveness.

One element of the model narrative of the comedy of forgiveness slighted by the stagings of the last scene of *Two Gentlemen* surveyed to this point is the alliance created between the Forgiven Comic Hero and the Authority figure by the marriage of Proteus's friend Valentine to Silvia, the Duke's daughter. Although many recent productions spotlight the conflicting claims of friendship and love, none of these performances give equal weight to the ways in which the play strives to reincorporate Proteus into the Duke's coterie of gentlemen at the cost of Silvia's and Julia's self-determination. The opportunity to underscore this aspect of Shakespeare's text occurs just before the end of the play, after the Duke, at Valentine's request, pardons the gentleman outlaws:

Duke. Come, let us go, we will include all jars,
       With triumphs, mirth, and rare solemnity.
Val.   And as we walk along, I dare be bold
       With our discourse to make your grace to smile.
       What think you of this page, my lord?
Duke. I think the boy hath grace in him, he blushes.
Val.   I warrant you, my lord, more grace than boy.
Duke. What mean you by that saying?
Val.   Please you, I'll tell you, as we pass along,
       That you will wonder what hath fortuned.
       Come, Proteus, 'tis your penance but to hear
       The story of your loves discovered.

(5.4.158–69)

At the start of my projected staging of this sequence, the Duke, from center stage, calls to Valentine, who leads Silvia over to her father, where both men place one arm around her shoulders from either side in a gesture that links the Duke and his future son-in-law through the body of Silvia. As they "walk along," Valentine guides all three toward the side of the stage where Proteus stands with Julia, who blushes at being introduced to the Duke for the first time dressed in her disguise. Valentine and Proteus share a condescending laugh at Julia's embarrassment and the Duke's inability to perceive her femininity, forgetting that they themselves were similarly ignorant until only moments ago. At "Come, Proteus," Valentine calls his friend over to join him and the Duke, and the three men proceed offstage together, followed by the Outlaws, as they happily anticipate the prospect of "one mutual happiness." Watching the clan of gentlemen exit, Silvia and Julia stare after them, flabbergasted at being left behind without a thought. Julia then looks at Silvia, and, recalling the manner in which both of them have been treated, removes the ring given to her by Proteus and hands it over to Thurio, who has been left behind as unfit for the company of gentlemen. Silvia, after a moment's hesitation and a mischievous smile at Julia, takes off Valentine's betrothal ring, presses it upon Thurio, then urges him with a gesture to return both bands to the two gentlemen. Thurio exits. Julia grabs Silvia's hand, and the two giggling women run offstage together in a different direction from the men. After a moment

of empty stage time, Valentine and Proteus race across the platform after the ladies, holding out the rings, and the lights
quickly fade to black.

This blocking, as opposed to those described in reviews of
other versions of the play's conclusion, recognizes that the Duke
plays an active role in the dialogue of the closing segment and
in the formation of bonds between men achieved through matrimony. Such a staging stresses that Valentine's marriage to Silvia binds him to his lord, while his friendship with Proteus also
brings the Forgiven Comic Hero into the elite society of gentlemen. Silvia and Julia, although they serve as crucial links in the
chain of affiliation, are largely ignored in the construction of this
alliance, and a feminist production might try to elicit an adverse
reaction to this oversight rather than to reproduce it without
interrogation. But unlike performances that cloud the ending of
the play, the enactment I offer maintains a more humorous
tone, attempting to draw satirical laughter at the men's insensi-
tivity to the women's dismay at being taken so thoroughly for
granted. The business with the rings at the end of the sequence
also reframes the status of the marriages between the two couples. Julia and Silvia's giggling exit implies that they are playing
a prank on their future husbands as punishment for their inat-
tentive behavior, and the double wedding will occur only after
Valentine and Proteus endure a more extensive penance for
their tactless behavior. This sort of enactment, I would assert,
more closely approaches a conclusion to a comedy of forgiveness in that it illuminates the main features of the model narrative without sacrificing either the promise of marriages or the
ironic comic spirit that pervades the play.

Stage productions of *The Two Gentlemen of Verona* need not
whitewash the character of Proteus in order to present a theatrical experience that will delight and instruct their audiences. A
more complex portrayal of the Forgiven Comic Hero, one that
gives equal weight to his vices and virtues, can elucidate the
ways in which an overvaluation of male bonds creates problems
for women in heterosexual relationships, and an ironic attitude
toward male follies can also prevent such an emphasis from
becoming oppressive or polemical. As an example of this desirable balance, I present Schlueter's description of the ending of
Langham's 1957 revival at the Bristol Old Vic: "The play's difficult dénouement was to provide the climax for satiric laughter,
a climax that was not reached when Valentine offered to
renounce his bride but when Proteus formulated his newly won

insight that man would be perfect if only he were constant" (1990, 43). Although this production predates the advent of feminism, its satiric treatment of Proteus's acknowledgement of his primary shortcoming accomplishes some aspects of a feminist project. The emphasis on Proteus's acceptance of constancy underscores a crucial aspect of the play as a comedy of forgiveness, while the concurrent disparity between Proteus's long list of faults and his otherwise "perfect" self-evaluation raises the biggest laugh of the scene. The ridicule directed at Proteus's foolish self-estimate discourages spectators from reenacting in their own lives the type of self-deception that allows a man to betray so severely both friendship and courtship practices.

Chapter 3

"Get thee a wife, get thee a wife!":
Much Ado about Nothing

> Shakespeare must have been a strange sort of dramatist to
> give the lovely and innocent Hero to an unworthy person; . . .
> then either Shakespeare was an inept dramatist, or Claudio
> should appear . . . an admirable hero on the evidence of the
> play itself, with no other witness needed, then or now. . . .
> Claudio . . . is not a brazen figure, but a golden one. Thus a
> genuinely happy ending of the comedy is possible. . . . We
> wreck Shakespeare's work if we fling mud at Claudio.
>
> (Schoff 1959, 12, 22)

THE PROBLEM OF CLAUDIO DIVIDES CRITICS OF *MUCH ADO ABOUT Nothing* into two camps. On the one hand, Claudio's detractors assert that Shakespeare intends to create a typical romantic hero who is deceived, acts badly, repents his error, and earns forgiveness. But Shakespeare, they argue, makes the Count far too callous in his repudiation of Hero and less than convincing in his apology, with the result that one can neither sympathize with Claudio nor rejoice at his reacquisition of his bride.[1] On the other hand, Claudio's supporters postulate that Shakespeare successfully creates a congenial romantic lead whose actions, though not entirely blameless, have been unfairly condemned by modern readers and audiences unfamiliar with Elizabethan social and literary conventions that excuse his behavior. Consequently, one may easily misjudge Claudio unless one witnesses a performance attuned to these conventions or imagines the details of such a production as one reads.[2] As A. R. Humphreys summarizes the pro-Claudio position: "He is doubtless meant for a brave, inexperienced youth, shocked out of romantic devotion by an unsuspected and cunning enemy and, himself a wounded victim, not overblameworthy for his appalling error, and so not disqualified for future happiness. Yet to convey this needs sensitive skill" (1981, 54).

76

A variety of circular reasoning creeps into this argument when performance is used to justify the portrait of Claudio that is "doubtless meant." Critics on both sides agree that the Count's words and actions have the potential to alienate readers and viewers, but Claudio's defenders assert that, if performed with "sensitive skill," these same words and actions can instead draw sympathy to Claudio and accomplish his redemption.[3] Theater history provides ample evidence that such a staging may indeed attain this objective, but the fact that a particular characterization of Claudio "works" on the stage does not prove that such a portrayal was "intended" by Shakespeare. When directors assume that *Much Ado* is a romantic comedy with a clear-cut happy ending, and that any textual matter running counter to this assumption must be neutralized or removed, they will inevitably produce a script with the same comfortable closure that they presuppose. However, it is not necessarily a desecration of Shakespeare (as Francis G. Schoff asserts above) to portray Claudio as something less than a "golden" figure. Lovely and innocent women do sometimes marry unworthy men, in real life as well as in the theater, and *Much Ado* can be performed in such a way that the forces that orchestrate such matches are revealed and questioned.

Of the four comedies of forgiveness, *Much Ado* comes closest to matching the patterns outlined in the model narrative, but there are a few important areas of dissimilarity that distinguish it from the other plays. First, the Forgiven Comic Hero never experiences any sort of romantic attraction to the Shrew. Unlike Proteus, who forsakes Julia for Silvia, Claudio's repudiation of the Griselda, Hero, is not caused or followed by a competing attachment to her cousin Beatrice. Second, the traits of the Authority figure, represented in *Two Gentlemen* by the Duke of Milan, are divided in *Much Ado* between Don Pedro, the Prince of Aragon, and Leonato, the Governor of Messina and father of Hero. In contrast to the Duke, neither the Prince nor the Governor resembles the Senex of romantic comedy; instead, Don Pedro and Leonato both operate as matchmakers, striving originally to bring Hero and Claudio together in marriage and then later to reunite them after their broken nuptials. Finally, in *Much Ado*, Hero suffers just as much shame and degradation as her counterparts in the other comedies, but it is not as clear as it is in the other plays that the Griselda's love for the Forgiven Comic Hero is what gives her the strength to endure these indignities. On the contrary, Hero's dutiful obedience to her father may be the primary cause of her willingness to endure public humiliation and eventual marriage to the man who has disgraced her. These features, (especially Hero's unarticulated motives for matrimony) require different theatrical strategies for the recuperation of Claudio than were necessary to gain the audience's forgiveness of Proteus. Although productions commonly endeavor to reduce the Count's level of blameworthiness for his actions and to amplify the emotional intensity of his penitence, they also attempt to insinuate, on Hero's part, both a depth of feeling for Claudio and an overt acceptance of his repentance that are absent from the printed text.

Moreover, the thematic focus of *Much Ado* proceeds on to the next stage in the channeling of male erotic desire toward socially sanctioned objectives. While *Two Gentlemen* accents Proteus's difficulty in displaying constancy toward a single object of affection, the male characters in *Much Ado* have no trouble settling on one romantic partner. Rather, the changeability exhibited by Claudio consists of a failure to remain constant in his trust for the woman upon whom he has fixed his affections. [Claudio, like all the males of Messina, mistrusts women due to their ability to emasculate and dehumanize men by turning them into cuckolds.] Therefore, the Count and his mates, as they reach marriageable age, face contradictory social imperatives, similar to the mimetic double bind encountered by Proteus and Valentine. If Claudio and Benedick wish to enter the male hierarchy as patriarchs, they must marry and produce legitimate heirs to perpetuate the status quo.[4] However, by marrying, a man places his masculinity in the keeping of a woman, who has the power to unman him by turning him into a horned beast or eunuch. As Coppélia Kahn notes,

> For a Shakespearean hero, to be betrayed by a woman . . . is to be humiliated and dishonored, and thus placed in a position of vulnerability that makes him psychologically like a castrated man. . . . To defend against the fear of such castration, men anticipate it in fantasy, and turn it against women by calling them whores. (1981, 132)

Claudio's ready acceptance of Don John's Vice-like slanders against Hero's virtue demonstrates the fragility of the Count's trust in the sexual fidelity of women.[5] To combat this suspicion, Claudio must be returned to a state of confidence in Hero's virginity sufficient to allow him to brave the threat of cuckoldry and become a patriarch. Furthermore, the play stresses that, even though the wives of Claudio and Benedick may still play them false, they may take solace in the renewal of their male bond, lodged in what Kahn calls "the brotherhood of all married men as potential if not actual cuckolds" (124).

The opening sequence of *Much Ado* establishes the atmosphere of male camaraderie between the Forgiven Comic Hero and his Friend, Benedick, within a military context. Beatrice asks Don Pedro's messenger about Benedick: "Who is his companion now? He hath every month a new sworn brother." The messenger replies, "He is most in the company of the right noble Claudio" (1.1.65–66, 76–77). Beatrice also questions Benedick's success in the recent defeat of Don John's rebellion, characterizing Benedick as a type of *miles gloriosus*: "I pray you, how many hath he killed and eaten in these wars? But how many hath he killed? For indeed I promised to eat all of his killing" (1.1.38–41). The phrase "eat all of his killing" proverbially evokes the figure of the braggart soldier,[6] and although Benedick's later courageous actions prove the untruth of this characterization, he does swagger through the first half of the play with an inflated military disdain for affairs of the heart. Once Claudio betroths himself to Hero, Benedick laments his friend's new preference for "the tabor and the pipe" to "the drum and the fife" and "the fashion of a new doublet" to a suit of "good armour" (2.3.13–18). Claudio's decision to wed poses a serious danger to the male camaraderie of war, and Benedick's jibes against marriage represent an effort to defend these male bonds against female insurgence.

Therefore, when Claudio first reveals his desire to make Hero his wife, Benedick warns him against it, citing the fear of cuckoldry as one of the drawbacks of marriage. According to Benedick, any man who weds will "wear his cap with suspicion" (1.1.184), plagued by doubts that his wife has entertained other lovers. If Claudio marries, Benedick says, the Count will effectively "thrust [his] neck into a yoke, wear the print of it and sigh away Sundays" (1.1.186–87). The yoke, part of the traditional emblem of matrimony (see Figure 2), represents the way in which marriage robs a husband of his manhood by turning him into an animal, for "what joins husband and wife together is also what degrades the man to the level of a dumb, yoked beast—the destiny of being a cuckold" (Kahn 1981, 125). Benedick claims to disdain such a fate for Claudio and for himself as well:

M A T R I M O N I O.

Figure 2—Matrimonio, with yoke and clog, a woodcut from Cesare Ripa's
Iconologia **(1603).**

D. Pedro. "In time the savage bull doth bear the yoke."
Bene.   The savage bull may; but if ever the sensible Benedick
          bear it, pluck off the bull's horns and set them in my
          forehead . . . and in such great letters as they write,
          "Here is good horse to hire," let them signify under my
          sign, "Here you may see Benedick, the married man."
          (1.1.241–45)

The "savage bull" is the play's image for the virile, unmarried
man who follows his sexual impulses without restraint. In time,
however, all men are expected to "bear the yoke," to enter the
state of matrimony and confine their sexual activity to one
approved partner.[7] "The sensible Benedick" resists this social
imperative, he says, because marriage, by making him liable to
become a cuckold, reduces him to a domesticated beast, the
equivalent of a "good horse to hire."

Benedick's fears of cuckoldry and emasculation through marriage tend to be confirmed by Beatrice, whom Don Pedro has picked out as "an excellent wife for Benedick" (2.1.329). Unlike her modest cousin Hero, Beatrice speaks openly and sharply of her preferences in a spouse, which draws the disapproval of her uncles Leonato and Antonio, who complain that she is "shrewd of [her] tongue" and "too curst" (2.1.17–18). These remarks clearly cast her, within the model narrative, in the part of the Shrew, whose scolding voice alienates (and yet provokes) potential suitors. Beatrice herself implies that, were she to marry, she would make her partner a cuckold, for she claims that she will have "no horns" only if God sends her "no husband" (2.1.23–24). Beatrice swears that she "could not endure" a masculine spouse, "a husband with a beard on his face" (2.1.26–27), but "a husband that hath no beard," who is therefore "less than a man," is only fit to be dressed in women's apparel and employed as her "waiting-gentlewoman" (2.1.29–33). Here Beatrice envisions herself as a version of Omphale, the mythological queen into whose service Hercules was sold as a slave and with whom he fell in love. Omphale is most notorious for dressing Hercules in women's garments and setting him to spin among her maids while taking from him his lion's skin and club (Mares 1988, 75n; Humphreys 1981, 122n). Therefore, despite the fact that Hercules serves as Messina's paragon of masculinity,[8] he also stands as a prominent example of a man effeminized and debased through the act of falling in love with a woman and putting his manhood under her control.

[Benedick's tirades against Beatrice as a potential spouse demonstrate that he perceives her in much the same fashion that she describes herself, a danger to her husband's masculinity.] His contention that Beatrice "would have made Hercules have turned spit, yea, and have cleft his club to make the fire too" (2.1.236–38) echoes Beatrice's allusion to herself as Omphale by evoking a similar image of Hercules, emasculated and degraded to the lowest of household servants, the turnspit (Humphreys 1981, 122n). Although Benedick claims that he "cannot endure my Lady Tongue," who, like a shrew, "speaks poniards" (2.1.257–58, 231), Beatrice's ability to match verbal wits with Benedick also arouses his desire for her. Nineteenth-century producers, troubled by the fact that Benedick, without any prompting, suddenly declares, "I would not marry her" (2.1.234–35), sometimes inserted a command from Don Pedro ("Benedick Marry her") before this vow to provide the speaker with a "logical" reason for his puzzling non sequitur.[9] Surely, however, this addition obscures the main point, that Benedick has been thinking about marrying Beatrice all along.

Don Pedro's plot to match Benedick with Beatrice turns out to be easier to carry out than he expects because, not only does Benedick harbor a secret love for Beatrice, but he also places more confidence in the sexual fidelity of women than his anti-feminist remarks would suggest. Alone among the soldiers, Benedick maintains a steadfast faith in Hero's virtue when her honor is called into question by Don John's slanders. This disparity derives from the fact that Benedick's misogyny is merely a verbal stance assumed for the pleasure of his companions. In response to Claudio's inquiries about Hero, Benedick's criticisms of her spring more from "custom" than from natural inclination (Mulryne 1965, 52), for as he admits, he simply poses as a "professed tyrant to their sex," in opposition to his "simple true judgement" (1.1.155–57). Beatrice's later depiction of Benedick as "the Prince's jester" cuts him so deeply because it borders so closely on the truth: he *is* a type of allowed fool in that he regularly makes Don Pedro (and Claudio) laugh by expressing his scorn for the institution of marriage. The Prince endures this criticism of the social structure partly out of eager anticipation that Benedick will "fall from this faith" and "prove a notable argument" against future nonconformity (1.1.236–37). Benedick's outward insubordination offers Don Pedro a chance to display his power to enforce submission, which he accomplishes through his authoritative role as a matchmaker.

Don Pedro has less success, however, in compelling the conformity of his brother Don John, who acts as a "matchbreaker" (Mueschke and Mueschke 1967, 54), aggressively undermining the patriarch's power to arrange matrimonial bonds. Alison Findlay suggests that Don John's unprovoked opposition to the union of Claudio and Hero "smacks of an antipathy to the institution of marriage. As a bastard, he is naturally inclined towards the unnatural destruction of social and spiritual bonds" (1994, 104). Himself a product of an illegitimate birth, Don John is living proof of women's proclivity for sex outside of marriage.[10] He also "really holds that view of marriage which Benedick only 'professes' ": the notion that matrimony inevitably brings with it the hazard of cuckoldry (Craik 1953, 300). When informed by his man Borachio of an impending wedding, Don John asks, "What is he for a fool that betroths himself to unquietness?" (1.3.44–45). Before he knows the identities of the bride and groom, Don John presumes that the husband has bound himself to a life of constant anxiety over the faithfulness of his wife. Despite the similarity of this sentiment to Benedick's claim that a married man must "wear his cap with suspicion," Don John's cynicism derives from a sincere antagonism to wedlock, in contrast to Benedick's pretended opposition to marriage, which he ultimately discards.

Don Pedro's matchmaking plot offers Benedick an opportunity to disavow his professed aversion to marriage while promoting his sense of masculinity. In an analysis of the gulling scenes (2.3 and 3.1), Jean Howard demonstrates how the strategies employed by Don Pedro and his conspirators in their attempts to fool Benedick and Beatrice into falling in love complete "their successful interpolation into particular positions within a gendered social order." While Beatrice is chastised for shrewish disdain and pride, which preclude her proper submission to the male authority of a husband, Benedick is persuaded to become the protector and master of his beloved. As Howard argues,

> Leonato and his friends construct [Beatrice] as a vulnerable, pitiful victim. Her tears, her sleeplessness, her indecision—all are dwelt on in loving detail. The role mapped for Benedick is to be her rescuer, to become more "manly" by accepting his duty to succor women as well as to fight wars. (1987, 178)

Despite the threat of emasculation posed by cuckoldry, marriage offers men various avenues to "become more 'manly,'" including the mastering of a woman and the fathering of legitimate heirs. Benedick justifies to himself the apparent hypocrisy of his sudden resolution to marry by disguising his straightforward desire for love as the acceptance of a higher social duty to procreate: "Shall quips and sentences and these paper bullets of the brain awe a man from the career of his humour? No, the world must be peopled" (2.3.231–34). The irony of this passage derives partly from the way in which Benedick characterizes his about-face as an individualistic choice that he will pursue in spite of the ridicule of his friends, even though readers and audiences know that Don Pedro and company have themselves initiated Benedick's determination to wed and reproduce. Benedick's pompous self-deception humorously illustrates the means by which society convinces men to confront the perils of marriage in fulfillment of their masculine obligation to perpetuate the social system.

After a brief encounter with Beatrice at the end of the gulling scene, Benedick exits with the parting remark, "I will go get her picture" (2.3.254). Editors usually take this comment literally and assume that Benedick intends to "commission an ornamental miniature" of Beatrice (Zitner 1993, 138n). Director Michael Kahn, in his 1992 production of *Much Ado*, reinforced this interpretation by introducing the picture as a prop in 5.2: "Benedick appeared sporting an enormous medallion containing a portrait of Beatrice around his neck. He showed it to the audience and gestured confidently, as if to say, 'This'll wow her!' " (Johnson-Haddad 1992, 461). Such a reading equates Benedick's resolution with the desire of Proteus in *Two Gentlemen* to possess the "picture that is hanging in [Silvia's] chamber" (4.2.118); but unlike that portrait, which figures in the exchange between Silvia and Julia in 4.4, the picture of Beatrice is never mentioned again. Instead, Benedick may be speaking in metaphorical terms about his newfound determination to marry and procreate. Elsewhere in the play, the word "get" sometimes serves as a shortened form of the verb "beget," as in Beatrice's reply to the Prince's offer to "get" her a husband: "I would rather have one of your father's getting" (2.1.302–3). Shakespeare also occasionally uses the word "picture" to refer to the notion, common in the procreation sonnets, that a male child may resemble a parent so strongly as to be a type of copy of him or her.[11] Given these alternative denotations, Benedick's vow to "go get her picture" may express his awakened ambition to beget upon Beatrice an heir who will look just like his beautiful mother.

Of course, the perpetuation of a patriarchal society through procreation also depends upon the fitness and willingness of women to cooperate in the birth of legitimate offspring. A cuckolded husband lives with nagging doubts that his wife's children are not his own; therefore, a nobleman like Claudio must protect against illegitimate succession by certifying that the chastity of his future wife is beyond reproach.[12] When Claudio begins to consider Hero as a marriage partner, he first inquires of Benedick, "Is she not a modest young lady?" (1.1.153). The Count clearly recognizes his obligation to procure a virginal wife, but Benedick's frequent aspersions against the chastity of married women apparently shake Claudio's confidence in the ultimate reliability of female modesty. The Count is so easily convinced of Hero's faithlessness because he truly holds the same deep-rooted assumption of women's promiscuity that Don John expresses in his slanderous characterization of the bride as "Leonato's Hero, your Hero, every man's Hero" (3.2.95–96). Don John formulates his accusation to chill the heart of any man who observes a woman passing from her father's hands into his own and dreads her inevitable passage into the arms of another. As Howard summarizes, "Don John lies about Hero, but his lie works because it easily passes in Messina as a truthful reading of women" (1987, 175).

Like Claudio, Benedick announces before the gulling scene that any woman he might love must be "virtuous, or I'll never cheapen her" (2.3.31). His resolve not to "cheapen" (bargain for) an unchaste female hints that only a virtuous woman may serve as acceptable tender in the transaction that seals the bond between the male parties joined through marriage. As Gayle Rubin points out, "If it is women who are being transacted, then it is the men who give and take them who are linked, the women being a conduit of a relationship rather than a partner to it" (1975, 174). Applying this concept to *Much Ado*, Claire McEachern asserts, "Claudio and the Prince invite Leonato, through the transfer of Hero, to join their own privileged company" (1988, 272). This exchange, along with the resulting male alliance between Leonato and Claudio (and through him, Don Pedro), provides both sides with extremely attractive acquisitions. In addition to a chaste wife, Claudio receives her dowry and the expectation of her father's wealth, while Leonato gains a place for his house in the ranks of the nobility. An awareness of this drive toward a mutually beneficial male bond elucidates certain aspects of the play as a comedy of forgiveness that frustrate a romantic reading of the Hero/Claudio relationship. For instance, when the eligible bachelor Don Pedro arrives in Messina, Leonato immediately maneuvers him within sight of his marriageable daughter to promote an attraction. By the next scene, Leonato busily prepares for Don Pedro's proposal, in case the rumor of its imminence is true. Leonato clearly hopes and expects to become father-in-law to the Prince, but he demonstrates no disappointment at all when it turns out that the offer of marriage comes from Claudio instead. Although Leonato never states the reasons for his willingness to accept this alternative alliance, it may be noted that this match is only slightly less profitable. Claudio can make Hero a countess, and his intimate affiliation with Don Pedro provides Leonato with another avenue for the advancement of his standing.

On the other side of the arranged match, Claudio expects some pecuniary advantage from his link to Leonato.[13] Before he admits his interest in Hero to Don Pedro, he first determines that she is Leonato's only child and heir to all his wealth. Such expectations make her a "rich and precious gift" (4.1.27) from the father to the son-in-law to seal their new association. Leonato is also fully aware that this agreement has its financial component; at the moment of Claudio's betrothal to Hero, the Governor says to the Count, "take of me my daughter, and with her my fortunes" (2.1.284–85). In reply, Claudio swears to his bride, "Lady, as you are mine, I am yours; I give away myself for you and dote upon the exchange" (2.1.289–91). Here, the elements of value pass *through* Hero rather than *to* her; it is the exchange that Claudio dotes upon rather than his future wife herself. In excusing his silent joy on this occasion, Claudio does not distinguish between its two sources, Hero's hand and her father's wealth, but over the years, most stage productions have discounted Claudio's monetary interest by implying, through loving embraces between Claudio and his bride, that romantic affection is the single cause of his tongue-tied delight. However, given the fact that Beatrice and Benedick also express strong interest in the potentially advantageous financial aspects of matrimony,[14] Claudio's concern for the riches that an alliance to Leonato can bring him must be viewed as a commonplace consideration for the marriageable inhabitants of Messina.

The male ties formed through the betrothal of Hero and Claudio are then dissolved in the church scene, where Hero's supposed crimes force Claudio to break off the arrangement. Only a small percentage of the dialogue in this segment passes between the bride and groom, the two people who are ostensibly being joined together; the greater portion proceeds among the three men who are party to the larger contract. The Count first addresses Leonato directly as "Father" (4.1.22), but he reverts to using the old man's first name once he dissolves the family bond by returning the gift given to secure their alliance: "There, Leonato, take her back again. / Give not this rotten orange to your friend" (4.1.30–31). From Claudio's perspective, Leonato, by trying to pass off contaminated goods as a pure commodity, has violated the terms by which their houses are to be joined, and the Count therefore has no choice but to cancel the transaction. In disbelief, the Governor appeals to Don Pedro for help, but the Prince considers himself disparaged by his role in the aborted proceedings: "I stand dishonour'd, that have gone about / To link my dear friend to a common stale" (4.1.64–65). Don Pedro's shame stems not only from his embarrassment at having arranged Claudio's match with a promiscuous woman, but also from the disgrace he personally would have suffered by his own alliance through Claudio to the family of "an approved wanton" (4.1.44).

Hero's presumed unchastity prevents, for the time being, the formation of male familial bonds; indeed, Claudio's response to Hero's "treachery" throws his future participation in the institution of marriage into doubt. Claudio's condemnation of his bride also reveals a repugnance toward female sexuality uncharacteristic of the Forgiven Comic Hero. Although Claudio still reveres Hero's chaste appearance, his disgust at her "savage sensuality" (4.1.61) casts suspicion on his ability ever to initiate a productive sexual relationship with a woman. The Count's vow to "lock up all the gates of love" (4.1.105) presents a barrier to the fulfillment of his masculine duty to marry and procreate; it also cuts him off from the creation of male bonds through the matrimonial exchange of women. For Claudio's own good and the best interests of society, he must eventually be reassured of the possible coexistence of female sexuality and chastity within marriage, despite the enduring threat of cuckoldry.

Benedick's opposite response to the accusations against Hero discloses his contrary values and increasing alienation from the world of male bonding. Even Leonato manifests no pity, and a great deal of inconsideration, toward Hero's suffering, but Benedick expresses sincere concern for her well-being and an atypical faith in her innocence. One crucial piece of evidence for such an attitude often passes unremarked in reading because it deals with a foreseeable action that does *not* occur. As Anne Barton remarks, Benedick "does not leave the church with Claudio, Don Pedro, and the Bastard, as might be expected. He chooses, instead, to remain behind with Hero, Leonato, the Friar, and Beatrice. In doing so, he breaks with that little all-male society of soldiers which has hitherto claimed his allegiance" (1974, 329). Unless a production does something to call attention to this pivotal nonexit, spectators will be unlikely to register Benedick's continued presence in the church as a significant rupture in his bond with Claudio and Don Pedro. For example, when Don John takes Hero's swoon as his cue to usher Claudio out of the church, the Prince may signal for Benedick to accompany them. If Benedick takes a step in that direction, then pauses and looks toward Hero and Beatrice, the audience will perceive his sense of divided loyalties. If, at that moment, the Prince once again indicates that Benedick should exit with the rest of the groom's party, but Benedick drops his eyes and remains in place while Don Pedro tosses his head in disapproval and stalks out, viewers will be more likely to understand Benedick's choice to stay put as a revelation of his belief in Hero's virtue and a momentous step in his estrangement from his companions.

This fissure splits wide open when Benedick accepts Beatrice's command to "Kill Claudio" (4.1.288). As Janet Adelman notes, "Beatrice's demand and Benedick's stunned response to it re-enact in compressed but very powerful form the full fantasy of woman as murderous to the male bond" (1985, 80). Benedick challenges the Count to a duel and informs the Prince, "I must discontinue your company" (5.1.186–87). Initially, Don Pedro and Claudio respond to Benedick as if he were still playing "the Prince's jester," railing against the frailty of women for the pleasure of his cohorts, and they fail to recognize the significance of his serious demeanor. However, as Claudio soon observes and informs the Prince, Benedick is in "most profound earnest, and, I'll warrant you, for the love of Beatrice" (5.1.192–93). Benedick's choice of Beatrice's cause over his friendship with both the Prince and Claudio plays out in miniature the masculine obligation to put aside resentment against women for their part in the dissolution of male camaraderie and to join with them in fruitful matrimony.

Before Benedick issues his challenge, Leonato informs Claudio that Hero, like the other Griseldas, has "died" as a result of his mistreatment of her. The Friar has predicted that this information will cause Claudio to regret his accusations and to love Hero more than ever before, but the Count displays no such sorrow in response to this news. Rather, he callously jokes at the grief of Leonato's family and maintains the righteousness of his own behavior. Only when Borachio's confession vindicates Hero's chastity does Claudio admit to any remorse over his part in her public disparagement: "Sweet Hero! Now thy image doth appear / In the rare semblance that I lov'd it first" (5.1.245–46). Once Hero's virginal image is restored, Claudio regrets his missed opportunity to marry her and forge a profitable bond with Leonato. When the old man appears, however, Claudio's direct apology falls something short of a full acknowledgement of his degree of culpability. As many critics have complained, Claudio's defense, "yet sinn'd I not / But in mistaking" (5.1.268–69), grossly underplays his vindictiveness in publicly ruining

her reputation.[15] At a point where one might expect Shakespeare, if he wants an audience to exonerate Claudio, to provide
him with a penitent apology for his cruelty, the text offers him
instead a lame excuse, which suggests that the unqualified
acquittal of Claudio by the audience may not be the goal of
Much Ado as a comedy of forgiveness.[16]

Instead, the play illustrates the extent to which the patriarchal matchmaker will go to secure the type of union that will
establish profitable links for himself within the male hierarchy.
Once the marital bond arranged by Don Pedro collapses, Leonato takes over the role of the authority figure to insure the continuation of the institution of marriage threatened by Claudio's
promise never to love again. Despite the rage Leonato vents
against Claudio for his hand in the "death" of his daughter, the
Governor quickly welcomes the Count back into his family with
three stipulations. First, Claudio must "Possess the people in
Messina here / How innocent she died" (5.1.275–76). This restoration of Hero's virtue both recovers the honor of Leonato's
house and renders Hero once again an acceptably chaste partner for Claudio in the match that Leonato has ultimately in
mind. Second, the Governor insists that the Count "Hang her
an epitaph upon her tomb, / And sing it to her bones" (5.1.278–
79), a ritual designed to offer Claudio the opportunity to express
publicly his penitence for his sins. Finally, Leonato offers Claudio a second chance to become his kinsman by marrying his
brother's "daughter." To induce Claudio to accept this final
aspect of his proposal, Leonato stresses that Antonio's girl is
"Almost the copy of my child that's dead, / And she alone is heir
to both of us" (5.1. 283–84). Being nearly identical to Hero, the
second bride must also be beautiful and modest, but her monetary value as heir to both Leonato and Antonio exceeds that of
her dead cousin. Claudio's critics, looking for the response of a
romantic lover, are disappointed by his hasty abandonment of
Hero's memory in favor of a woman whom he has never seen,
but this response should hardly be surprising. The woman functions merely as the channel through which the male exchange
flows, so any agreeable female who can serve in this capacity
pleases the Count. To Claudio, who does not know that Hero
still lives, the Governor's pardon seems unbelievably generous.
However, Leonato only appears overkind to viewers if they
ignore that the Governor has everything to gain by refashioning
a marriage between his "niece" and Claudio. Such a match
cements Leonato's alliance with the nobility, in return for which

he writes off the bad behavior of the Count as an honest "error" (5.4.3) provoked by the Bastard. As Robert Grams Hunter observes, in Don John, "Shakespeare has provided a scapegoat on whom to heap Claudio's misdeeds at the end of the play" (103).[17]

The scapegoating of Don John occurs most prominently in the following scene, when Ursula announces: "It is proved my Lady Hero hath been falsely accused, the Prince and Claudio mightily abused, and Don John is the author of all" (5.2.89–91). Since the Bastard engineered the scheme to interrupt the wedding, he surely deserves most of the blame, but Claudio and the Prince, however mightily they were abused, also acted poorly in believing Don John's flimsy accusations and disgracing Hero with malice aforethought. The inhabitants of Messina, however, elect to condemn Don John for *all* of the wrongdoing because such a choice allows them to rebuild the alliance between Leonato, Claudio, and Don Pedro. The Prince's brother, a sincere proponent of the antimatrimonial position, also serves as a scapegoat for Benedick, who can once again be welcomed into the male hierarchy, his crime of opposing marriage vicariously expiated through the punishment of the Bastard. As Richard A. Levin sums up the conduct of Leonato's clan: "By not properly investigating the crime that took place and by accepting perfunctory repentances, the family is able to celebrate two marriages, as it has long desired to do" (1985, 113).

Before the wedding ceremony itself, at Leonato's instigation, Claudio reconstitutes the betrothal ceremony originally solemnized in 2.1 and later undone by the Count's repudiation of his bride in the church scene: "Give me your hand before this holy friar. / I am your husband if you like of me" (5.4. 58–59). Just as Valentine reenacts the handfasting between Proteus and Julia at the end of *Two Gentlemen*, Leonato repairs the damage to the institution of marriage through a reinscription of the social ritual of betrothal. Once Claudio formally assents to the implications of this rite, Hero may unmask and declare her true identity. The Count's shocked response, "Another Hero!" (5.4.62), contains no words of apology, which prevents Hero's next speech from supplying any sense of her emotional attitude toward Claudio's cruelty or his later penitence. Hunter argues that the dénouement of *Much Ado* as a *romantic* comedy of forgiveness "comes when the heroine is discovered to be alive and the *humanum genus* figure awakens from his nightmare to be pardoned by the woman whose worth he has doubted" (1965,

88). But when Hunter tries to show that "Claudio is unreservedly forgiven" at the end of the play (104), he can only quote Leonato's pardon, not Hero's, since her speeches express no such idea.

Significantly, the play as written never considers the question of Hero's willingness to reaccept Claudio as a husband. She cooperates fully in the restoration of her bond with the Count, but the text does not indicate the degree to which she does so out of charitable love for Claudio or a sense of duty to her family, whose best interests take precedence over any personal resentment she may understandably feel. Whatever the case, she agrees without protest to the rematch and thereby resumes her role as the conduit of the bond between her husband and her father.[18] In place of a speech of reproach, such as the one Julia delivers to Proteus, or an expression of forgiveness for the Count's sins, Hero emphatically declares her primary qualification for wifely status: "One Hero died defil'd, but I do live, / And surely as I live, I am a maid" (5.4.63–64). Having already proclaimed the virtue of the Hero who died innocently, Claudio now receives his deceased bride back again, reborn as an immaculate version of the tainted goods he once rejected.

With the chastity of Hero reestablished, one might anticipate that the specter of cuckoldry would fade from prominence as the play concludes in double marriage. However, the issue of wifely promiscuity reappears with a vengeance when Claudio and the Prince greet Benedick as they arrive for the promised wedding:

> *Claud.* I think he thinks upon the savage bull.
> Tush, fear not, man, we'll tip thy horns with gold,
> And all Europa shall rejoice at thee,
> As once Europa did at lusty Jove,
> When he would play the noble beast in love.
> *Bene.* Bull Jove, sir, had an amiable low,
> And some such strange bull leap'd your father's cow,
> And got a calf in that same noble feat
> Much like to you, for you have just his bleat.
>
> (5.4.43–51)

Claudio imagines that Benedick, contemplating marriage with Beatrice, laments his upcoming transformation from an unfettered sexual being, a savage bull, to a yoked beast, destined to wear the cuckold's horns. Benedick replies testily that the Count's father was also a cuckold, and that Claudio is the illegitimate child of his mother's extramarital union. This reference to bastardy recalls the antimatrimonial position of the bastard Don John, whose reminders of the hazard of female promiscuity have been challenged by the virtue of Hero and Beatrice, but never effectively eliminated.

The men of Messina ultimately reconcile themselves to the threat of cuckoldry in marriage with recourse to the notion of "kinship in horns" (Williamson 1986, 40). They rationalize, from the misogynistic premise of female duplicity, that even though women may reduce them to horned beasts, such a condition ironically links them to other husbands and therefore enhances the formation of male bonds that is at the root of matrimony in the first place.[19] Despite the animosity between Claudio and Benedick at the beginning of 5.4, the marriages sealed at the end of the play bring the two comrades back together in amity. As Benedick remarks, "For thy part, Claudio, I did think to have beaten thee, but in that thou art like to be my kinsman, live unbruised, and love my cousin" (5.4.107–10). The family ties created by matrimony restore the male friendship between the soldiers, which is reinforced by their common status as potential cuckolds. When Benedick exhorts Claudio, "Come, come we are friends. Let's have a dance ere we are married, that we may lighten our own hearts and our wives' heels" (5.4.116–18), he hints at the "savage sensuality" of women previously so abhorrent to the Count, but Benedick explains away the danger to manliness posed by female sexuality by claiming that a man is paradoxically most worthy of respect when he has been cuckolded: "There is no staff more reverend than one tipped with horn" (5.4.121–22). A patriarch deserves reverence for his courage in braving cuckoldry's threat to his masculinity, and just as Benedick and Claudio have faced the perils of war side by side, they now enlist together in the army of husbands, carrying staffs tipped with horn.

Benedick, once he has agreed to marry, assumes a leading role in the communal male hierarchy. He overrules Leonato on the question of dancing before the wedding ceremony, and he eventually speaks the final lines of the play, usually reserved for the highest ranking character. When a messenger brings word of Don John's capture to the Prince, Benedick interjects, "Think not on him till tomorrow; I'll devise thee brave punishments for him. Strike up pipers!" (5.4.125–26). The "professed" opponent of matrimony takes charge of the discipline of the true matchbreaker and concludes the play by calling upon pipers to play the music of love. Furthermore, Benedick takes over the role of the matchmaker from Don Pedro and Leonato, ushering the Prince himself toward matrimony with the injunction, "get thee a wife, get thee a wife!" (5.4.121). Now that Don Pedro has maneuvered his companions into the ranks of the patriarchs, Benedick urges the Prince to join them in a reconstituted version of their battlefield fraternity. [Claudio weds Hero, and Benedick marries Beatrice, but above all, the men of Messina reunite with each other.]

*   *   *

Stanley Wells, in a study of the editorial treatment of foul-paper texts, chooses *Much Ado* as a "test case" because the play contains so many instances of the inconsistencies in stage directions, speech headings, and character names that typify such texts (1980, 1). In most cases, the disputed designations Wells identifies do not arise from a disagreement between the Quarto and Folio (since F derives from Q and repeats many of its curious features) but from a discrepancy between what Q and F both read and what modern editors believe Shakespeare must have meant. Humphreys, the Arden editor, claims that most of his corrections of QF are "self-evident" (1981, 81), and in many cases they are (such as when he adds a speaking character's missing entry direction); but not all of his reattributions of speech headings or emendations of stage directions rely on similarly "practical" reasoning. At some points, he and other editors of *Much Ado* alter QF readings based on interpretive assumptions, yet the rhetoric of their justifications characterizes these emendations as "obvious" reconstructions of Shakespeare's intent rather than the products of critical judgments. Moreover, as A. R. Braunmuller points out, editorial practices tend to construct a play as either a "literary" or a "theatrical" artifact:

> Either the editor ignores the text as a theatrical script . . . or the editor creates a performance of the play in notes, stage directions, and other commentary according to the theatrical conventions of the editor's own time. . . . No matter which avenue an editor follows . . . there are occasions when the imagined staging of a scene will actually influence what the editor chooses to print, and I do not mean simply what stage directions the editor chooses to add or modify, but how the editor construes or distorts the ipsissima verba of the Bard himself. (1989, 139–40)

Beyond their modifications of the spoken lines, when editors provide additional stage directions in the form of notes or commentary that offer projected stagings and line readings, they in effect legitimize one particular significance of a scene or passage, sometimes in contradiction to what the text "seems" to say on paper.[20] Several of these interventions appear to be designed specifically to recuperate the dubious reputation of Claudio and thereby to make the text of *Much Ado* conform more closely to the conventions of romantic comedy.

To illustrate this phenomenon, I will draw evidence primarily from four chronologically varied editions of *Much Ado*: the acting edition published by J. P. Kemble (1810),[21] the New Shakespeare edited by Sir Arthur Quiller-Couch and John Dover Wilson (1923), Humphreys' Arden Shakespeare (1981), and the New Cambridge Shakespeare edited by F. H. Mares (1988). A comparison of the textual operations performed in these four editions reveals several points at which editorial practice appears calculated to insure the audience's full pardon of Claudio's offenses. In addition, I will refer repeatedly to productions of the play that enact the textual changes made or suggested within these editions.

One of *Much Ado*'s most puzzling passages occurs in 2.2, when Borachio counsels Don John to provide Claudio and Don Pedro with concocted evidence of Hero's unchastity: "offer them instances, which shall bear no less likelihood than to see me at her chamber-window, hear me call Margaret Hero, hear Margaret term me Claudio, and bring them to see this the very night before the intended wedding" (2.2.41–45). Mares identifies the enigmatic aspect of this passage by quoting Theobald, who notes that if the Count heard Hero call another man "Claudio, he might reasonably think her betrayed, but he could not have the same reason to accuse her of disloyalty" (1988, 81n). Theobald, Mares recalls, proposed to emend "Claudio" to "Borachio," as did Kemble, who printed the text as it reads in Q and F, but added a handwritten notation substituting "Borachio" for "Claudio" in his promptbook (7:25). Alternately, Humphreys accepts the passage as it stands and offers the explanation (dating back to Dyce [1857]) that "Borachio means to persuade Margaret to disguise as her mistress, and to act with him a love-scene in which the servants masquerade as their 'betters' " (1981, 131n). Quiller-Couch and Wilson assent in principle to this annotation, but they attribute the curious nature of the passage to the "fact" that *Much Ado* represents Shakespeare's recasting of an old play that originally included the balcony scene, which was cut in the process of revision. In his introduction to the play, Quiller-Couch laments that we only hear of this staged interview at second-hand: "The omission of the window-scene weakens our sympathy with Claudio in the chapel-scene. We cannot put ourselves in his place, deprived as we have been of the visual evidence that convinced him" (1923, xiii).

Although the New Shakespeare editors do not go so far as to print a balcony scene in their edition, their comments have helped to perpetuate the notion that such a scene, which once existed, is now lost. In an effort to "restore" this missing segment, modern directors have periodically introduced some version of the interlude at Hero's chamber-window into their productions.[22] Michael Langham's 1961 Stratford-upon-Avon revival, which used the New Shakespeare as its playtext, inserted the following sequence at 3.3.92:

> Claudio, Don Pedro, and Don John entered and saw [Borachio] entering from the pit, with a ladder which he put up to the balcony. . . . He went up the ladder and was joined on the balcony by "Hero." In fact, the actress on stage was not Margaret disguised as Hero but Hero herself, "heavily cloaked" [promptbook's phrase], pretending to be Margaret pretending to be Hero. (Mason 1976, 59)[23]

To cap this segment, Langham transported a passage carved from one of Claudio's speeches in the previous scene (3.2.112–14). Skipping the phrase, "If I see anything tonight why I should not marry her," the Count said, "tomorrow, in the congregation, where I should wed, there will I shame her" (Mason 60).

These alterations provide a degree of vindication for Claudio's actions that Q and F significantly omit. In Shakespeare's text, Claudio is ready to disgrace Hero publicly before he sees evidence of her infidelity, but Langham's version postpones this vow until after the Count has witnessed the exchange on the balcony. Furthermore, Langham makes Claudio's deception more "believable" by employing the actress portraying the real Hero instead of dressing the actress playing Margaret "in Hero's garments" as the text demands (5.1.233). As the reviewer for the *Morning Advertiser* (10 April 1961) writes approvingly:

> So cunningly staged and lit is the scene at the window on which the false accusation of Hero's lapse from virtue on the eve of her wedding is based, that the Don John conspiracy and the subsequent denunciation of the bride in the middle of the ceremony does not impose quite so heavy a strain on credulity as usual. (Mason 1976, 61)

Langham's enactment makes it far easier for the audience to observe Hero from Claudio's point of view and to pardon him for his erroneous allegations. Ten years later, William Hutt achieved a comparable effect by incorporating a dumb-show version of the balcony scene into his Stratford, Ontario production. Berners W. Jackson found this "innovation" effective and commented that Claudio "was helped by our actually seeing him shaken by the spectacle of Borachio with Margaret at Hero's window" (1971, 370). That these enactments of the balcony scene "help" Claudio reinforces Quiller-Couch's assumption that the text, which intends to present Claudio sympathetically, fails to do so only because it has lost in revision the crucial segment which draws viewers' sympathy to him.[24]

The premise that the play aspires to represent Claudio attractively in performance has permitted editors to proceed beyond theories of textual revision to otherwise unwarranted alterations of Q and F, particularly in 5.3, commonly known as the tomb scene. There, Claudio fulfills Leonato's injunction to "Hang an epitaph upon [Hero's] tomb, / And sing it to her bones." The Count and his entourage duly perform this rite, but readers and theatergoers have often expressed dissatisfaction with the brevity and coldness of the scene at Hero's monument.[25] The epitaph, for example, concentrates solely on Hero's "glorious fame" (5.3.8) and omits any heartfelt declarations of grief, love, or remorse. Rather than concluding that Claudio's penitence is designed to be perceived as a hollow gesture (an effort to placate Leonato), editors and critics have often suggested that music, lighting, and stage business should compensate in performance for the sincere emotion which the scene lacks in other respects. As Humphreys contends, "Short though the scene is, a conviction of religious grief and awe is to be evoked, creating depth and dignity of emotion more by non-verbal than by verbal means" (1981, 210n).

In his introductory comments, Humphreys elaborates on his conception of the way in which nonverbal elements of performance accomplish the "spiritual expiation" of Claudio and redeem him in the eyes of spectators:

> The effects about to be described are all in the text, not interpolated, and should receive full weight. The numinous impressiveness of the monument, the silent black-robed procession with tapers flickering in the darkness, the elegiac verses (on the deeply felt delivery of which much depends), the grave music and slow dirge to which the

mourners circle the tomb . . . all this, legitimately present in the
scene, warrants its acceptance not as a superficial formal rite but as
a fundamental turning-point. (1981, 57–58)

Humphreys's assertion that the theatrical effects he outlines are
"all in the text, not interpolated" overstates his subsequent
observation that these effects are "legitimately present in the
scene." A monument of some kind, for instance, is indicated by
the dialogue, but the editor detects a "numinous impressive-
ness" which is not demanded by the text. Humphreys also attributes a large part of the redemptive effect of these "elegiac
verses" to their "deeply felt delivery." Presumably, if Claudio
reads the epitaph with deep feeling, the audience will acknowledge his sorrow and pardon his offenses. In practice, spectators
do usually forgive Claudio if he speaks penitently at the tomb,
yet this staging is grounded, not in the text, but in editorial tradition, which assigns the reading of the epitaph and two other
important lines in the scene to Claudio despite the fact that Q
and F allot them to another character.

Here are the first twenty-one lines of 5.3 as they appear in the
Quarto (1600):

> *Enter Claudio, Prince, and three or foure with tapers.*
> Claudio   Is this the monument of Leonato?
> Lord   It is my lord. *Epitaph.*
>   Done to death by slauderous tongues,
>   Was the Hero that heere lies:
>   Death in guerdon of her wronges,   [5]
>   Giues her fame which neuer dies:
>   So the life that dyed with shame,
>   Liues in death with glorious fame.
>   Hang thou there vpon the toomb,
>   Praising hir when I am dead.   [10]
> Claudio   Now musick sound & sing your solemne hymne.
>   *Song* Pardon goddesse of the night,
>   Those that slew thy virgin knight,
>   For the which with songs of woe,
>   Round about her tombe they goe: [15]
>   Midnight assist our mone, help vs to sigh & grone.
>   Heauily heauily.
>   Graues yawne and yeeld your dead,
>   Till death be vttered,
>   Heauily heauily.   [20]
> Lo.   Now vnto thy bones good night, yeerely will I do this
>   right.

In a note to the first line of the epitaph, Mares summarizes the traditional emendations: "Nearly all editors follow Capell in inserting a speech heading for Claudio at this point in spite of the fact that he is given one in Q [and F] at 11. Similarly the couplet after the song . . . which has the heading *Lo.* in Q and F is given (following Rowe) to Claudio" (1988, 139n). Since the arrangement of Q and F indicates that an attendant Lord is to speak both the epitaph and the vow following the song, editors are forced into a number of speculative and rhetorical strategies to defend their augmentation of Claudio's role. Quiller-Couch and Wilson refer to Elizabethan theatrical and printing practices:

> Q. heads the verses "Epitaph" and does not assign them to Claudio. The player was of course intended to read them from a scroll on the stage, and by thus marking them "Epitaph" perhaps Shakespeare wished to indicate that they did not belong to his "part" but were to be copied out on to a separate piece of paper. (1923, 151n)

Concerning the night/right couplet, the coeditors hypothesize that "Shakespeare wrote 'cla.' so carelessly in the margin that the compositor took it for 'lo.' " (151n).[26] Humphreys, however, does not offer a "logical" reason for the "error" and merely obscures the machinery of interpretation with an appeal to Nature: "It seems natural that Claudio should himself deliver the epitaph, and Capell's arrangement is therefore adopted" (1981, 210n).[27]

Mares, who prints the passage substantially as it occurs in Q and F, protests that the emendations of his predecessors are "hard to justify textually: it does not seem out of character for Claudio to do his grieving by proxy, as he did his wooing" (1988, 139n). While the claim that the QF reading is acceptable involves no less interpretation than the opposing view, Mares bases his decision on textual evidence, from which he develops his assessment of Claudio's character, rather than assuming the nature of the Count's portrayal by the performed text and working backward to reshape the printed text to fit this characterization. On stage, Claudio has a better chance to recover a viewer's good graces if he delivers the epitaph and vows to repeat the penance in his own voice. But given the criticism he has suffered for wooing Hero through Don Pedro, one may speculate that if Claudio mourns Hero almost exclusively through a spokesman, the verses and vow will not seem as deeply felt, and the scene will not be as likely to induce spectators to forgive the Count. Rather, they will observe the disparity between their own reluctance to pardon Claudio and the eagerness of Leonato's family to absolve the Count of his offenses.

In addition to Claudio's reading of the epitaph, other elements of stagecraft have often been called into service to generate the Count's "depth and dignity of emotion" at Hero's gravesite. Whereas nineteenth-century producers, including Kemble, generally omitted the tomb scene entirely,[28] twentieth-century directors have tended to amplify the scene's ritual elements with elaborate stagings in a religious or military style. For example, Jörg Hasler recalls Ronald Eyre's steps to bolster the emotional force of the Count's repentance:

> In the 1971 Stratford production, in addition to the solemnity engendered by the liturgical chants, somber lighting and candles, Claudio was made to prostrate himself after delivering his "epitaph." Furthermore, the numerous attendants (not "three or four") revealed themselves, after Don Pedro and Claudio had left, to be none other than Leonato, Hero and their whole household. Thus Hero actually witnessed Claudio's act of penitence. (1974, 212n)[29]

The desired effect of Hero's interpolated presence at the tomb is evident in Mason's account of John Barton's variation on this business five years later:

> Beatrice and Hero, heavily cloaked in black, entered . . . unseen by the mourners. When the military had left, Beatrice and Hero threw back their cloaks and joyfully carried the wreaths off stage, while Hero delighted at the sentiments expressed in the inscription Claudio had placed with the wreath. (1976, 137)

This staging implies that if Hero is satisfied by Claudio's act of atonement, so should we be, but Q and F provide no such direct expression of her delight. On the contrary, Hero's almost complete silence on this issue has allowed centuries of editors, directors, and critics to impose upon her a legitimate but nonetheless speculative reaction to Claudio's penance which coincides with their conception of the Count's fall and regeneration.

Those who edit or stage *Much Ado* commonly assume that Hero's actions are motivated primarily by her love for Claudio. However, Hero says almost nothing about her feelings for the Count, and the statements she does make are open to question. For example, Beatrice prompts Hero, at her betrothal to Claudio, to make a declaration of her love for her fiancé: "Speak, cousin, or, if you cannot, stop his mouth with a kiss, and let not him speak neither" (2.1.292–93). Curiously enough, Hero speaks no words of devotion aloud; Beatrice presumes that she tells Claudio of her love—"My cousin tells him in his ear that he is in her heart" (2.1.292–98)—and the Count confirms this message, but the play shows both characters to be prone to misread Hero, especially in situations involving overheard conversations. Certainly, the scene in performance may include an embrace which signifies Hero's abiding affection, but the written text goes out of its way to avoid letting an affirmation of such feelings escape her lips in our hearing. In fact, the closest Hero ever comes to proclaiming her love for her future husband is actually a compliment to Benedick offered during the gulling of Beatrice: "He is the only man of Italy, / Always excepted my dear Claudio" (3.1.92–93). Although Humphreys discovers "kindly feeling" in this comment (1981, 50), "my dear Claudio" seems far too minimal to carry the emotional intensity ascribed to Hero by editors and critics. Furthermore, Hero tells so many white lies designed to deceive Beatrice during this segment that her remark about Claudio remains equivocal at best.

Lacking a clear statement of Hero's motivation for her generosity toward the Count, one might reason from her behavior that she *must* love Claudio, or she wouldn't agree (twice) to marry him. The logic of this claim is problematic, however, because Hero also silently acquiesces to a match with Don Pedro (whom no one argues that she loves) at the request of her father Leonato: "Daughter, remember what I told you: if the Prince do solicit you in that kind, you know your answer" (2.1.61–62). Leonato's confusion over the identity of Hero's suitor stems from 1.2, when Antonio, misinformed by an eavesdropping servant, mistakenly reports that the Prince intends to woo Hero for himself. This misunderstanding has often been viewed as an unnecessary complication of the plot,[30] and nineteenth-century producers like Kemble commonly excised the scene, transporting the bare essentials of the exchange to the beginning of the banquet scene (2.1) with the important change that Antonio correctly anticipates Don Pedro's role as a matchmaker.[31] In Kemble's acting edition, Antonio's first speech consists of one sentence derived from 1.2 and another carved from a passage of Borachio's cut from the previous scene (1.3.54–60):

> I tell you, the prince and count Claudio, walking in the thick-pleach'd alley of the orchard, were overheard by a man of mine. It

was agreed upon, that the prince should in a dance woo Hero as for
himself; and, having obtain'd her, give her to count Claudio. (7:15)

Kemble's modifications streamline the plot and eliminate a possible source of audience confusion, but they also change the significance of Leonato's later admonition to Hero, which now
means, "If the Prince solicits you to marry Claudio, you had better say yes." In Kemble's version, Hero's assent to this command is less enigmatic than it is in Q and F, where she first
agrees to marry Don Pedro and then without a word consents to
a match with Claudio. Thus, Kemble's alterations increase the
likelihood that spectators will perceive Hero's acceptance of the
Prince's proposal on Claudio's behalf as a sign of her love for
the Count rather than as an act of obedience to her father.

Later, in the church scene, Kemble inserts crucial stage directions that guide readers and viewers to attribute Hero's emotional collapse entirely to Claudio's harsh public repudiation
and not at all to her father's betrayal of his trust in her. Our
three twentieth-century editions print the segment substantially as it appears in Q and F with two interpolated stage directions:

Claud.	And on my eyelids shall conjecture hang, To turn all beauty into thoughts of harm, And never shall it more be gracious.
Leon.	Hath no man's dagger here a point for me? [*Hero swoons.*]
Beat.	Why, how now, cousin! Wherefore sink you down?
D. John.	Come, let us go. These things, come thus to light, Smother her spirits up. [*Exeunt Don Pedro, Don John, and Claudio.*]

(4.1.105–12)[32]

At the end of Claudio's harangue against Hero's beauty, Leonato speaks for the first time as if he believes the charges
against her are true. Modern editors place the stage direction
"*Hero swoons*" after this lament on the basis of Beatrice's next
line, which indicates that Hero has begun to "sink down." Don
John's exhortation ("Come, let us go . . ."), which comments on
Hero's fainting spell, then prompts the interpolated exit for the
Prince, the Bastard, and the Count. Kemble, however, reverses
the order of these two stage directions and gives the exchange
as follows:

> *Claud.*   And on my eye-lids shall conjecture hang,
> To turn all beauty into thoughts of harm,
> And never shall it more be gracious.
> > [*Exeunt* Claudio, Pedro, *and* John.
> > [Hero *swoons.*]
> *Leon.*   Hath no man's dagger here a point for me?
> *Beat.*   Why, how now, cousin? wherefore sink you down?
>
> > (7:46)

Kemble's revision appears calculated to allow Claudio and the others to leave the stage immediately before Hero swoons, as evidenced by the fact that Don John's lines, which establish the opposite sequence of events, are cut.[33] In this version, Hero faints *before* she hears her father abandon his faith in her virtue, collapsing solely as a result of Claudio's cruel desertion. Such an arrangement inhibits the expression of a notion that Q and F insistently suggest: that Hero's actions and reactions are motivated as much by devotion to her father as they are by any affection she may feel for Claudio.

The editorial interventions I have described are all present in the most widely viewed version of *Much Ado*, Kenneth Branagh's 1993 film adaptation. Among numerous other changes to the text, Branagh makes frequent cuts, interpolations, and rearrangements of events in an effort to simplify the character of Claudio and increase the possibility that audiences will forgive him for his brutal treatment of Hero. Some reviewers, such as James Bowman, appreciate Branagh's efforts to eradicate the interpretive difficulties Claudio causes:

> I also like the fact that [the film] all but ignores the problem of Claudio. . . . There is every reason to think him a thoroughly discredited character in any plausible modern reading of the play and at the same time to believe that Shakespeare didn't care about that, or want it to appear in performance. For the play to come off on stage, he needed Claudio himself to remain, as well as to marry, a Hero. (1993, 57)

Bowman asserts that, for the play to "come off" (as a romantic comedy), the Count must be portrayed as a heroic figure whose discreditable actions are ignored or minimized. As Harry Pearson points out, Branagh accomplishes this rehabilitation by altering or removing those parts of the text that emphasize his premeditated cruelty and by highlighting his youth and immaturity:

One of Branagh's key decisions is to edit Claudio out of a quite genuine macho nastiness . . . and into a kind of thoughtless boyishness, in which inexperience masks the good heart. This [actor Robert Sean] Leonard plays to a song, and so believably that it underlines what many critics think was the playwright's basic intent with this comedy, i.e., how we are misled by flaws in our communications with each other. (1993, 261)

By editing out the Count's "macho nastiness," Branagh presents a Claudio who is merely "misled" by the human flaw of miscommunication and therefore may be genuinely exonerated by the excuse that he "sinn'd . . . not / But in mistaking." The question that both Bowman and Pearson raise but do not answer here is why Branagh must undertake such an extensive revision of Shakespeare's text to achieve what Pearson calls "the playwright's basic intent with this comedy."[34]

Despite Bowman's claim that Shakespeare did not intend the portrayal of Claudio that "any plausible modern reading of the play" would demand, Branagh does incorporate into his film a contemporary view of gender dynamics through the characterization of Beatrice, played by his then-wife Emma Thompson. Branagh reveals how his spouse enlightened him on the play's sexual politics:

Shakespeare's attitude toward the sexes is very much the attitude of our own time. He's very subversive. Beatrice and Benedick are equals, and in many ways she is a far more highly developed creature. I have to be reminded sometimes—and, God knows, my wife does it for me—that, although the women in the piece are strong presences, they are in effect powerless. Hero, for example—Don Pedro woos her for Claudio and Leonato gives her away. One sort of accepts that until the chapel scene between Beatrice and Benedick. You understand what it means to be powerless when she gives vent to her anger and frustration: "Oh God, that I were a man! I would eat his heart in the marketplace." [4.1.305–6] (Stuart 1993, 91)

As David Denby notes, it is in the "Kill Claudio" scene, from which Branagh quotes above, that "Branagh and Thompson come as close to a feminist reading of the play as they can without altering the meaning of the text" (1993, 63). Indeed, as Richard Ryan argues, the film begins with a striking interpolation that leads spectators to believe that the film will pursue Shakespeare's examination of women's suffering caused by the "inconstancy" of men:

[T]he Shakespearean plot encourages us to think this is a play about how women feel about men. Branagh in his turn underlines this "feminist" reading by a clever maneuver. . . . As the movie opens, we hear Emma Thompson's silken voice slowly reciting the words to the song ["Sigh no more, ladies"] as they appear one after another on a black background. The force of this device is to make the lyric into the play's argument. Unfortunately, it is an argument whose implications . . . Branagh fails to pursue. (1993, 53)

Branagh elects not to follow through completely on a feminist reading of the play, I would argue, because to do so would require a more complex treatment of Claudio than the conventions of romantic comedy would allow. To represent the Count essentially as the text depicts him would be "to risk the dark side of the play" (Zitner 1993, 27), and Branagh does not appear to be ready to take that sort of artistic and financial chance with a comedy of forgiveness.

Branagh's introduction to his published screenplay hearkens back to the emphasis of Quiller-Couch on the importance of the "missing" balcony scene to Claudio's reception by the audience:

The deception of Claudio was most important in this screen adaptation. . . . Hero's alleged infidelity (her "talking" to a man at a window) is described as happening offstage. It seemed that if we saw this occur on screen, it would add a new dimension to our understanding of Claudio. (1993, xv)

In order to increase spectators' "understanding" of Claudio's predicament, Branagh, like several directors before him, interpolates a version of the balcony scene into his production, printed here as it appears in the screenplay:

DON JOHN, DON PEDRO, and CLAUDIO'S point of view. In silhouette, we can see BORACHIO and MARGARET making love. CLAUDIO lets out a cry and makes to run at them but is held by DON PEDRO and DON JOHN. All three are shaking.
   DON JOHN [Intense, emotional]
   The lady is disloyal!
   If you love her, then, tomorrow wed her. But it would better
   fit your honor to change your mind.
Close on CLAUDIO. Tears in angry eyes. DISSOLVE. (56)

To encourage viewers to sympathize with Claudio and excuse him for his mistaken apprehension, Branagh employs a camera angle that portrays the episode on the balcony from Claudio's perspective, prompting spectators to perceive how easily Margaret "in silhouette" might be taken for Hero. Claudio's anguished cry and the close-up on the tears in his angry eyes also foster an emotional identification with his pain at Hero's betrayal. Moreover, Branagh transports Don John's lines from Shakespeare's 3.2, which occurs *before* the incident at Hero's window, in order to show how convincing his accusation of Hero's disloyalty can be made to appear after Claudio has been presented with ocular proof. Anne Barton sums up the general effect of this interpolation: "A movie audience . . . that has been allowed to join Claudio, Don John, and the Prince as they watch a particularly lusty Borachio . . . making vigorous love to . . . Margaret on Hero's balcony (a scene Shakespeare calculatedly did not stage) is far more likely to forgive the violence of Claudio's response" (1993, 12).

In recompense for his mistaken apprehension, Branagh's Claudio, along with the Prince and dozens of hooded monks, travels to Leonato's monument. The screenplay describes this visual image as follows: "Point of view from the Villa of a wide shot of a cloaked, torched procession towards HERO'S tomb. Beautiful and sombre, a snake of lights against the hillside. We pull back to reveal ANTONIO and HERO in the foreground" (1993, 76). As in the stage productions directed by Ronald Eyre and John Barton, Branagh's film makes Hero an observer of Claudio's penitence, and by shooting this sequence from Hero's perspective, Branagh encourages viewers to share in her evident deep feeling at the Count's "beautiful and sombre" gesture of remorse. Once the procession arrives at the monument, the film follows the emendations of most editors by having Claudio read the epitaph, full of heartfelt regret and sorrow, eventually breaking into tears and collapsing to his knees as the attendant musicians sing their solemn hymn. The scene concludes at the end of the song, omitting Claudio's discussion with Don Pedro of the Count's upcoming wedding to Leonato's "niece" (5.3.30–33). These alterations reduce the likelihood that audiences will perceive Claudio's "mourning ostentation" (4.1.205) as a perfunctory rite designed to gratify Leonato, and they increase the probability that viewers will forgive him, as Hero apparently does, on the basis of his earnest repentance.

There is never any question, in Branagh's film, that Hero loves Claudio enough to suffer the abuse he heaps upon her and yet emerge with her affections unscathed. To compensate for the text's scarcity of opportunities to express such devotion ver-

bally, Branagh punctuates his version of the play's first scene
with occasional shots of Hero and Claudio exchanging loving
glances.[35] He also cuts Shakespeare's 1.2 in its entirety, which
removes any confusion about Don Pedro's marital intentions,
but the omission of Antonio's communication of the imminent
wooing of Hero to his brother renders Leonato's command to
Hero ("Daughter, remember what I told you: if the Prince do
solicit you in that kind, you know your answer") puzzling at
best. Leonato has no way of knowing that Don Pedro is about to
solicit Hero, either for himself or for Claudio, and therefore the
phrase "in that kind" remains ambiguous. Hero, in any case,
evinces no response to this injunction, neither duteous acquiescence to her father's behest nor eager anticipation of the
Prince's wooing on Claudio's behalf.[36] Branagh, like Kemble,
also adapts the printed text's arrangement of 4.1 to indicate that
Hero's distress at the moment of her swoon stems entirely from
her lover's condemnation of her wantonness and not at all from
her father's loss of belief in her chastity. After Don Pedro
announces Borachio's confession of his affair with Hero, the
screenplay includes this passage:

> THE CROWD is stunned. Reactions of BEATRICE, BENEDICK.
> LEONATO is beaten. HERO faints once more.
> {**BEATRICE**
> *How now, cousin?*}
> THE CROWD react as if this is some proof. DON JOHN acts
> quickly.
> **DON JOHN**
> *Come, let us go. These things, come thus to light,*
> *Smother her spirits up.*
> {**BEATRICE**
> *Cousin, cousin, wherefore sink you down?*}[37]
> The princes and the count leave. THE CROWD likewise starts to
> move away.
> **LEONATO** [Grimly, to himself]
> *Hath no man's dagger here a point for me?* (1993, 62)

Branagh's revision of this sequence differs from Kemble's in
that Hero's faint occurs before the Princes and the Count exit
the stage, but the swoon itself, which follows Leonato's acceptance of the charges against Hero in Shakespeare's text, here,
as in Kemble, precedes it. Also, Leonato's rhetorical question is
spoken "to himself" rather than to the assembly, so neither
Hero nor anyone else appears to hear it. No viewer of this seg-

ment could possibly attribute Hero's faint to her father's betrayal of trust; her true love's public repudiation of their betrothal would appear to be her only source of anguish.

Likewise, nothing in the film suggests that anything other than love for Claudio motivates Hero to pardon his offenses. In the final scene, Claudio's contrite attitude and Hero's overt forgiveness of the Count combine to insure that spectators will exonerate Claudio for his earlier mistakes. To accomplish this goal, Branagh cuts all of the Count's speeches that have troubled critics and editors over the years, including his vow that he will wed Antonio's daughter "were she an Ethiope" (5.4.38) and his badinage with Benedick on the subject of cuckoldry.[38] At the moment of Leonato's daughter's "resurrection," Branagh also eliminates Claudio's brief response, "Another Hero!" and replaces it with a closeup on the Count's face as he embraces Hero and weeps with joy. Claudio kneels at the feet of the veiled Hero as he takes her hand and swears to marry her, and when she removes her veil, she is also crying happy tears. The Count rises, and they embrace again while the assembled crowd cheers to endorse their reconciliation. After the less sentimentalized reunions of Benedick and Beatrice and the two soldiers (during which Branagh omits Benedick's claim that "There is no staff more reverend than one tipped with horn"), the film ends with a shower of white confetti and an exuberant dance that seems to rejuvenate the entire community. Clearly, this enactment of the finale of *Much Ado* depicts marriage wholly as the culmination of romantic, heterosexual desire and not at all as an institution that allies men. In this way, the film fails to persist in the feminist perspective with which it begins. As reviewer John Ottenhoff asserts, "A more daring director might have inquired into the connections between cuckold jokes and violence toward women and wondered about the resolution of sexual tensions in marriage. This *Much Ado* sweeps all such concerns away in a grand fit of dancing" (1993, 823).

Ottenhoff speculates that financial considerations led Branagh to abandon the feminist point of view that the play suggests: "*Much Ado* raises questions about the treatment of women as marriageable commerce and about the comic resolution of romantic norms, but the film only casually raises such issues and finally embraces (with good marketing sense, I concede) good feelings and warmth" (1993, 824). Branagh's "good marketing sense" is borne out by the negative reception accorded to the only major professional performance of *Much*

Ado that has approached the play from a feminist perspective: Di Trevis's 1988 RSC production, which was greeted, according to Smallwood, with a "chorus of disapproval of quite unusual unanimity" (1989, 83). Trevis reexamines the play with special attention to gender dynamics, eschewing the traditional whitewashing of Claudio and romanticizing of Hero so prevalent in previous theatrical incarnations of the play. As Smallwood discerns, Trevis's approach

> does sharpen one's awareness of the angularities and inadequacies of the Hero-Claudio relationship. Julia Ford's Hero is appropriately shallow, inept with words, conventional and unthinking as she betroths herself to Claudio. Ralph Fiennes's Claudio, stiff, immature, uncertain . . . lashes out in the church scene in a panic that is at once spiteful and grief-stricken. (84)

These portrayals seem sufficient to disappoint viewers expecting the orthodox treatment of lovers in a romantic comedy, but it is the production's conclusion that, according to Smallwood, provoked much of the annoyance of spectators by leaving them with a disturbed reaction to Claudio's reunion with Hero:

> At the end of the play, . . . black petals or bits of black confetti float down to the stage in what seems a macabre or ironic comment on the hollowness of the relationships being presented. . . . The production leaves one with the abiding image of Claudio and Hero achieving uneasy reconciliation as the black confetti wafts down upon their future. (84)

In light of Claudio's many positive attributes, this staging may convey an overly pessimistic outlook on the young couple's immediate prospects, but it also represents much more suggestively those vexatious aspects of Q and F that editors and directors have historically chosen to simplify. The foregrounding of such troublesome elements may not inspire spectators with vicarious satisfaction, but it does offer, in place of emotional identification, the pleasures of a multifaceted response to the play's Forgiven Comic Hero.

Another less "macabre" avenue toward a production of *Much Ado* as a comedy of forgiveness might involve more attention to moments in the play, such as Benedick's refusal to exit the church with his comrades, when the primacy of male bonds can be stressed through meaningful performance choices. Along these lines, some recent productions have established the priority of emotional ties between men from the moment of the soldiers' first appearance. For example, Gerald Freedman's 1988 New York Shakespeare Festival production featured Benedick and Claudio entering in the midst of a mock sword fight. Kevin Kline (Benedick) explains that Freedman was "using the sword fight to set up this battle to follow. . . . It's also about the male bonding of these guys, who are soldiers and doing what guys like that like to do when they're together" (Bennetts 1988, 15). Similarly, Kahn's Shakespeare Theatre production "solved the problem of Claudio" by having him and Benedick "enter playing at sword-fighting. It's playing all right, but there's an overlay of competitiveness to it, as though the younger Claudio would like, just once, to score a palpable hit on Benedick. Claudio wants the men to see him as a man, and he aspires to all of their values" (Timpane 1994, 9).[39] Later in the play, Claudio's aspiration to share the values of his military comrades leads him to place his duty to Don Pedro above his newly formed relationship with Hero. As Harry Berger notices at the beginning of 3.2, "Claudio clings to the Prince before his wedding, begging to escort him to Arragon as soon as the marriage is consummated" (1982, 312). Such a request illustrates the Count's desire to show his allegiance to a masculine, military ideology that puts alliances between men before intersexual ties.[40] On stage, if Claudio grasps the arm of the Prince when he announces his departure and displays evident disappointment when Don Pedro forbids him to remain in his company after the wedding, audiences may readily perceive the conflict between Claudio's loyalty to his liege and his new liaison with Hero.

In the theater, it is also possible to signal that Claudio's marriage to Hero primarily creates a familial affiliation between males. In 2.1, when Leonato first grants Claudio his daughter and his fortunes, the Count does not react verbally until Beatrice nudges him to respond. Before he speaks, should Claudio clasp and vigorously shake the hand of his future father-in-law, so that Beatrice's prompt comes as a reminder that he ought not to neglect his bride, spectators may understand that his happiness is elicited at least as much by his lucrative connection to Leonato as it is by his affection for Hero. Declan Donnellan's 1998 Cheek by Jowl production goes a step further by including Don Pedro's renewal of his bond with Claudio in the same stage action:

> When Don Pedro wins Hero's hand for Claudio . . . Claudio turns upstage, presumably to look upon Hero, and, visibly moved, he

rushes upstage, flying past the stunned Hero, to embrace Don Pedro. The staging is hilarious and pointed. After embracing Don Pedro, Claudio then moves on to Hero's father and embraces him. Finally, remembering Hero, he goes to her and calmly takes her hand. Clearly, Hero is a convenient link for her husband-to-be, one that connects him to other men. (J. Collins 1998, 11)

By the same token, the agreement to substitute Antonio's daughter for the "dead" Hero may be performed as a reforging of the family tie between Claudio and Leonato. As he intones the words, "I do embrace your offer" (5.1.288), Claudio may advance to Leonato and warmly grip the old man's hand with both of his own, shaking it in a subdued echo of the vigorous embrace he gives Leonato at the moment when Hero is first presented to him. This parallel undercuts the romantic notion that Claudio marries for love alone while simultaneously emphasizing his pursuit of beneficial connections within the male sphere.

The masculine hierarchy is not completely reunified until the end of the play, when Claudio's friendship with Benedick is restored and Benedick counsels Don Pedro to enter the brotherhood of cuckolds. One modern production, Bill Alexander's 1990 directorial effort for the RSC, placed considerable emphasis on the reunion of the Count and his wartime companion as the culmination of the play's action. According to Peter Holland, "the play's attitude towards women" was that "they were of far less importance than male-bonding and an awareness of social hierarchies." Holland claims that this attitude was most evident in the final scene, when the animosity between the two men finally subsided:

> By the end of this production the relationship of Beatrice and Benedick mattered much less than Claudio and Benedick, a relationship still as venomous after the rebirth of Hero as it had been after her death. . . . Only Beatrice's intervention stopped Benedick continuing the quarrel after Claudio's sneering delivery of his final speech in the play (5.4.111–15) and the play's climax was effectively the reconciliation of the two men with a handshake. (1991, 171)

At this point, Claudio and Benedick have rebuilt their battlefield camaraderie through their common status as husbands, which excludes their wartime companion the Prince. Therefore, several modern productions have chosen to focus on the isolation of Don Pedro as a means to add pathos to the otherwise joyful ending of the comedy. For example, Michael J. Collins records the Prince's forlorn detachment in Matthew Warchus's 1993 production at the Queen's Theatre: "As the company broke into couples for the final dance, Don Pedro crossed to the left edge of the stage and looked out, weeping at the audience" (1994, 17).[41] Such a staging is based on a modern reading of Benedick's observation, "Prince, thou art sad" (5.4.120–21) to mean that Don Pedro is unhappy, but in the early modern period, "sad" was commonly a synonym for "serious" without the connotation of sorrow, as in Don Pedro's remark, "pluck up, my heart, and be sad. Did he not say my brother was fled? (5.1.200–201).[42] Benedick's final cuckold joke—"get thee a wife, get thee a wife! There is no staff more reverend than one tipped with horn"—is designed both to tickle the somber Prince and to relieve his isolation by inducing him to join the ranks of the wedded males. In performance, Benedick may act out a figurative version of this encouragement by calling Claudio to assist him in dragging Don Pedro across the stage to pair him up with one of the waiting gentlewomen for the final dance.[43] This staging underlines the coercive nature of the social imperatives supporting matrimony, while it also highlights the transformation of cuckoldry from a severe threat to masculinity to a condition that happily binds men to one another.

In contrast to the stage history of *Two Gentlemen*, that of *Much Ado* reveals few concerted attempts to employ the critical observations of feminist scholarship in the theater. Perhaps because the plot does not demand that spectators observe Claudio performing any act approaching the heinousness of Proteus's rape attempt, directors (and editors) have almost inevitably opted to alter or concretize the text in such a way that Claudio's misdeeds are represented as understandable, forgivable mistakes that he sorely regrets and Hero lovingly pardons. Although one may discern an increased emphasis on male bonding in performances of the play since the advent of feminism, no production has offered a consistent treatment of the ways in which the drive to link men together shapes their attitude towards women and the social institution of marriage. *Much Ado* requires relatively little editorial and theatrical tinkering to render it in the spirit of romantic comedy, and perhaps for this reason, the option of performing it as a comedy of forgiveness remains largely unexplored.

Chapter 4
"Service is no heritage":
All's Well that Ends Well

Bertram also demands a good actor, if the spectator is to perceive that this is a man capable of rewarding efforts so great
on the part of a woman. . . . That this unsentimental youth
has a heart . . . is indeed *read* in his scanty words, but few
readers of the present day are free enough from sentimentality to believe such things on the credit of a few words. The
case is entirely different when, in the *acted* Bertram, they *see*
the noble nature, the ruin of his character at Florence, and
the contrition which his sins and his simplicity call forth.

(Gervinus 1903, 185–86)

G. G. GERVINUS OFFERS AN ARGUMENT THAT HAS NOW BECOME A
commonplace in the criticism of *All's Well*: the idea that, while
Bertram may appear irredeemable to readers of the play, in the
theater, his visible contrition will signify to audiences the "noble
nature" that the written text regrettably neglects to articulate.[1]
However, those like Gervinus who invoke performance to solve
the problem of Bertram's sudden repentance seldom acknowledge that they refer to only one of many possible versions of
"the *acted* Bertram," a single alternative that can neither establish the nature of the character once and for all nor explain
away the issue of his troublesome reversal. As Richard Levin
notes,

It is true that a talented actor can do a lot with Bertram's role, even
with that limp final couplet he has to speak. Indeed, if Shakespeare
had not given him any lines at all to express his conversion, the
actor might be able to mime it quite persuasively. I am not sure
what this proves, however, since we still have to acknowledge . . .
that the part presents a real difficulty that the performance must
strive to *overcome*. (1988, 34)

112

Implicit in the remarks of both Levin and Gervinus is the notion that one function of performance is to overcome the inadequacies of the text, to supply on stage whatever the play lacks to make it fit securely into a generic category like romantic comedy. And yet, because their attention is devoted to what is putatively "missing" from the text, neither critic considers the possibility that Bertram's sudden about-face, which appears so implausible to readers, might be designed to be performed with exactly the same effect on spectators. Although the Count vows to love the detested Helena forevermore, if viewers suspect, with good reason, that he may not fulfill this promise, they may also be drawn to observe the social forces that have maneuvered him into this predicament in the first place. An alternative goal for a performance of *All's Well* as a comedy of forgiveness (rather than a faulty romantic comedy) might be to instill an awareness of society's efforts to redirect the promiscuous sexual impulses of young men like Bertram towards marriage and legitimate procreation.

Of the three Forgiven Comic Heroes examined to this point, Bertram is the first to display no erotic desire for the Griselda, whom he eventually marries. While Proteus and Claudio freely confess their romantic affection for Julia and Hero, Bertram expresses only repugnance toward Helena until the final scene of *All's Well*, when he undergoes his problematic conversion. In an attempt to address this difficulty, theatrical personnel have typically employed stage business early in the play to suggest within Bertram a buried tenderness toward his mother's servant that the circumstances of the closing scene bring to the surface. For example, in Laird Williamson's 1996 Shakespeare Theatre production, the director appended a prescene described by Alan C. Dessen:

> A lengthy pre-show sequence started with a seated Lavatch and two children (younger versions of Bertram and Helena) who disappeared, to be replaced by their adult counterparts. . . . At the end of this sequence, an amorous Bertram made a move to seduce Helena, and she pulled away. This episode explained his displeasure with her in 1.1 and set up her virginity speech. (1997a, 5)

Such an interpolation presents an audience with visual evidence of the Count's sexual attraction to Helena, which the text conspicuously omits. Her rejection of his advances explains his open antipathy toward her, but the demonstration of his "amorous" feelings also paves the way for spectators' acceptance of the "fact" that, when Bertram promises to love Helena in act 5, he is merely swearing to do what he has wanted to do all along.

Commonly, performances of *All's Well* insinuate that Bertram's hidden love for Helena would have surfaced much sooner had it not been for the malevolent influence of Parolles, whose antimatrimonial and promiscuous attitude rubs off on the impressionable young Count. As opposed to *Two Gentlemen* and *Much Ado*, in which Shakespeare assigns the model narrative roles of the Friend and the Vice figure to distinct characters, *All's Well* unites the braggart companion with the Vice-like villain in the guise of Parolles. In *Much Ado*, the male Friend who opposes marriage but eventually enters the brotherhood of cuckolds (Benedick) is a separate character from the figure who disrupts the hero's wedding (Don John), which allows the Messinians to place the blame for Claudio's actions on the Bastard and to reestablish the bond between Claudio and Benedick at the end of the play. In *All's Well*, however, the hybrid nature of Parolles complicates the usual pattern because he serves as both the companion, with whom the hero is typically reunited, and the character who is scapegoated for the hero's indiscretions. Parolles, disgraced and impoverished, is no longer fit company for Bertram and can find no other place in the social formation aside from a debased role as Lord Lafew's fool. Bertram's marriage to Helena links him to the Authority figure, the King of France, who arranges the match and provides Helena's dowry, but the bond between the Count and Parolles must be severed so that Bertram may recapture his place in the male social hierarchy.

Significantly, although several characters in the play fault Parolles for leading Bertram astray, Shakespeare never dramatizes this negative influence to the extent that he enacts Don John's manipulation of Claudio. As Robert Grams Hunter states, "Parolles is unquestionably a low fellow and far from suitable company for the young, but we never see him actively misleading, tempting, or corrupting Bertram" (1965, 120). In fact, the scenes containing Bertram's most cruel and misguided resistance to marriage with Helena (2.3 and 2.5) show no evidence of the direct inducement to evil of which Parolles is later accused. Therefore, an argument can be made that those who charge Parolles with Bertram's misdeeds do so in a partisan attempt to exonerate the Count, in whose rehabilitation they have a considerable stake, at the expense of the social-climber

Parolles. Nevertheless, modern productions have tended to interpolate stage business, particularly in 2.3 and 2.5, to supply the proof of Parolles' maneuvering of Bertram that the written text pointedly omits. These additions help to absolve the Count of responsibility for his offenses against marriage and make it easier for spectators both to forgive him and to accept his sudden resolution to honor his marital vows in the final scene.[2]

By marrying off Bertram in the first half of the play, *All's Well* moves into step three of the channeling process: turning the erotic impulses of the Forgiven Comic Hero away from extramarital sex toward procreative sexuality within marriage. In particular, the play focuses on the ways in which society pressures young males to renounce a life of barren, licentious sexual activity and to embrace their obligation to people the world with legitimate offspring. For further references to this social drive, I would like to turn for a moment to Shakespeare's procreation sonnets, specifically Sonnet 9, which abandons the strategy of exhorting the young man to beget a son for the benefit of his own self-perpetuation and turns instead to the concerns of "the world," which maintains a keen interest in his failure thus far to produce an heir:

> Ah, if thou issueless shalt hap to die,
> The world will wail thee like a makeless wife.
> The world will be thy widow and still weep
> That thou no form of thee hast left behind
> . . . .
> No love toward others in that bosom sits
> That on himself such murd'rous shame commits.
> (lines 3–6, 13–14)

This social dimension of the procreative process takes the form of familial pressure on the young man to carry out his duty to pass down the honor of his house for others' sake as well as his own. Robert Crosman, who argues for Southampton as the target of Shakespeare's exhortations, suggests, "If the sonnets are not addressed to Southampton, then they are addressed to someone very much like him: a vain young aristocrat with a beautiful mother and a dead father, whose family was eager to see him marry and beget an heir, but who was not himself eager to put aside self-admiration, casual sex, and perhaps crushes on older men" (1990, 486). Such a description of the young man of the Sonnets also fits Bertram, who finds himself in a similar sit-

uation vis-à-vis his own recently widowed mother, who supports
the designs of Helena to become her son's wife. However, Bertram disdains Helena's lowly origins and flees with his mentor
Parolles to the Tuscan wars, where he attempts to seduce the
virtuous Diana. Here, the play goes beyond the situation
described in Sonnet 9 by enacting the triumph of the "makeless
wife," who beguiles the Count into unwittingly fulfilling his
ancestral responsibility by means of a bed trick. She conceives
a child through this union, and "the world" eventually has its
way.

Despite the fact that Helena's conspiracy achieves its desired
effect, *All's Well* does not resolve the original contradiction
between Bertram's desire to engage in unfettered sexual liaisons and his social obligation to father legitimate heirs. Indeed,
Bertram's interactions with the predominantly male society of
the court exacerbates this conflict by encouraging him in both
directions at once. The King urges Bertram to live up to the
example set by his father, a family man and a soldier, but the
sexual ethics associated with these roles, as the play presents
them, are seemingly incompatible. While marriage promotes
monogamous sexuality for the purpose of procreation, the code
of military behavior condones the illicit seduction of young
maids as analogous to the slaughter of enemies on the battlefield. At the end of the play, Bertram is first celebrated for his
service in the wars, then condemned by his king and mother for
his metaphorically equivalent act of military "service" performed, as Bertram thinks, upon Diana.[3] Helena's climactic
reappearance dramatizes the ostensible resolution of this contradiction, for it demonstrates to Bertram that a man may love
like a soldier and a father at the same time. Helena's bed trick
allows Bertram to experience the thrill of licentious sex, then
her pregnancy both legitimizes that experience and fulfills the
Count's lineal duty. Of course, this resolution is imaginary, for
as Janet Adelman points out, "the act imagined to have been
deeply illicit is magically revealed as having been licit all along"
(1989, 152).[4] Nevertheless, Bertram submits to this illusory solution and accepts his designated position as both soldier and
father.

In Althusserian terminology, the conclusion of *All's Well*
exemplifies the way in which ideology situates the subject (Bertram) in a " 'lived' . . . relation to the real" (1970, 233–34), which,
in the words of James Kavanagh, provides the subject with "a
set of pre-conscious image-concepts in which men and women

see and experience, before they think about, their place within a given social formation." Ideology, in this context, refers to "a system of representations that offer the subject an imaginary, compelling sense of reality in which crucial contradictions of self and social order appear resolved" (1985, 145). In Bertram's case, the bed trick and the resulting pregnancy offer him just such a "compelling sense of reality," which seems to resolve the conflict between his individual desire and the needs of the social order. However, the text also encounters difficulty attempting to reconcile the lustful, "wicked" intent of Bertram's act of seduction and the chaste, "lawful" meaning of his conjugal union with his wife. As Helena says before implementing the bed trick,

> Let us assay our plot; which, if it speed,
> Is wicked meaning in a lawful deed,
> And lawful meaning in a lawful act,
> Where both not sin, and yet a sinful fact.
> But let's about it.
>
> (3.7.44–48)

Faced with the ambiguity of the deed that she and Bertram are about to perform, Helena cannot avoid the conclusion that it is both "lawful" and "sinful" at the same time. Unable to resolve the conflict, she dismisses it in favor of direct action to reclaim Bertram for the social order: "But let's about it."[5] Helena inevitably falls silent when she encounters the notion that lascivious male desire may be turned to legitimate procreative use,[6] for such a paradox contradicts the cultural assumption that, as Sonnet 129 puts it, "lust in action" is "Th' expense of spirit in a waste of shame" (lines 1–2). Nevertheless, the play also highlights the biological truth that illicit copulation is no more "wasteful," in a reproductive sense, than married sexuality; the product of an extramarital coupling is simply not recognized by society as a legitimate heir.

Thus, the written text of *All's Well* manifests both the successful reconciliation of the subject to the social order and the unresolved contradictions that ought to impede such resolution. This counterposition of contrary ideological elements is a characteristic strength of Shakespearean drama, but the allowance of discursive space to opposed ideological components

also destabilizes the reconciliation effect that the text seeks to achieve within a given cultural ideology. The achievement of the

appropriate effect with a text that opens itself so to insurgent ideological positions becomes more heavily reliant on the context of
extra-textual ideological, political, and economic practices that sur-
round and enmesh the text, and manage its consumption. (Kavanagh 1985, 159)

Critical discourse represents one extratextual practice that
"develops and realizes the ideological effects of a literary text"
(Macherey and Balibar 1980, 56). When the text is dramatic,
however, *performative* discourse may also serve to manage its
consumption, providing a context in which the "reconciliation
effect" may achieve stability within a particular cultural ideology. As this chapter's examination of *All's Well* on the stage will
demonstrate, the performance choices of directors and actors
have tended to eliminate or distract attention away from conflicts present in the written text, thereby averting ideological
discord between the performed text and its spectators. This
practice will become most evident in a consideration of the production history of 5.3, with emphasis on the moment of Helena's
return, pregnant, to Rossillion, which offers various manifesta-
tions of the ideological function of performance.

Upon Bertram's arrival at the Court of France, the King comments on the young Count's physical likeness to his predeces-
sor: "Youth, thou bear'st thy father's face / . . . Thy father's moral
parts / Mayest thou inherit too!" (1.2.19, 21–22). This resemblance is at the heart of Bertram's conflict with society, for his
friends and family, "eager to see a potential for nobility in him
that he does not really possess . . . keep saying they hope he will
live up to the virtues and achievements of his famous father"
(Parker 1984, 100). The Count's responsibility to uphold the
family name is symbolized by his ancestral ring, which he later
hesitates to give to Diana as proof of his affection: "It is an honour 'longing to our house, / Bequeathed down from many
ancestors, / Which were the greatest obloquy i' th' world / In me
to lose" (4.2.42–45). This ring represents not only Bertram's
duty to emulate his honorable forbears, but also his link in a
chain of inheritance that has endured for generations. To avoid
disgrace, Bertram must both keep the ring (the honor of his
house handed down to him intact by his father) and eventually
produce a "sequent issue" (5.3.196) to whom he may bequeath
it. Thus, Bertram's responsibility extends to future generations
as well as to the past; he owes it to his father *and* his son to serve
as the intermediary between them. As the poet reminds the

young man in Sonnet 13, "You had a father; let your son say so" (line 14).

Despite his duty to his house, Bertram gives away the symbol of his honor to a woman who cannot produce for him a legitimate heir, thereby endangering his link in the generational chain in both directions at once. The discrepancy between Bertram's ancestral obligations and his wartime behavior is one symptom of the conflicts within and between the ideologies that dominate the civilian and military spheres. When Bertram first appears at Court, the King urges him to emulate his father, the famous soldier, but when the Tuscan wars arise, the King prohibits the very emulation he ordains. Bertram is "commanded here, and kept a coil with / 'Too young,' and 'The next year' and "Tis too early' " (2.1.27–28). Frustrated by this contradiction, Bertram must stand by and hear the King salute the other youths about to embark in their fathers' footsteps: "Whether I live or die, be you the sons / Of worthy Frenchmen" (2.1.11–12). The King's speech to the departing soldiers illustrates the conflicting codes of sexual ethics impressed upon the minds of the young French courtiers. Their sovereign's first command—"see that you come / Not to woo honour, but to wed it" (2.1.14–15)— employs the language of love and courtship to describe the acquisition of glory on the battlefield; honor is personified as a woman with whom the young soldier must not dally, but enjoy only within the confines of marriage. Later, the King reverses the metaphorical relationship between love and war and speaks of courtship as if it were battle: "Those girls of Italy, take heed of them; / They say our French lack language to deny / If they demand; beware of being captives / Before you serve" (2.1.10–22). Here, women are no longer personifications of honor, but enemies plotting to capture the soldiers. Contradicting his earlier mandate of committed sexuality, the King warns his lords to "serve," both literally in the field and metaphorically in the beds of the Italian girls, *before* becoming prisoners of war or love.

Looking back on his own military days, the invalid King nostalgically recalls the former Count Rossillion as a paragon of "service":

> He did look far
> Into the service of the time, and was
> Discipled of the bravest. He lasted long,
> But on us both did haggish age steal on,
> And wore us out of act.
>
> (1.2.24–30)

This passage refers, in one sense, to the elder soldiers' lack of corporal fitness for battle, but it also glances at their inability to perform the sexual "act," which the King blames on the advancement of "haggish age." Again, the soldier's enemy is personified as a woman, this time a sorceress who steals upon the unsuspecting warrior to sap his strength and virility. Plagued by this hag, the King now languishes of a fistula, an ailment described by Lafew as a form of impotence that may be cured by Helena, "whose simple touch / Is powerful to araise King Pippen, nay, / To give great Charlemain a pen in's hand / And write to her a love-line" (2.1.74–77). Old Lafew himself, in conversation with Parolles, laments the fact that age has also stolen away his own potency:

> Par. My lord, you do me most insupportable vexation.
> Laf. I would it were hell-pains for thy sake, and my poor doing eternal; for doing I am past, as I will by thee, in what motion age will give me leave. *Exit*. (2.3.227–30)

Arthur Kirsch speculates that Lafew's "compulsive interest" in Parolles stems in part from the old lord's exasperation with his own "declining sexual powers" (1981, 129); Lafew is well past "doing" while the younger soldier is not. This envious scorn of youthful sexual capacity characterizes the elder generation's disdain for younger men in the play, especially Bertram and Parolles.[7]

Faced with diminished capabilities, the old Count, as the King recalls, found no more purpose to his life: " 'Let me not live,' quoth he, / 'After my flame lacks oil, to be the snuff / Of younger spirits' " (1.2.58–60). This wish eventually comes true, for the old Count's death clears the way for his son to possess the "oil" or potency his father's flame of desire came to lack. The Countess, speaking to the King in the final scene, excuses her son's earlier disobedience as "Natural rebellion done i' th' blade of youth, / When oil and fire, too strong for reason's force, / O'erbears it and burns on" (5.3.6–8). According to Bertram's mother, the fire and oil of youth (its will and its ability to put that will into action) works unreasonably against its own self-interest. Helena clarifies the sexual component of this metaphor when she explains to the Widow that Bertram's lust for Diana burns more intensely than his devotion to the symbol of his family's honor: "This ring he holds / In most rich choice; yet, in his idle fire, / To buy his will it would not seem too dear, / Howe'er repented after" (3.7.25–28). Such youthful "abuse" of sexual capacity particularly angers the impotent Lafew, who observes Helena's choice of a husband from a distance and remarks on her suitors' apparent rejection of her proposals, "Do they all deny her? And they were sons of mine I'd have them whipp'd, or I would send them to th' Turk to make eunuchs of" (2.3.86–88). In Old Lafew's mind, any young man who foolishly passes up the chance to enjoy Helena's physical charms within the context of marriage does not deserve to possess sexual capability in the first place.

Angered by the youthful misuse of sexual potency, the King and Lafew pressure the young lords to apply their virile energies toward the reproduction of the elder generation's version of the social order. Helena's cure, although it seems to restore the King's own sexual vigor,[8] cannot remove the class barriers that disqualify her as a partner in the propagation of his royal name. He may, however, bestow enough wealth upon Helena to make her what he considers an eligible match for Bertram, through whom the King may vicariously experience a legitimate consummation with Helena and thereby perpetuate the current social structure of the Court.[9] The King's concern with procreation, not merely sexuality, as the matchmaking patriarch is evident in his description of Helena's fitness to produce offspring for the house of Rossillion:

> She is young, wise, fair;
> In these to nature she's immediate heir,
> And these breed honour; that is honour's scorn
> Which challenges itself as honour's born
> And is not like the sire.
>
> (2.3.131–35)

After praising Helena's ability to "breed honour" for Bertram, the King moves in the other direction along the chain of inheritance and criticizes Bertram's failure to uphold his father's example of honorable behavior. Ironically, the Count's own notion of honor, with its emphasis on class, forbids the type of "humility" for which his father has been commended (1.2.44). Given Bertram's present refusal to act as the link between generations, the King tries to ensure the continuation of the house of Rossillion by asserting his power to enforce the Count's cooperation in the reproductive process: "It is in us to plant thine honour where / We please to have it grow" (2.3.156–57). As if by artificial insemination, the King intends to plant the seed of Bertram's honor in Helena's womb, but the Count foils this plan by running away without bedding his wife. Like the other Forgiven Comic Heroes, Bertram cruelly rejects the woman who loves him, and until the contradiction between the sexual roles of soldier and father are resolved, he cannot be compelled to behave towards her or his family according to the King's notion of honor.

Despite Bertram's heartless treatment, Helena, like Griselda, never waivers in her devotion to him.[10] In contrast to Hero, whose affection for Claudio cannot be accurately gauged, Helena discloses an obsession with Count Rossillion in her first soliloquy: "my imagination / Carries no favour in't but Bertram's. / I am undone; there is no living, none, / If Bertram be away" (1.1.80–83). This all-encompassing love emanates unmistakably from an erotic attraction to its object. Bertram's devastating good looks—"His arched brows, his hawking eye, his curls" (1.1.92)—inspire in Helena a sexual passion that impels her to hazard everything, even her life, in order to achieve its consummation: "The hind that would be mated by the lion / Must die for love" (1.1.89–90). By envisioning herself as a deer willing to risk death to mate with a wild cat, Helena picks up an image from the earlier comedies of forgiveness whereby the Comic Hero is associated with a murderous, ravenous lion. At the beginning of *Much Ado*, the Messenger commends Claudio for his service in the wars: "He hath borne himself beyond the promise of his age, doing, in the figure of a lamb, the feats of a lion" (1.1.12–14). Similarly, near the end of *Two Gentlemen*, Silvia contrasts Proteus's unwelcome heroics with an attack by a savage and famished creature: "Had I been seized by a hungry lion, / I would have been a breakfast to the beast, / Rather than have false Proteus rescue me" (5.4.33–35). Proteus's ensuing sexual assault on Silvia, coupled with the deadly consequences of Helena's imagined erotic union with the lion, links this beast to the dangerous carnal impulses of the Forgiven Comic Hero. Like the "savage bull" of *Much Ado*, who represents the untamed sexual desires of the unmarried male, the ferocious lion symbolizes for Helena the wild sexual urges of Bertram that she must domesticate, possibly at the cost of her own survival.

Chancing death to cure the King's disease, Helena wins the right to choose Bertram, against his will, as her husband. After their wedding, in the spirit of Griselda, she proclaims her subservience to her husband with such fervor that even Bertram becomes uncomfortable at her self-debasement:

> Hel.   Sir, I can nothing say
> But that I am your most obedient servant.
> Ber.   Come, come; no more of that.
>
> (2.5.71–76)

Back at Rossillion, when she receives his letter disavowing their marriage and imposing the impossible tasks, Helena's ardor is not quenched; rather, she blames herself for Bertram's self-imposed exile and resolves to expiate her sins by making a pilgrimage to Saint Jacques le Grand.[11] In Florence, she discovers the Count's attempts to seduce Diana, but Bertram's adulterous longing neither curbs her own affection nor dissuades her from carrying out the impossible tasks by arranging the bed trick. Faking her own death, Helena deceives her husband into returning to France, where her conspiracy with the Widow and Diana brings out the worst of Bertram's duplicitous and scornful nature. In spite of his contemptuous behavior, Helena holds Bertram to the bargain in his letter and restores him to the favor of the King through her conception of an heir to continue the honorable house of Rossillion.

Bertram cannot, by himself, successfully reenter the male hierarchy because he fails to reconcile, until the play's end, the conflicting expectations of the Court and the military domain, where the concept of "service" governs battlefield and bedroom activity. In both arenas, the object is to kill one's enemy: either to slay the soldier in the field or to be the death of a maid's virginity. While civilian society openly glorifies the first type of service, it publicly condemns (yet privately winks at) the second, branding illicit seduction a barren, sterile pursuit that does not serve social ends. However, a competing military ideology espoused primarily by Parolles temporarily resolves this contradiction for Bertram by asserting that "Loss of virginity is rational increase" (1.1.125). In other words, all copulation, even "service" performed outside marriage, is potentially procreative; therefore, a man may kill and bring life in the same sexual act. Although Parolles' own soldiership is debatable, as a voluble *miles gloriosus*,[12] he functions as the spokesman for an exaggerated version of the military ideology that "true" soldiers, like the brothers Dumaine, secretly disparage. Bertram shares the braggart soldier's attitude until his exposure in act 4, which invalidates Parolles' construction of reality and prepares the Count for his reacceptance into civilian society.

Helena first introduces Parolles as "a notorious liar" and "a coward" with "some stain of soldier" in him (1.1.98–99, 109). As part and parcel of his military braggardism, Parolles affects a disdain for marriage that resembles that exhibited by Benedick and Don John in *Much Ado*. Within that play, the professed tyrant and the true opponent to matrimony threaten to merge into one figure, particularly when Beatrice and Leonato say of the Prince's brother,

> *Beat.* He were an excellent man that were made just in the mid-way between him and Benedick: the one is too like an image and says nothing, and the other too like my lady's eldest son, evermore tattling.
>
> *Leon.* Then half Signior Benedick's tongue in Count John's mouth, and half Count John's melancholy in Signior Benedick's face. (2.1.6–12)

Parolles in *All's Well* represents such a cross between the voluble Benedick and the taciturn Don John, for Parolles is both a talkative character whose name means "words" and a soldier who affects a silent and "melancholy" resolution to his fate (3.5.85). Leaving the stage, ostensibly to undertake the recovery of his company's drum, he avows, "I love not many words" (3.6.80), echoing Don John's first speech in *Much Ado*: "I thank you: I am not of many words, but I thank you" (1.1.146–47). Other characters' remarks about Parolles misleading Bertram have led critics to compare him, as I have done with Don John, to the medieval Vice,[13] but as John M. Love notes, "Unlike every Vice from Newgyse to Iago, Parolles never confides in the audience any plot against the hero" (1977, 518). While Don John directly informs viewers of his plan to prevent Claudio's wedding, Parolles merely abets Bertram's own ploy to escape his enforced marriage.

After Bertram agrees to marry Helena in reluctant obedience to the King of France, the Count unhappily endures the offstage wedding ceremony, then returns to bemoan his fate with his closest comrade:

> *Ber.* Although before the solemn priest I have sworn, I will not bed her.
>
> *Par.* What, what, sweetheart?

> *Ber.* O my Parolles, they have married me!
> I'll to the Tuscan wars and never bed her.
>
> (2.3.263–69)

Although Bertram has sworn to love Helena, this exchange with Parolles clearly exhibits their competing emotional investment in each other; the braggart calls Bertram "sweetheart" while the Count refers to his friend as "my Parolles." This bond may inhibit Bertram's capacity to form a meaningful male-female relationship, but Parolles does not initiate the Count's separation from his wife. As Jules Rothman notes, "Parolles supports, applauds, foments if you will, but does not instigate what Bertram has decided for himself" (1972, 185–86): to escape the consummation of his marriage by running off to the Tuscan wars, "those Italian fields where noble fellows strike" (2.3.286–87). Bertram's desire to experience battlefield camaraderie with men endangers his marriage, just as the sexual component of marriage, according to Parolles, drains the masculine juices that would qualify him to join his fellow soldiers on the battleground:

> To th' wars, my boy, to th' wars!
> He wears his honour in a box unseen
> That hugs his kicky-wicky here at home,
> Spending his manly marrow in her arms,
> Which should sustain the bound and high curvet
> Of Mars's fiery steed.
>
> (2.3.274–79)

Since marital relations sap the potency that allows a man to perform as "Mars's fiery steed," matrimony imperils Bertram's identity as a soldier; in Parolles' proverbial wisdom, "A young man married is a man that's marr'd" (2.3.294).[14] Like Benedick, who envisions a married man yoked to his wife, sighing away Sundays, Parolles imagines a husband remaining "here at home," hugging his kicky-wicky while his former companions face the hardships of battle together. Near the end of the scene, Bertram reveals a preference for war over marriage which coincides closely with that of Parolles: "Wars is no strife / To the dark house and the detested wife" (2.3.287–88).

At the Tuscan wars, Bertram discovers the male comradeship he seeks, but he also pursues an intersexual liaison with the Florentine maid Diana. His object, however, is not to form a lasting bond with the woman; rather, he means to seduce and abandon her, to achieve a conquest that will earn him recognition among his male peers. Bertram shares with his friend the second Lord Dumaine his intent to try Diana's virtue: "Now will I lead you to the house and show you / The lass I spoke of . . . . / She's a fair creature; / Will you go see her? (3.6.106–7, 112–13). Bertram is not content to bed Diana merely for the sake of the act itself; the seduction is incomplete unless he can also display his prize before an appreciative male audience. Thus, in the wartime context, male bonds also depend upon a camaraderie of the sexual battlefield, where women and their virtue represent an enemy to be despoiled.

Unlike conjugal relations, extramarital sex (because it resembles military combat) does not threaten to diminish the martial capabilities of the soldier; in fact, Bertram's victories on the battlefield and the bedroom seem to progress along parallel courses. Diana recounts that "the French count has done most honourable service," and her mother adds, "It is reported that he has taken their great'st commander, and that with his own hand he slew the duke's brother" (3.5.3–7). Just as Bertram's "service" in war involves the slaying of the duke's brother, his supposed seduction of Diana is described privately by the second Captain Dumaine as the slaughter of her virginity: "He hath perverted a young gentlewoman here in Florence, of a most chaste renown, and this night he fleshes his will in the spoil of her honour" (4.3.13–15). As G. K. Hunter notes, "To 'flesh a hound with the spoil' was to give it some of the flesh of the hunted animal to eat, to stimulate its hunting instincts. So, Bertram's *will* (lust) is to be *fleshed* (rewarded and stimulated) with the honour of the girl it has hunted down" (1959, 105n). Dumaine, who has himself accompanied the Count on the hunt for Diana, now somewhat hypocritically censures Bertram for tracking down his innocent prey, then killing and devouring her honor. In Dumaine's view, the Count has taken the first step toward demonstrating the violent and voracious sexual appetite ascribed to him by Parolles: "I knew the young count to be a dangerous and lascivious boy, who is a whale to virginity, and devours up all the fry it finds" (4.3.211–13).

All's Well insistently portrays Bertram's pursuit of Diana as a martial campaign with sexual conquest as its objective.[15] As Helena tells the Widow, "The count he woos your daughter, / Lays down his wanton siege before her beauty, / Resolv'd to carry her" (3.7.17–19). Diana herself reproaches Bertram for attempting to carry out this form of military service:

Ber.   I love thee
     By love's own sweet constraint, and will for ever
     Do thee all rights of service.
Dia.   Ay, so you serve us
     Till we serve you; but when you have our roses,
     You barely leave our thorns to prick ourselves,
     And mock us with our bareness.

                                         (4.2.15–20)

As Diana knows, Bertram intends to pluck the rose of her chastity and leave her bare of honor, an image which John F. Adams argues represents the "barrenness" of dishonorable sexual union (1961, 267).[16] The Clown Lavatch agrees that carnal service outside of marriage is unfruitful: "Service is no heritage, and I think I shall never have the blessing of God till I have issue a' my body; for they say barnes are blessings" (1.3.21–24). As Elizabeth Sacks comments,

> The word "service" is double-edged, referring both to domestic servitude and sexual service, and the Clown's speech thus acquires a second meaning: "There is no future in sexual dalliance; I must marry and found a family." The sexual pun on "service" points up the ["fact" that] illicit sexual encounter is sterile, offering no promise of children. Only marriage assures survival—"heritage," "blessing of God"—through procreation. (1980, 52)

The Clown's proverbial phrasing ("Service is no heritage"— "they say barnes are blessings") suggests that Lavatch articulates the civilian social order's ideology of procreation. Bertram, as a subject, must also come to accept the sterility of service if he is to assume his place within that social formation.

However, Parolles' military code offers Bertram a different ideology that resolves for the time being the conflict between his desire for uncommitted sex and the wastefulness of such activity. According to Parolles (and biological fact), illicit sex is potentially no less procreative than conjugal relations, so a soldier's brief encounter with a maid will not necessarily leave her barren. When Helena asks Parolles to unfold some "warlike resistance" to man's assault against virginity, the braggart replies, "There is none. Man setting down before you will undermine you and blow you up" (1.1.141–17).[17] A soldier "setting down" before a virgin, like Bertram laying down his "wanton siege" before Diana's beauty, may easily swell her womb with his unborn child. The military context of these remarks implies that Parolles refers to martial service, but he does not specify that such a loss of virginity takes place outside of marriage; indeed, the question of marriage does not arise. Parolles merely argues against virginity as an impediment to the natural, fruitful process of procreation: "Virginity, by being once lost, may be ten times found, by being ever kept it is ever lost. . . . There's little can be said in't; 'tis against the rule of nature. To speak on the part of virginity is to accuse your mothers, which is most infallible disobedience" (1.1.128–35). Bertram's identification with this sense of reality is evident in the reasoning he uses to talk Diana into bed with him: "And now you should be as your mother was / When your sweet self was got" (4.2.9–10). Like Parolles' appeal to the mothers of virgins,[18] Bertram's encouragement of Diana to follow in her mother's sexual footsteps affirms procreation while avoiding the issue of marriage altogether.

Nevertheless, Diana will not allow Bertram to disregard the fact that her mother's procreative sex act occurred within the bonds of matrimony:

> *Dia.* My mother did but duty; such, my lord,
>   As you owe to your wife.
> *Ber.*   No more a' that!
>
>   (4.2.12–13)

Diana's reminder of the unpalatable truth provokes in Bertram an outburst that reveals his irritation with Diana's spoken resistance, as well as his mounting desire for her.[19] Such a response identifies her as the Shrew of the model narrative, a role she plays most clearly in the final scene of the play. Under the King's interrogation, her riddling answers to his inquiries about the Count enrage her questioner: "She does abuse our ears. To prison with her" (5.3.288). Diana's paradoxes and verbal evasiveness irritate her male listeners, and the angry King orders her removed from his presence.

Contrary to Bertram's expectations, his "conquest" of the Shrew does not raise him in the eyes of his military fellows. The brothers Dumaine condemn his ruination of Diana's good name and hatch a plot to separate the Count from Parolles, the proponent of the antimatrimonial position, whom they now blame for Bertram's indiscretions. To show Parolles' untrustworthiness, the Dumaines arrange to have him captured and questioned by soldiers posing as the enemy. During this scene, Parolles' interrogator finds in the braggart's pocket a set of verses written to Diana, warning her of the Count's disreputable intentions and pressing his own claim to her love. In the corresponding scene of *Much Ado*, in which Benedick overhears Leonato, Don Pedro, and Claudio speak of Beatrice's concealed love, Benedick betrays his hidden affection for Leonato's ward, which is later proven, again, through the discovery of verses: a "halting sonnet of his own pure brain / Fashion'd to Beatrice" (5.4.87–88). In both gulling segments, the Friend of the Count is exposed as a fraud, a traitor to the military ideal of sexual service and disdain for love and marriage.

The revelation of Parolles' double-dealing drives a wedge between Bertram and his companion, which leads the Count to disavow his allegiance to his former mentor. As Bertram later portrays Parolles to the King, "He's quoted for a most perfidious slave / With all the spots a' th' world tax'd and debosh'd, / Whose nature sickens but to speak a truth" (5.3.204–6). Having recognized Parolles' duplicity, Bertram disputes the truth of anything the braggart soldier might claim, particularly his valorization of sexual service, which the Count now views as mere debauchery. Thus, the conclusion of the play demonizes Parolles' alternative ideology with an *ad hominem* argument rather than a refutation of its principles, and residual conflicts persist. When we see Bertram in act 5, he is eager to please the King by marrying and assuming his position within the civilian social order, but traces of Parolles' version of the military ideology still remain within his "lived relation to the real."

In Bertram's eyes, his sojourn in the wars succeeds on all fronts: he lives up to his father's example as a soldier, and he achieves what he believes to be a sexual conquest in the tradition of military service. His own reputation as a warrior secured, Bertram tries to make peace with the civilian social order by accepting a match with Lafew's daughter, which would allow him to emulate the old Count once again, this time as a producer of legitimate heirs.[20] Bertram's battlefield success has already led to one metaphorical pregnancy; the Duke of Florence, promoting Bertram to the command of his cavalry, ordains, "The general of our horse thou art, and we, / Great in our hope, lay our best love and credence / Upon thy promising fortune" (3.3.1–3). The Count's match with Maudlin is arranged so that he may make *her* "great" with child as well, but this marriage does not resolve the conflict between the codes governing the sexual behavior of the soldier and the father. Until Helena's reappearance, Bertram merely assigns these contradictory ethics to different spheres: he keeps the lustful, uncommitted copulation acceptable within the military context separate from the lawful, monogamous sexuality appropriate to the bonds of matrimony. Only Helena's legitimate pregnancy, engendered through an hour of "illicit" passion, can unite these two standards and fully reconcile Bertram to his social position. The visual revelation of Helena in a pregnant state embodies this resolution, fusing together in one form the chaste woman who has provided him with sexual stimulation and the wife who will bear him a child.

Before this match can be arranged, the members of civilian society must rehabilitate Bertram's wounded reputation by scapegoating Parolles for the Count's reprehensible conduct toward his spouse and King. When the Countess and Lafew prepare to greet her wayward son, they openly shift responsibility for his transgressions and the demise of his wife to Parolles' shoulders:

> *Laf.*   No, no, no, your son was misled with a snipp'd-taffeta fellow there.... Your daughter-in-law had been alive at this hour, and your son here at home, more advanc'd by the king than by that red-tail'd humble-bee I speak of.
>
> *Count.*   I would I had not known him; it was the death of the most virtuous gentlewoman that ever nature had praise for creating. (4.5.1–10)

Vivian Thomas points out that "despite Parolles' bad influence on Bertram, the audience can't take Lafew's rationalisation at face value. As Lafew goes on to inform the Countess that the King has agreed to a marriage between his daughter and Bertram, the scene has all the flavour of an exercise designed to restore social harmony and reintegrate Bertram into the community" (1987, 155). Since Lafew stands to profit from a marriage between the Count Rossillion and his child Maudlin, he is willing to exaggerate the extent of Parolles' culpability to clear the path toward this match. Leonato in *Much Ado* at least requires Claudio to perform a brief rite of penance at Hero's tomb before he will allow him to marry his "niece," but neither Lafew nor the King require anything more from Bertram by way of atonement than a simple request for pardon. In both cases, a hasty wedding welcomes the Count back into the social formation and appears destined to cement his relationship to his future father-in-law.

Once the male bonds impeding marriage have been broken, Bertram offers no resistance to the idea of matrimony, particularly as it will connect him to one of the prominent males in his community. To make amends with Leonato in *Much Ado*, Claudio agrees to marry, sight unseen, the old man's niece; Bertram, by contrast, maintains that he has loved Maudlin for some time, but the fact that he never mentions her until the play's final scene, when to do so may excuse him in the eyes of the King and Lafew, casts some doubt on the truth of his declaration. Furthermore, Bertram claims that, since he has lost Helena, he has come to love her (5.3.54), but such a sentiment, even if genuine, more likely represents an appreciation of her virtuous qualities than an erotic attraction toward a woman he now believes is dead.[21] In any case, both Count Rossillion and Count Claudio reach a point at which they are poised to wed, but as they are about to take the hands of their wives, conspirators spring a trap upon them; the woman never materializes, and the original bride is resurrected to take her place. After Claudio swears before the Friar to marry Leonato's niece, she reveals that she is actually Hero, the woman he has earlier refused to accept as his wife. Similarly, Diana appears to contest Bertram's marriage to Maudlin, whose father then withdraws his consent to the match, and Maudlin is never mentioned again. Helena returns from the dead moments later and claims Bertram as her husband, having fulfilled his tasks and consummated their marriage by means of the bed trick. Thus, in both plays, the severing of male bonds discredits the antimatrimonial position and releases the hero to approve marriage in general, which then allows him to be manipulated into accepting the particular wife whom society has picked out for him from the beginning.

When Bertram first runs away from Helena to the wars, his mother insists that "his sword can never win / The honor that he loses" (3.2.92–93), but the Count's brave service on the battlefield restores him to the good graces of the King, who accepts Bertram's excuses for his disobedient conduct and approves his upcoming engagement. When Diana's charge of a prior claim to Bertram's hand threatens to disrupt this match, the Count downplays his attachment to her as a mere youthful indiscretion: "Certain it is I lik'd her / And boarded her i' th' wanton way of youth" (5.3.209–10). Here Bertram displays vestiges of the military view of sexuality advocated by Parolles: Diana is simply a vessel "boarded" by the young soldier during his allowably wanton service in the wars. Bertram's excuse assumes, with some justification, that the King shares his distinction between the codes of sexual behavior appropriate to military and civilian life, but Lafew, the enemy to youthful carnal abuses, now rejects the Count as a match for Maudlin: "Your reputation comes too short for my daughter; you are no husband for her" (5.3.175–76). The elder generation, which rules the civilian social order, simultaneously exalts and condemns Bertram's "service" in the wars, and his reconciliation with society now appears to be in jeopardy.

At this point, Helena miraculously returns to salvage Bertram's reconcilement to the civilian society. Her pregnancy represents a change from the play's source, in which Giletta of Narbona delivers twin sons, then waits years for them to grow up to resemble their father before offering them to him as evidence that she has fulfilled one of her assigned tasks.[22] The translation from prose fiction to drama may have occasioned the foreshortening of events here, but the demand for dramatic economy cannot also account for the curious deceleration of the plot at the beginning of act 5. In reference to this slackened pace, R. B. Parker complains of "the apparently unnecessary scene at Marseilles" (1984, 111) during which Helena laments the rigors of her "exceeding posting day and night" with Diana and the Widow (5.1.1). One of the functions of this scene, however, may be to create the illusion of the passage of time between the bed trick and Helena's arrival at Rossillion, time enough for her condition to begin to show.[23] Helena's obvious pregnancy, unmentioned by the text until seconds before her appearance, may provide in performance a surprising dimension of visual significance for both the audience and Bertram.

Parker asserts that "there has certainly not been time for the pregnancy to be so advanced" (1984, 112), but Diana's prelude to Helena's entrance states specifically that her condition has progressed to the stage at which she can sense Bertram's child moving in her womb: "Dead though she be she feels her young one kick. / So there's my riddle: one that's dead is quick, / And now behold the meaning" (5.3.294–98). According to Diana's riddle, Helena is both dead and alive, lifeless yet bearing life. In a similarly paradoxical way, she is now two women to Bertram: the virgin he has killed in the line of service and the wife he has impregnated with his child. Tellingly, we must "behold" the meaning of this riddle; its significance is embodied by the visual image of Helena's pregnant form. After she appears, the text continues to direct attention to what Bertram and the others "see" when they look at her:

> King.   Is there no exorcist
> Beguiles the truer office of mine eyes?
> Is't real that I see?
> Hel.   No, my good lord;
> 'Tis but the shadow of a wife you see;
> The name and not the thing.
> Ber.   Both, both. O pardon!
>
> (5.3.298–302)

Helena claims to appear as a wife in "name" only and not as "the thing" itself, Bertram's spouse by law alone and not by practice. But when the Count views her, he sees "both" at the same time: the "shadow of a wife" whose chaste bed he has not entered and the "real" wife with whom he has conceived an off-spring. Through the bed trick, Helena portrays simultaneously the two diverse sexual partners Bertram seeks: the virgin illic-itly deflowered and the spouse who will help him fulfill his ancestral duty to procreate. Finding both coalesced into one woman, Bertram accepts this resolution, however imaginary it may be, and assumes his designated place at Helena's side, vow-ing, "If she, my liege, can make me know this clearly / I'll love her dearly, ever, ever dearly" (5.3.310). The fact that Bertram directs this conditional offer to reform toward the King rather than to his wife reveals the extent to which the Count's acknowl-edgement of the marriage represents a renewed political alli-ance with his liege at least as much as it does an emotional tie with Helena.

Since the dialogue at the end of the play allots more discourse to the reconciliation between Bertram and the King than to the reunion of the Count and his wife, a significant portion of the text's sense of comic closure derives from Bertram's reentry into the male social order. Like Claudio in *Much Ado*, the For-given Comic Hero finds himself back in the Authority figure's favor when he accepts marriage to the proper woman. However, Bertram differs from Claudio in that his bond with his friend Parolles is not restored. As Don John must be excluded from the closing festivities in the earlier play, so the scapegoat Parolles cannot be allowed by society to recontaminate Bertram. The construction of *Much Ado*, which splits Parolles' function between two characters, permits Messina both to expel the scapegoat Don John and to welcome the renewal of the hero's bond with his male friend Benedick, which results in a conclusion less fraught with complications than that of *All's Well*. Although the play brings Bertram and Helena together in fruitful matrimony, the text also provides considerable reason to view their alliance as something less than the joyous merging of souls typical of a romantic comedy.

*   *   *

From Bertram's point of view, the conflict between his individual desire and the needs of the civilian social order is resolved, but readers of *All's Well* have often found the Count's reconciliation with his wife and his society more open-ended and disturbing than one would expect in a traditional comedy. At least four sources of tension remain unresolved. First, although Parolles himself is disgraced as a coward, his alternative ideology of procreation receives some degree of persuasive articulation that is never directly refuted. Contrary to cultural beliefs, sexual service does possess a reproductive capability equal biologically to that of conjugal relations. To support the competing cultural imperative of procreation solely within marriage, productions frequently intensify the play's demonization of Parolles by altering or augmenting the text to make his supposedly evil influence over the Count more evident. If viewers can be led to believe what Lafew and the Countess claim, that the honorable Bertram would have welcomed his alliance to Helena had it not been for Parolles' interference, they will be more likely to forgive Bertram's resistance to matrimony and his sexual indiscretions as products of perverse manipulation. Stage business inserted for this purpose can be found in the stage history of 2.3, the scene of Bertram's enforced union with his wife, as well as 2.5, which includes Helena's reluctant departure for Rossillion.

Second, Helena's dual role as a virgin sinfully seduced and a wife lawfully impregnated is merely illusory; readers are fully aware, in a way that Bertram is not, that the excitement of his "illicit" act was not in the deed itself but in his mind. Recalling the tenderness of Bertram's passion when he thought he was making love to Diana, Helena admits, "when I was like this maid / I found you wondrous kind" (5.3.303–4), but the question remains whether Bertram can desire Helena for herself and not simply as a body substituted for Diana's. Therefore, performances of *All's Well* have often deployed elements of stagecraft in an effort to encourage audiences to accept a romantic basis for the relationship between Bertram and Helena that will allow them to believe in his resolution to love her "dearly, ever, ever dearly" at the end of the play. Productions generally underplay the preservation of male bonds as a motive for Bertram's behavior and devise enactments of crucial segments, such as Helena's request for a kiss in 2.5, which suggest that the Count's disdainful exterior disguises a true affection for his wife. This tendency is motivated, I would argue, by a modern preference for the intersexual and emotional aspects of the marital bond over the male homosocial and political ties accented by the written text. However, the play also offers the potential for a production that foregrounds the significance of male bonding to the institution of marriage in distinct contrast to the modern ideological inclination toward romantic ties.

The third source of tension arises, as Joseph Westlund points out (1984, 144), because Helena makes a subtle change in the tasks assigned to her by Bertram when she reads them aloud at the end of the play: "*When from my finger you can get this ring / And is by me with child, &c.*" (5.3.306–7). Technically, Bertram is not yet "doubly won" (5.3.308), for Helena's pregnancy does not fulfill the second condition as it is originally stated in his letter: "*show me a child begotten of thy body that I am father to*" (3.2.57–58). Unlike Giletta of the source, Helena still must convince Bertram that the child in her womb is his. Moreover, there is no guarantee that the baby will turn out to be the male heir to the house of Rossillion that Bertram is obliged to produce. To avoid these impediments, productions that portray Helena as visibly pregnant often provide gestures that indicate both Bertram's acknowledgement of the child as his own and his gratitude toward his wife for helping him fulfill his lineal duty.

Finally, as in the other comedies we have examined, the Forgiven Comic Hero speaks very little by way of apology to the Griselda. His ejaculation, "O pardon!" may be entirely sincere, but stage performances have so keenly felt its lack of verbal power that they have almost always accompanied it with some form of physical prostration or, in rare cases, an amplification of Bertram's speech of repentance. All of these trouble spots could potentially disrupt what Kavanagh calls "the reconciliation effect that the text seeks to achieve within a given cultural ideology," but in production, the performance choices made by actors and directors have served to manage the consumption of the text and to resolve contradictions between the text's sense of reality and that of a particular audience. My conclusion will raise the question of whether or not such contradictions *ought* to be resolved in the first place.

Act 2, scene 3 begins with Bertram, Lafew, and Parolles discussing the miraculous recovery of the King. For the next 130 lines, while Helena plays out her selection of Bertram, who vehemently rejects the match until the King threatens to abandon him, the text makes no mention of Parolles' activities. This indeterminate area of the script forces directors to choose something for Parolles to do, and a few, like Michael Benthall in his 1953 Old Vic production, have elected to make Parolles an active participant in the proceedings. Richard David recalls this strategy as an attempt to exculpate the Count:

> Bertram, however, was given every assistance by the producer who, taking a hint from Lafeu's "No, no, no, your son was misled with a snipt-taffeta fellow there," made Parolles responsible for all Rousillon's misbehavior. Bertram . . . was shown taking his cue at every step from his unsavoury pedagogue. It was Parolles whose nods and becks strengthened Bertram in his first resistance to the King's command that he should marry a commoner. (1955, 136)

Alan Dessen, in a review of Jon Jory's Oregon Shakespeare Festival production in 1975, points out how Parolles "whispers in Bertram's ear during the youth's dilemma before the King in II.iii; significantly, Bertram capitulates to royal authority in this scene only when he has been cut off from his mentor" (1976, 84). Although both stagings interpolate, without textual authority, Parolles' direct intervention to account for Bertram's reluctance to marry, Jory's version also draws attention to the way in which the male bond between Parolles and the Count must be severed, at least temporarily, if the male-female alliance is to be arranged. However, both stagings provide unwarranted justification for Lafew's contention that Bertram was misled by Parolles, which conceals the extent to which the scapegoating of the braggart soldier is a partisan attempt to return Bertram to his place in the male social order.

Shortly after the enforced wedding, we witness what J. L. Styan calls "the cruelest scene in the play" (1984, 73), Helena's reluctant leave-taking from her husband, which includes the following exchange:

> *Hel.*   Strangers and foes do sunder and not kiss.
> *Ber.*   I pray you, stay not, but in haste to horse.

(2.5.86–87)

Since the text gives no indication whether Bertram grants Helena the kiss for which she pleads, directors must choose between countless viable possibilities for the staging of this segment. However, one option, which exploits the fact that (as in 2.3) Parolles is present but has no lines, has been selected more often than all others. As David's account of Benthall's production resumes:

> Having married her, [Bertram] appeared to soften towards her, and would have given her the kiss she so pathetically begs at parting had not a "Psst!" from Parolles recalled him to his previous resolution. Shakespeare makes Parolles the factotum in Bertram's arrangements for the disposal of his wife; Benthall made him the prime mover as well. (1955, 136)

In the promptbook for Noel Willman's 1955 revival at Stratford-upon-Avon, at line 86, there appears the handwritten notation: "Par. makes a small move U. S. as bert goes to kiss Helen—when he hears Par. move he stops and turns to Par." Likewise, Charles Frey remembers that, in the 1982 Seattle Actor's Workshop production directed by Michael J. Murnin, "When Helena asked Bertram for a kiss . . . he started to kiss her and was restrained by Parolles, again suggesting that Bertram's coldness was hardly his own" (1982, 408). Some version of this stage business has been used so frequently that Sylvan Barnet writes that it has "very nearly become standard operating procedure" (1988, 208).[24] Aside from encouraging an audience to fault Parolles for Bertram's "coldness," this choice also implies that Bertram feels some degree of romantic attraction to Helena that he simply denies at Parolles' bidding. Although the text offers no evidence of Bertram's affection for his mother's servant (and strong indications to the contrary), this suggestion of repressed fondness on Bertram's part prepares spectators to accept that the Count will love his wife, according to a modern conception of marriage, once Parolles' influence has been neutralized.

Significantly, since the mid-1970s, there has been a competing tendency to move away from using elements of performance to blame Parolles at these critical points, but the suggestion lingers that Bertram is denying a buried tenderness toward his new wife. Roger Warren offers an account of 2.5 from David Jones's 1977 Stratford, Ontario, production:

> Bertram bent and brushed her *hand* with his lips, whereupon she seized him and held him in a prolonged kiss; his response was to

break away (though not immediately) with "I pray you, stay not, but in haste to horse" [2.5.87] and she, a first intimacy achieved, ran lightly from the stage. (1978, 145)

Bertram's failure to break away immediately from Helena's kiss discloses that the Count is suppressing a physical attraction to her that may serve as a basis for the sexual intimacy of marriage. A similar effect was achieved in the 1989 RSC production directed by Barry Kyle. Bertram "seemed to steel himself to deny Helena her kiss on his departure from court and momentarily to be tempted to hug her when she wept at the refusal" (Smallwood 1990, 494). Although this version does not imply a hidden sexual attachment on Bertram's part, the fact that he must both "steel himself" to deny her the kiss and resist the temptation to comfort her with a hug evinces an emotional tie between the two young people that viewers may perceive as a foundation for conjugal affection.

By contrast, in an earlier RSC production (1981–82), director Trevor Nunn chooses not to sentimentalize Bertram with suggestions that his indifference is merely a facade. Robert Smallwood writes, "The sequence in which he humiliates her by coldly ignoring her request for a farewell kiss and, after her departure, gleefully flings his arms around Parolles, memorably demonstrates his callousness and immature emotional dependence on his companion" (1982, 29).[25] Unlike most other directors, Nunn refrains from using this segment to establish a textually unwarranted warmth in Bertram's feelings toward Helena and instead uses Parolles' presence, not to exonerate the Count, but to highlight the strength of his bond with his male friend. Of all the enactments of 2.5 examined in this chapter, Nunn's alternative to traditional performance choices stands the best chance of conveying to an audience a feminist perspective on the importance of male bonding to marriage and procreational practices.

The issue of procreation arises most conspicuously in 5.3 with the revelation of Helena's pregnant body. Historically, stage productions of *All's Well* have approached the paradoxes created by the bed trick with strategies of omission and misdirection designed to draw viewers' attention away from the contradictory elements of the final scene. According to Joseph G. Price, the precedent for nineteenth-century revivals was set by J. P. Kemble's 1811 acting edition, which contained several major cuts, including the virginity dialogue between Parolles and Helena, the passage from Bertram's letter mentioning the conception of a child, and all overt references to the bed trick (1968, 24–26). Samuel Phelps's production at Sadler's Wells in 1852, which probably followed the Kemble text, featured the same expurgations but went a step further by eliminating the bed trick altogether (Price 37). These bowdlerizations are clearly intended to remove possibly offensive material, but they also resolve potential ideological conflicts for the audience by omitting their foundations. The deletion of the virginity dialogue eliminates the most articulate expression of Parolles' competing ideology of procreation, which no longer challenges the notion that "service" is barren. The obfuscation or elimination of the bed trick blurs the contradictory roles of seduced virgin and lawful wife that Helena plays for Bertram upon her reappearance, and the loss of the condition of the child removes pregnancy (and the indeterminate sex of the baby) from its central position in the visual scheme of the conclusion.[26] As Price sums up the thrust of these changes, "Everything in the play is directed to the delicate sensibility of the heroine and to the bliss of the reconciliation" (134).

While twentieth-century productions of *All's Well* have restored most of the passages deleted during the previous century, some modern directors have also incorporated stage business that focuses attention on Bertram's newfound romantic attachment to Helena. For example, at the end of John Barton's 1967 RSC revival, "Helena's entry was a moving event to which Bertram responded with a passionate cry on the words, 'Both, both. Oh pardon!'; his 'ability to collapse' . . . was 'his salvation' " (Fraser 1985, 35).[27] Photographs of this scene in performance show Bertram on his knees, grasping Helena's hand as he gazes lovingly into her eyes, but she is not visibly pregnant (see Figure 3).[28] Such a staging highlights Bertram's remorse over his shabby treatment of Helena and his awakening love for her, and these emotions overshadow questions about sexuality and reproduction that linger in the written text. The visual element of Helena's pregnancy is also effaced from the best known version of the play, Elijah Moshinsky's BBC television production, which employs a dramatic shift in perspective at the moment of her entrance. G. K. Hunter recalls,

As the cast looks through the door music begins to play. "Behold the meaning," says Diana. But the camera does not allow us to behold. Instead it does what the camera does best—it shows us a set of

Figure 3—Bertram (Ian Richardson) kneels to Helena (Estelle Kohler) while the King of France (Sebastian Shaw) looks on in John Barton's 1967 RSC production of _All's Well_. Photo courtesy of the Shakespeare Birthplace Trust, Stratford-upon-Avon.

> mouths and eyes. As it tracks along the line, we are made witness to
> a series of inner sunrises, as face after face responds to the miracle
> and lights up with understanding and relief. (1988, 187)

Moshinsky's manipulation of the audience's point of view directs our attention away from the visual image of Helena's body to the faces of the onlookers, particularly Bertram, whose apprehension of the event as a miraculous resurrection the viewer is invited to share. The rest of the scene is shot in tight close-ups, only briefly offering a glimpse of Helena's torso (which has not yet begun to show) moments before Bertram expresses his newly discovered love with a kiss. Moshinsky opts to allow the emotional power of Helena's reunion with her husband to take precedence over the troublesome meaning one might behold in her pregnant body, a choice that precludes potential conflict between the spectator's perception of reality and the version offered by the performed text.

When directors do provide audiences with the visual image of Helena in an observably pregnant state, they also tend to use stage business to foreground Bertram's attachment to the unborn child. Muriel St. Clare Byrne's review of Tyrone Guthrie's 1959 revival at Stratford-upon-Avon recalls that, at the moment of Bertram's concluding couplet, the Count knelt and clung to Helena in a "gesture of contrition" (1959, 557–58). A photograph accompanying this review depicts Bertram down on one knee, his head pressed to Helena's side, with one hand resting gently on her slightly swollen womb (556–57). A variation on this business occurs in the 1989 production directed by Edward Gilbert at Boston's Huntington Theatre. Helena enters slowly, wearing a dress with an empire waist, which emphasizes her expectant state. As she concludes her reading of the conditions of Bertram's letter, she takes her husband's hand and places it on her stomach, allowing him to feel the palpable life within her. Bertram's expression of love for Helena is prompted by the powerful feelings evoked through this gesture, which signals the beginning of the bond between the father and child. Similarly, in Sheldon Epps's 1993 production at San Diego's Old Globe Theatre, as Bertram speaks his final couplet, "he puts his

Figure 4—In Tyrone Guthrie's 1959 production of *All's Well* at the Shakespeare Memorial Theatre, Bertram (Edward de Souza) senses his child in the womb of Helena (Zoë Caldwell). Photo courtesy of the Shakespeare Birthplace Trust, Stratford-upon-Avon.

hands on Helena's nearly flat belly and seems, from his expression, to have felt the fetus move. Falling to his knees, he kisses her belly, before rising to kiss her lips" (Deese 1994, 39). In all three performances, the spectator's focus on the affection of Bertram for his unborn offspring, regardless of its sex, distracts attention from the Count's contradictory vision of Helena and the possible unfitness of the child to become the next Count Rossillion.

As these modern examples show, Helena tends to be portrayed visually in 5.3 as either the object of Bertram's passion or as the mother of his child, but not "both," as the text demands. When Helena's pregnancy is not visible, she may easily fit the conventional role of the object of male sexual desire, but when directors choose to make her condition obvious, they also tend to rechannel Bertram's ardor directly toward his child and only indirectly toward Helena in gratitude for conceiving his baby. What performances have not yet provided us is a picture of Helena as Bertram sees her, simultaneously his illicit lover and pregnant wife. The fact that there are practical difficulties involved in fusing these two parts convincingly on the stage is precisely the point; the union of the two roles is purely imaginary, and spectators unconvinced by the illusion that they have coalesced will become aware of the contradictions involved in their fusion, even if Bertram himself does not. These contradictions arise in the first place because Shakespeare's contrived solution, the bed trick, requires Bertram's reconciliation to the civilian social order to depend upon the facilitation of military "service," with which the Court's ideology of procreation is ultimately incompatible. The sexual ethics of the soldier and the father are, in the end, mutually contradictory, and the play cannot hope to "resolve" them without residual conflicts.

Dissonance also lingers between the play world's easy reacceptance of Bertram and the historically less generous responses of readers and playgoers. R. G. Hunter argues that Shakespeare's obligation to "give his play a happy ending" forces him to attempt to bring the reaction of audience members in line with the forgiving attitude displayed by Bertram's family and the King:

> Within the play, Bertram has offended Helena. The strength of her love for him makes her forgiveness of him a foregone conclusion. Bertram has also offended the world of his play, the society of which he is a member. This society, represented by his king and his

mother, must also forgive him and it does. If the play is to succeed
fully as a work of art, however, the audience must acquiesce in these
forgivenesses. We, too, must forgive Bertram. Whether or not this,
in fact, happens, and why it does or does not, have been the subject
of a great deal of speculation. (1965, 5)

According to Hunter, this debate arises because Elizabethan
viewers believed in "the descent of grace upon a sinning
human" as "an everyday psychological possibility" and would
not have suspected the credibility of the Count's complete alteration at the end of the play (131). Since that time, Hunter
asserts, contemporary spectators have lost their faith in spiritual transformation:

> Critics of this play have felt (as far as I know, without exception)
> that the final scene of the play fails because Bertram's regeneration
> is unconvincing. There can be no doubt that, indeed, the scene does
> so fail for a modern audience. We do not believe in regeneration. It
> is not communicated to us. (130)

Here Hunter fails to distinguish between a monolithic belief (or
lack of belief) in regeneration and a specific regeneration that
"is not communicated to us." He neglects the possibility that an
audience of any era might accept the conversion of Bertram if
the play were to contain a convincing demonstration of a significant change in his demeanor. On the page, however, it does
not. The only textual indication of the Count's penitence—the
bare phrase, "O pardon!"—has not appeared to be sufficient to
manifest the internal reformation of Bertram that a romantic
reading of the play requires.

Faced with this textual feature, one might conclude that the
final scene of *All's Well* is designed to *provoke*, rather than to
ease, audience resistance to the forgiveness of Bertram. More
often, however, scholars and theatrical professionals have
resorted to Gervinus's argument that Shakespeare left the
responsibility to communicate Bertram's conversion up to the
actor, upon whose vocal and physical talents the success of any
production rests. Yet, as Oxford editor Susan Snyder remarks,
"There is a limit to how much transformation the actor can project into his brief 'Both, both. O pardon!' [and] his lines of conditional acceptance addressed to the King . . . even with assistance
from stage business" (1993, 27). This limitation has not pre-
vented productions from enhancing the credibility of Bertram's
sudden repentance and willingness to love Helena through

stage action. As we have seen, Bertram's "ability to collapse" in Barton's 1967 revival earned the Count's "salvation." A minimum of four other productions at Stratford during this century have also sent Bertram to his knees. Snyder's edition features a photograph from one of them with the caption: "Edward de Souza kneels to Zoë Caldwell at the end of Guthrie's 1959 Stratford-upon-Avon production, filling out with gesture Bertram's too-brief words of penitence" (29).[29] To persuade spectators of the truth of the Count's newfound love for his wife, several performances have also incorporated a kiss between the two young people at the culmination of Bertram's final couplet.[30] For instance, Frey's account of Murnin's version of this climactic embrace records that "Bertram's fervid sincerity at 'I'll love her dearly, ever, every dearly' . . . was capped with a long kiss that greatly helped the audience to become 'reconciled' (to use Dr. Johnson's term) to Bertram" (1982, 408).

Director Laird Williamson, who introduced the prescene of Helena and Bertram as children described at the beginning of this chapter, also expanded the conclusion of his 1996 Shakespeare Theatre production. Clearly concerned about the brevity of Bertram's penitence, Williamson interpolated lines from another Shakespearean work to give the Count additional raw material with which to convince the audience of his repentance and reformation:

> [G]iven the inadequacy or ambiguity many readers have found in Bertram's four words [—"Both, both. O pardon!"—Williamson] had the actor deliver Sonnet 109 (which starts with "O, never say that I was false of heart" and ends with "For nothing this wide universe I call / Save thou, my rose; in it thou art my all"). The choice eliminated a lot of ambiguity, greatly diminished the potential hurt or pain of the ending, and, in effect, transformed the final moments. What many find to be the most provocative problem in the play— how to deal with the comic "resolution"—has here been "solved" by an infusion of new material from elsewhere. (Dessen 1997a, 5)

The speaker of Sonnet 109 assures the young man that, despite his "absence" (his affairs with other lovers), his affections, like a traveler, will always return to his beloved, his "home of love" (lines 2, 5). Relocated to the end of *All's Well*, these lines signify that Bertram has always loved Helena deeply, and in spite of his attempted seduction of Diana during his travels in Italy, his affections have reverted to their original object back home in Rossillion. Williamson's interpolation of this poem allows the actor portraying the Count to overcome the "inadequacy" of the text and offer a clear and convincing display of Bertram's remorse and reawakened ardor.

The preceding instances from the performance history of *All's Well* demonstrate that the stage has traditionally attempted to resolve for its audiences the generic and ideological conflicts present in the text rather than to allow them to trouble the guarded optimism of the conclusion. They achieve their effects, as do all performances, by foregrounding certain aspects of the text while obscuring others, but it seems significant that the aspects that are generally obscured are those that could draw notice to the opposed ideological elements of the text and disrupt harmonious comic closure. As Sheldon Zitner remarks, "Music, dance, lighting and gesture and all the determination of actors and directors in league with audience susceptibilities can make *All's Well* seem [to be] a [traditional] comedy in the theatre. But the text has other directions" (1989, 149). To follow in these other directions, a contemporary performance of the play might enlist elements of production to expose sites of generic and ideological tension rather than conceal them. Contrary to popular belief, performance has no obligation to make consistent and definitive what the text presents as contradictory and ambiguous; indeed, the revelation of the text's perplexing inconsistencies may represent the most effective means toward a theatrically arresting version of the play.

This claim is borne out by a further examination of Trevor Nunn's 1981–82 RSC production, which Roger Warren called "the finest and most illuminating interpretation of a Shakespeare play for many years" (1983, 79).[31] Nunn's production, which featured Bertram's cold humiliation of Helena in 2.5, is one of three versions of *All's Well* that represent a countertrend against the romanticization of Helena and Bertram's relationship, especially at the end of the play. Along with productions directed by Henry Woronicz at the Oregon Shakespeare Festival in 1992 and Sir Peter Hall at the RSC's Swan Theatre in the same year, Nunn's version makes no attempt to establish a secret affection for Helena on Bertram's part. As the King forcibly engages him to Helena, Nunn's Count leaves no doubt about his contempt for the physician's daughter:

Bertram looked Helena straight in the eyes to say very deliberately "I cannot love her, nor will strive to do't" [2.3.145]. . . . And Bertram's very emphatic delivery of "she, which late / Was in my nobler thoughts *most base*" [2.3.170–71] made it quite clear that he had not changed his attitude, even in the act of capitulating to the King. (Warren, 80)

This segment also highlights the way in which the Count out-wardly submits to the King's control of his marital affairs while stubbornly maintaining the independence of his affections. In act 5, when Bertram swears to the King that he has come to love Helena now that she is dead, audiences will likely believe such a man capable of another deceptive speech of this kind in the interest of renewing his bond with his monarch. And as Warren adds, "this was demonstrably the same man who could say, '*If* she, my liege, can make me know this clearly, / I'll love her dearly—ever, ever dearly' " (80).

Nunn's enactment of the final scene avoids the uncomplicated happy ending suggested by the play's title in favor of the more tentative assessment implied by the opening of the King's final couplet: "All yet *seems* well" (5.3.327). Bertram and Helena achieve a reconciliation, but Nunn shifts the emotional focus of her resurrection away from the reunited husband and wife to Helena's restored bonds with her surrogate mother and father, the Countess and the King:

> [Helena] stands motionless, framed in a doorway upstage. . . . After a few moments, the statue moves and advances towards Bertram. . . . "Both, both. O Pardon!", says Bertram, reaching out towards the outstretched hand of the slowly advancing Helena. But just as their hands are about to touch he withdraws his and it is Helena's resto-ration to the King and the Countess that produces the tears of joy from Lafeu and Parolles. (Smallwood 1982, 30)

Bertram's unwillingness to grasp his wife's hand sidesteps the potential sentimentality in their reunion, which, in this staging, is not a primary source of joy. The Count's hesitation may also reduce the level of sincerity that spectators perceive in his repentance, making it less likely that they will forgive him for his previous emotional brutality. The production also offers no sure indications that the wounds once opened have now healed:

> [T]he mood of the final exit of Bertram and Helena remains sub-dued. The production began with a graceful circling dance of a young couple in silhouette. . . . Here, after the final scene of his return, Helena and Bertram seem about to begin a similar dance, answering our wonderings about the identity of those first two

dancers. But the dance does not quite manage to start, and the couple walk slowly from the stage, side by side but not quite hand in hand; and we are left wondering. (Smallwood, 31)

Warren refers to this exit as "the final image of an unequal marriage" (1983, 80); Smallwood calls it a "combination of timid hope and threatening uncertainty" (31). In either case, Nunn's production leaves strongly in doubt the eternal happiness implied by those stage versions of *All's Well* that strive for an unambiguously positive conclusion for Helena and Bertram.

An unsure future for the Count and his wife also lies ahead at the end of Woronicz's Ashland production. Like Williamson, Woronicz inserts material from the Sonnets into the performance, but he associates the sentiments of the speaker with the hopeless love of Helena at the beginning of the play rather than the apologetic affection of Bertram at the conclusion. The production opens with Lavatch as an itinerant poet, reading Sonnet 87 ("Farewell! Thou art too dear for my possessing"). This interpolation anticipates the seemingly unattainable desire of Helena for the Count, whose failure to return her erotic attraction to him is emphasized by the "brotherly peck on the cheek" he gives her at his parting from Rossillion (Armstrong 1992, 26–27). This gesture is one of a series of kisses that "punctuated the action," including, in the middle of the play, "a fumbling, inept kiss upon request in 2.5" and "a lusty, confident kissing of Diana in 4.2" (Dessen 1993, 36–37). While Woronicz's version of 2.5 lacks the cruelty displayed by Nunn's Bertram, the contrast between the Count's chaste and awkward approach to Helena and his "lusty" kissing of Diana focuses attention on the disparity between his passion for the Florentine maid and his lack ardor for the woman who adores him.

Like Nunn, Woronicz complicates an audience's response to Bertram's brief speech of repentance. As in many productions that do not highlight Helena's pregnancy, this enactment plays down the visual element of her reappearance: "Helena . . . entered and moved to the King, so that Bertram, with his back turned to her, heard rather than saw her entrance, at which point he rose (after saying 'Both, both'), made a slow circle to his left (with no audible 'O'), and then addressed 'pardon' directly to her" (Dessen 1993, 37). Alan Armstrong maintains that spectators "cannot certainly judge" the frankness of Bertram's apology here (1992, 27); it is plain, however, that they do not attribute his assertion that Helena is now a wife in both name and practice to his visual apprehension of her pregnant state, for in this embodiment, he does not even see her until after making that statement. After she reads Bertram's letter, the couple engage in a third and final kiss, which Dessen describes as "gentle rather than passionate," and "soulful, yet ambiguous" (37). Unlike the long kiss that helps the audience to become reconciled to Bertram in Murnin's Seattle production, this equivocal embrace fails to recuperate the Count or to predict with assurance the outlook for his marriage to Helena:

> They sit downstage, at opposite sides, intermittently regarding each other with expressions compounded of hope, doubt, and despair. The audience remains uncertain of their eventual success or failure, confident only of their standing yet at the virtual beginning of a relationship still to be forged. (Armstrong, 27)

Dessen concurs that the playgoer retains the image of "Helena and Bertram in the light, with their 'reconciliation' uncertain and the emphasis upon separation, not union" (37). To cap this unromantic closing, Woronicz cuts the Epilogue and transfers the King's final couplet to Lavatch, "whose voice thus frames the play" (Armstrong, 27). Emanating from the mouth of the same poet who spoke Sonnet 87, the tentative assessment that all yet seems well assumes the status of a choric commentary by Shakespeare himself.

Though Sir Peter Hall's staging of the conclusion of *All's Well* in his 1992 RSC production differs from Woronicz's version, their overall approaches are similar in that "both directors left open a sense of problems to come without eliminating all hope" (Dessen 1993, 37). Helena entered wearing a white gown, visibly pregnant, and sank to her knees by the already kneeling Bertram. Despite her obvious condition, reviewers record no stage business dealing with her pregnancy; nor do they recall a kiss between husband and wife (Dessen, 37; Smallwood 1993, 358). Instead, they emphasize Hall's inventive enactment of Helena's reminder of the Count's impossible tasks:

> Then she was on her knees with Bertram, reading out in her quiet but deliberate and resolute little voice the appalling conditions of his letter . . . as if the public enunciation of it all were some essential ritual expiation for them both. . . . And then she tore the letter in two. The gesture released him from his bond, leaving him free, if he wished, to reject her again. It also released them both from their

past, a past that had done great, perhaps irreparable damage to any hope of a relationship. (Smallwood, 358)

Peter Holland agrees that this staging "marked the possibility of change, the possibility of forgiveness," but he also cites Paul Taylor's review in *The Independent*, which calls Helena's ripping of the letter "a wonderfully double-edged gesture. On the one hand, it seems to be saying that all this can now be put behind them; but the thickened intensity of the action suggests that damage has been done that cannot be so easily forgotten and forgiven" (1993, 167). Instead of presuming Helena's immediate pardon of Bertram, Hall's production implies that she experiences a difficult time overlooking his transgressions against her. Such an inference ratifies a contemporary spectator's own difficulty in excusing Bertram but does not preclude the prospect that Helena, as well as audience members, will eventually overcome this barrier.

Whether or not viewers forgive Bertram in this sort of enactment may depend on his response to Helena's gesture. If, after she releases him from his bond, Bertram clearly begins to act like a loving husband, spectators may believe in his reformation. However, Hall's staging provided no such evidence of the Count's amenability toward the match. After the letter sequence, Helena moved toward the Countess, and "mother, son, and daughter-in-law then joined hands and formed a circle, the final image for the playgoer. . . . The circle of three provided more physical contact than the separation highlighted in Oregon, but the absence of a kiss forestalled any upbeat ending" (Dessen 1993, 37). Holland refers to this triangular Rossillion family portrait as "a tentative nervous grouping with Bertram still unable to look at Helen" (1993, 167). Bertram's failure to embrace his wife, or make eye contact with her, suggests that his dominant emotion at this point is not love but guilt; indeed, Taylor characterizes him as "a head-hanging, penitent wreck" while Benedict Nightingale calls him "an abject, shattered husband" (Coursen 1993, 10). While Bertram's obvious remorse may count in his favor with an audience, the best that Hall offers for the future of the Count's marriage to Helena is "the glimmer of a chance of a new beginning" (Smallwood 1993, 358).

Assessing the productions of Hall and Woronicz, Dessen comments (1993, 37) that both "provided little sense of romantic climax or love fulfilled or Helena as victor (although neither fully ruled out such a conclusion for the romantics in the audience)."

Like Nunn's open-ended version, these productions stake out a middle ground between the cynicism of a reading that denies the possibility of the Count's conversion and the optimism of an interpretation that insists on Bertram and Helena attaining eternal bliss. Until the 1980s, the fairy-tale ending ruled the stage, while the antiromantic treatment was limited to literary criticism, but since that time, a compromise position has come to seem the only viable approach to *All's Well* on the stage. As Holland writes in response to the conclusion of Kyle's 1989 production:

> I never thought to see again an *All's Well* in which Bertram and Helen (and, in this case, the Countess) embrace at the end of the play in a full reconciliation, as if nothing very much has happened and all will live happily after. I suppose that in this production nothing very much had happened and in the tradition of good children's stories everything could be glibly resolved. But that is only a small fragment of the play. (1991, 161)

Any production that ignores the play's troubling aspects reduces *All's Well* to something less substantial than it can be, while a production that denies any hope of Bertram's reformation offers a correspondingly distorted rendition. The text clearly indicates that Helena has won Bertram's conditional agreement to love her dearly; thus, one key to a feminist production of the play as a comedy of forgiveness might be found in renewed attention to the issue of "Helena as victor" over her reluctant husband at the conclusion of the action.

The fact that Helena so desperately desires her marriage with Bertram complicates a feminist perspective on matrimony in the performance of *All's Well*. With *Two Gentlemen*, Julia and/or Silvia's resistance to marriage can be viewed as an appropriate feminist response to their treatment by Proteus and Valentine; at least one female director (Di Trevis) has also cast doubt upon the felicity of the matches sealed at the conclusion of *Much Ado*. However, a director who presents the marriage between the Count and his bride at the end of *All's Well* as an entirely hopeless union risks the demonization of female sexual desire by stressing the negative consequences of its fulfillment. If, in a particular stage version, Helena's choice of her life's partner spells disaster for herself and her husband, such a production reinforces the wisdom of female passivity in marital affairs. To oppose such a notion, a feminist performance might endorse

Helena's marriage, not only as the triumph of her independent will, but also as the defeat of those predatory sexual impulses in men that lead to the seduction and ruination of women. Helena's bed trick successfully turns "service" against itself, but such a ruse cannot plausibly induce Bertram to "love" her in the romantic sense. At best, Helena offers the Count an imaginary resolution of his incompatible desire for both marriage and illicit sexual conquest, which he accepts partly for the sake of his alliance to the King and partly for the sake of his nascent heir. Although spectators may remain unsettled by their inability to rejoice at such a match, a feminist production may still hold out the hope that, over time, the marriage of Helena and Bertram may evolve into a mutually satisfying relationship. In such an enactment, the audience's own forgiveness of Bertram at the end of the play remains as conditional as Bertram's promise to love his wife forevermore.

Through their refusal to confirm or deny a happy future for the Count and his wife, the performances directed by Nunn, Woronicz, and Hall approach the mixture of cautious optimism and freedom from sentimentality necessary for such a version of the play. Yet none of these directors interrogates the formation of male bonds as a factor in the renewal of Bertram's marriage, and while Hall does feature an obviously pregnant Helena, he does not clarify the visual importance of her condition. Beyond an open-ended treatment of the conclusion to the play, a director may adapt certain choices made in previous performances of *All's Well* to convey a feminist reading that focuses on the channeling of male sexual desire. For example, after Helena arrives in Florence, the Widow informs her daughter Diana that she has mentioned Parolles' solicitations on Bertram's behalf to her neighbor Mariana, who extends the following warning:

I know that knave, hang him! one Parolles; a filthy officer he is in those suggestions for the young earl. Beware of them, Diana: their promises, enticements, oaths, tokens, and all these engines of lust, are not the things they go under; many a maid hath been seduced by them; and the misery is, example, that so terrible shows in the wrack of maidenhood. (3.5.16–22)

Richard Jones's 1993 New York Shakespeare Festival production featured "a very pregnant Mariana . . . as an object lesson to all virgins *not* to make much of time" (Ranald 1993, 17). Such

152   "THE WORLD MUST BE PEOPLED"

a choice hints that Mariana's condemnation of male profligacy flows from personal experience; viewers may even assume from her bitterness toward Parolles, the champion of service, that he is responsible for her miserable condition. In 5.3, if Helena is also portrayed as being in the later stages of pregnancy (as she was in Jones's production [Ranald, 16]), her appearance will echo Mariana's predicament and remind the audience that Helena's legitimate pregnancy depends for its creation on a pandering to the same extramarital lust that has ruined "many a maid."[32] However, the Count's agreement to honor his wedding vows after viewing his wife's expectant state holds out the promise that his sexual urges may continue to be directed toward authorized procreation rather than illicit service.

Male bonding as another crucial factor in Bertram's marital affairs may be highlighted at two separate points in the final scene. The first concerns Lafew's daughter Maudlin, who is nearly betrothed to the Count before Diana's revelation of his indiscretions. Although there is no entry direction for Maudlin in the text, Roger Wood and Mary Clarke recall that Benthall's Old Vic production elected to bring Maudlin on stage as "a simpering and quite pathetically ugly damsel," a sight which "won gales of easy laughter," but also struck these observers as "a cruel and unnecessary joke" (1954, 58). A feminist production would likely avoid this sort of humor at a woman's expense, but a version of this choice might be employed with a more serious effect. The performer depicting Maudlin need not be played as "pathetically ugly"; if her garments, features, and body language contrast sharply with the beauty and vivacity of Diana, whom we may presume to be "Bertram's type," this disparity will imply to viewers that the Count's eagerness to marry Maudlin is based, not on romantic love, but on the beneficial connection to her politically potent father that such a match would afford him. As for Lafew, portraying his daughter as, in herself, an unattractive candidate for marriage increases his motivation to overstate Parolles' influence over Bertram and thereby exculpate the man who may represent Maudlin's only chance for a socially advantageous match.

The other opportunity to stress the function of ties between men in the Count's attitude towards wedlock occurs during the exchange including Bertram's infamous final couplet:

    Ber.   If she, my liege, can make me know this clearly
           I'll love her dearly, ever, ever dearly.

Hel. If it appear not plain and prove untrue
Deadly divorce step between me and you!
O my dear mother, do I see you living?

(5.3.309–13)

Although many productions provide an embrace between Bertram and Helena along with the Count's vow, a director could easily bring the issue of same-sex bonds to the forefront of the audience's attention by having Bertram turn away from his wife and deliver his lines directly to the King, thereby demonstrating his ultimate concern that his marriage reestablish him in his monarch's good graces. Subsequently, Helena may turn her attention to the Countess—"O my dear mother, do I see you living?"—and embrace her instead, celebrating the female bond between them made official through matrimony. Helena's evocation of the possibility of "deadly divorce" for the young couple may be reflected in their separation from one another, while their stage grouping with the elders of their own sex may make manifest the notion that their marriage represents, not the triumph of youthful romantic love over the elder generation, but the victory of society over the unruly sexual impulses of the Forgiven Comic Hero.

Chapter 5

"We shall have all the world drink brown and white bastard": *Measure for Measure*

> Our modern feeling may be that Angelo gets off altogether
> too lightly, but the pardon of the repentant villain and his
> union to a heroine was a commonplace in Elizabethan
> drama, and would certainly have been readily accepted by a
> contemporary audience. . . . The same miraculous processes
> which lead to the forgiveness of erring male characters . . .
> also automatically make them perfect husbands. The audi-
> ence in the Globe Theatre, we may be sure, did not worry
> their heads over the illogicalities of the situation. They knew
> that the raptures of reunion and the music of marriage bells
> were a prologue to the good old story-book ending, "And so
> they lived happily ever after."
>
> (Lawrence 1931, 116–18)

TODAY, FEW WOULD AGREE WITH WILLIAM W. LAWRENCE'S CONFI-
dent assertion that the problem of Angelo's forgiveness may be
solved simply by distinguishing the skepticism of modern readers from the conventional acceptance of the repentant villain's
pardon displayed by Shakespeare's audience. No evidence of
such a contemporary response exists, and from the eighteenth
century onward, a contrary sense of outrage against the whole-
sale pardons offered to all offenders, particularly Angelo, at the
end of *Measure for Measure* pervades the history of the play's
reception.[1] Moreover, the text provides scant basis for the
notion that Angelo's forgiveness automatically renders him a
perfect husband for Mariana, nor does it plainly support the
idea that their marriage represents a happy ending for either
one of them.[2] Even Bertram, at the conclusion of *All's Well*,
explicitly vows, however weakly and conditionally, to love his
wife. But Angelo, in contrast to all three of his counterparts,
never speaks a word of affection for his bride; indeed, his
repeated demand for capital punishment even after his wedding

154

sparks no confidence in his prospects for a successful marriage. This textual feature poses a difficulty for productions that, in the spirit of Lawrence's fairy-tale romantic vision, aim to present "the raptures of reunion" between the deputy and his wife. As Alexander Leggatt observes of Mariana and her mate, "It is clear that she wants him. . . . But it is equally clear that all Angelo wants is death. It is up to the actor to suggest otherwise, making what he can of the 'quick'ning in his eye' the Duke claims to see" (1988, 89). Like Gervinus in his remarks on Bertram, Leggatt assumes that the role of the performer is to make up for the text's failure to conform to the generic expectations of romantic comedy by providing visual signs of Angelo's awakened desire for Mariana. The production history of *Measure* does in fact reveal various attempts to supply some sort of indication, in the final scene or earlier in the play, that Angelo will cherish his bride now that the Duke has granted him a reprieve.

In addition to Angelo's lack of stated affection for his partner, the text of *Measure* manifests two other deviations from the model narrative of the comedy of forgiveness that influence the staging strategies employed to ensure the audience's assent to the pardon of Angelo. First, although the Duke's substitute exhibits most of the traits and behaviors associated with the Forgiven Comic Hero, Shakespeare assigns crucial elements of this figure, those aspects associated with male bonding, to Isabella's brother Claudio (who shares his name with the Forgiven Comic Hero of *Much Ado*). Therefore, the character whose love affair separates him from his Friend (Lucio), and whose relationship to the Authority (the Duke) is sealed by marriage at the end of the play, is distinct from the character who abandons the Griselda (Mariana), fixes his affections on the Shrew (Isabella), and later apologizes for his offenses. However, the play also establishes a parallel between the two men (both characters violate the law by sleeping with their betrothed brides before any religious ceremony), and by the conclusion, their lives have become interchangeable: "An Angelo for Claudio; death for death" (5.1.407). Once Claudio is revealed to be alive, the Duke must pardon the prisoner alongside the deputy, as if both men together constitute the whole figure of the Forgiven Comic Hero.

This division of the traits of the model narrative's central character between two individuals affects the way in which the Forgiven Comic Hero relates to both the Friend and the Vice, who are joined, as with Parolles in *All's Well*, in the figure of

Lucio.[3] Given that there are, in *Measure*, two Forgiven Comic
Heroes, Lucio serves as the Friend in relation to Claudio and as
the Vice figure chiefly with regard to Angelo. In his latter role,
Lucio exhibits *Measure*'s second deviation from the model narrative, for in this play, the Vice figure cannot be blamed for the
Forgiven Comic Hero's separation from the Griselda. Angelo's
desertion of Mariana occurs five years before the action begins,
long before Lucio and Angelo ever meet, and nothing in the text
suggests that Lucio had anything to do with Angelo's cancellation of his betrothal. Instead, Lucio fulfills the morality play
figure's role of leading the Comic Hero into temptation, particularly by bringing Isabella, in search of mercy for her brother, to
Angelo, who conceives a lustful passion for her. In Shakespeare's primary source, George Whetstone's two-part play *The
Historie of Promos and Cassandra* (1578), Angelo's counterpart,
the deputy Promos, appears "in the company of Phallax, a Vice-
like evil counselor" (Lever 1965, xli), who encourages Promos to
pursue his desire for Cassandra by trading the life of her condemned brother Andrugio for her virginity.[4] Even though, as
J. W. Lever notes, the part of the evil counselor disappears from
Shakespeare's version of the story (xli), there is evidence to suggest "that Phallax lies behind Shakespeare's invention of
Lucio" (Hillman 1993, 105). Mathew Winston illustrates the
manner in which Lucio, in 2.2, unintentionally plays the tempter's part consciously performed by Phallax:

> His interspersed comments contain more than a suggestion of the
> sexual—"You are too cold"; "To him"; "Ay, touch him: there's the
> vein"—which is consistent with the Vice's love of bawdry, of
> obscene puns, and of verbal equivocation. . . . Moreover, although
> Lucio is unaware of it, he is helping to inspire Angelo's lust for Isa-
> bel. (1981, 239)

As a proponent of lust, Lucio carries out another of the standard
functions of the Vice, to serve "as a dramatic symbol for that
attitude or force within the kingdom which the dramatist wishes
to single out as a basic cause of contemporary evils" (Dessen
1971, 16). This force is the vice of lechery, which infects both
Angelo and Claudio, the play's Forgiven Comic Heroes.[5]

Lucio functions as a dramatic symbol for the general vice of
lechery, but not as the intentional provocateur of Angelo's lustful acts. Therefore, the scapegoating of Lucio in the final scene
of the play does not effectively shift blame away from Angelo, as

the demonization of Don John and Parolles can do for *Much Ado*'s Claudio or *All's Well*'s Bertram. Although some productions of *Measure* have tried to intensify the scapegoating of Lucio by using stage business to emphasize the negative effects of illicit sexuality,[6] the theatrical recuperation of Angelo seems to require two auxiliary strategies: increasing the audience's sympathy for him in his dilemma, particularly during his three major soliloquies, and providing a stronger sense of punishment for his crimes through actions that highlight his initial anguish and his humiliation later in the play. In this way, orthodox stage productions compensate for the absence of official retribution enacted by the Duke at the play's conclusion.

Angelo's lecherous impulses lead him to commit his transgressions, just as Claudio's passionate desire to consummate his betrothal to Juliet leads him to anticipate his wedding vows and perpetrate the capital crime of fornication. Claudio and Juliet's act of intercourse results in her conception of a child, so her teeming presence in 1.2 picks up, near the beginning of the play, the same visual image of pregnancy presented by Helena at the close of *All's Well*. *Measure* then proceeds to the final stage in the channeling of male sexual desire by taking up the issue of childrearing. Juliet, I will argue, goes into labor and delivers her bastard child before her reappearance at the end of the play, so when the Duke orders Claudio to make reparations to Juliet by marrying her, he exemplifies Vienna's social pressure to force men who have engaged in illicit sex to take responsibility for any children they have fathered. Lucio's enforced marriage to Kate Keep-down in act 5 mirrors Claudio and Juliet's more willing union in that the Duke mandates Lucio's wedding to force him to acknowledge his own illegitimate child conceived in lust two years previously. Angelo's equally coerced marriage to Mariana may also be viewed, at least in part, as the Duke's means for insuring that any child resulting from the bed trick has a father charged with financial responsibility for it.

In this way, *Measure* dramatizes the social contrivances by which the state seeks to contend with the negative consequences of unrestrained sexual behavior at the expense of the individual desire of young males prone to reckless promiscuity. Robert N. Watson observes how Vincentio's behind-the-scenes maneuvering of his subjects into matrimony bridles their illicit sexual urges and diverts them toward what he perceives as the greater good of Vienna:

The Duke's complex plot serves to remind us that the procreative impulse can be seen as essentially a mechanism of biology manipulated as a ploy of the state, a way of preserving social structures rather than individual consciousness. The state is merely doing its best to harness, rationalize, even sentimentalize, the relentless directionless march of nature. (1990, 424)

Although the state of Vienna may attempt to "sentimentalize" its manipulation of the procreative impulse by forcing the Forgiven Comic Hero into a "loving" marriage, *Measure* brings the artificial quality of these pairings so far to the forefront of the audience's consciousness that even the multiple marriages that conclude the action cannot reclaim the play for the genre of romantic comedy. As Watson also points out, "The comic triumph here belongs not to love or to the hero but instead to . . . the need of the state, under the guise of personalized benevolence, simply to keep the procreative machine running" (415). This "procreative machine," in the words of Alberto Cacicedo, "requires the sacrifice of male sexual license in order to run effectively" (1995, 190).[7] Thus, the play endeavors to justify this sacrifice by portraying Claudio's overeager erotic desire as well as Angelo's perverse compulsion to despoil a novice as two forms of the same sociosexual malady that the Duke of Vienna must cure.

After the Duke delegates power to Angelo, Lucio appears in conversation with two nameless gentlemen. All three appear to be military men, for the First Gentleman states, "There's not a soldier of us all that, in the thanksgiving before meat, do relish the petition well that prays for peace" (1.2.14–16). Later in the same act, Lucio cannot resist bragging to Isabella about his fictitious military connection to the Duke: "The Duke is very strangely gone from hence; / Bore many gentlemen—myself being one— / In hand, and hope of action" (1.4.50–52). Despite these hints at the figure of the *miles gloriosus* in the early stages Lucio's portrayal, the traits that identify him as a braggart soldier drop out of his character after act 1; henceforth, the play limits his braggardism to sexual, rather than military, service. In dialogue with his disguised ruler, Lucio boasts of impregnating one of Mistress Overdone's girls, Kate Keep-down, and forswearing his paternity when called to account before the Duke (4.3.167–72). Perhaps Vincentio's leniency in Lucio's case leads him to believe that the Duke understands the pleasures of extramarital sexuality from personal experience; as Lucio tells the Friar, the Duke "had some feeling of the sport; he knew the service; and that instructed him to mercy" (3.2.115–17). Lucio's reference to the sex trade as "the service" is reinforced by the bawd Pompey's assurances to Mistress Overdone that the closing of the brothels in the suburbs will not lead to her ruin: "courage, there will be pity taken on you; you that have worn your eyes almost out in the service, you will be considered" (1.2.101–3). As in *All's Well*, illicit sexuality goes by the name of service, but in *Measure*, the sport reaches beyond the seduction and abandonment of a virgin (as practiced by Angelo) to include premarital sex (as pursued by Claudio and Juliet) and the patronage of prostitutes (as conducted by Lucio).

Claudio's sensual indulgence with Juliet leads to his death sentence under the old law against fornication, the news of which causes Lucio suddenly to adopt an uncharacteristic seriousness:

> *Lucio.* But, after all this fooling, I would not have it so. Art thou
> sure of this?
> *Mis.* O. I am too sure of it: and it is for getting Madam Julietta
> with child.
> *Lucio.* Believe me, this may be: he promised to meet me two
> hours since, and he was ever precise in promise-keeping.
> (1.2.64–70)

With deft dramatic shorthand, Shakespeare sketches in the relationship between Lucio and Claudio. Lucio's abrupt somber tone indicates his genuine concern for his companion, and his knowledge of Claudio's habits suggests a friendship of intimate standing. Significantly, Claudio's alliance with Juliet comes between the two men: Claudio misses his appointed meeting with Lucio because of his arrest for impregnating his betrothed bride. This threat to the male bond, along with Lucio's early resemblance to the *miles gloriosus*, establishes him in the role of the Friend within the model narrative.

Lucio's ensuing conversation with his comrade specifies sexual license as the vice at the heart of Claudio's predicament:

> *Lucio.* What's thy offence, Claudio?
> *Cla.* What but to speak of would offend again.
> *Lucio.* What, is't murder?
> *Cla.*   No.
> *Lucio.*   Lechery?
> *Cla.*   Call it so.
> (1.2.126–29)

Although Claudio hesitates to refer to his premarital coupling as an immoral act, he admits that society considers sexual activity before a religious wedding ceremony to be a form of lechery. While Claudio and Juliet's offense is relatively benign, by calling it lechery, the play links their transgression to the more serious wave of unrestrained sexuality plaguing Vienna with sin, disease, and illegitimate procreation. Later in the play, Lucio complains to the disguised Duke about Angelo's Draconian methods for dealing with this epidemic:

> *Lucio.* A little more lenity to lechery would do no harm in him. Something too crabbed that way, friar.
> *Duke.* It is too general a vice, and severity must cure it.
> *Lucio.* Yes, in good sooth, the vice is of a great kindred; it is well allied; but it is impossible to extirp it quite, friar, till eating and drinking be put down. (3.2.94–99)

Vincentio's response to Lucio brands lechery as the force within Vienna that is responsible for its ills, while Lucio's defense of sexual indulgence as an inescapable human trait identifies him as the Vice figure who symbolizes that frailty. Indeed, when Claudio asks his "good friend Lucio" (1.2.182) to prompt Isabella to use her powers of persuasion to seek her brother's pardon, Lucio hopes for her success as an inspiration to similar offenders: "I pray she may: as well for the encouragement of the like, which else would stand under grievous imposition, as for the enjoying of thy life, who I would be sorry should be thus foolishly lost at a game of tick-tack" (1.2.177–81). Lucio's speech of compassion for his comrade's plight combined with his desire for the encouragement of lechers joins his two roles as Friend and Vice figure, but the play does not imply that Lucio might be held directly responsible for Claudio's acts. Here, *Measure* contrasts with *Much Ado*, which clearly suggests that the Vice figure Don John is largely to blame for the sins of Count Claudio.

Lucio shares with Don John an opposition to marriage, but only for himself. He does not speak against the institution per se or discourage others from entering it; rather, like Parolles in *All's Well*, he considers it irrelevant to the necessary process of procreation.[8] Conveying to Isabella the news that Claudio has impregnated his partner, Lucio couches his description in agricultural imagery reminiscent of the procreation sonnets that characterizes this illegitimate conception as a natural and fruitful act of generation:

> Your brother and his lover have embrac'd;
> As those that feed grow full, as blossoming time
> That from the seedness the bare fallow brings
> To teeming foison, even so her plenteous womb
> Expresseth his full tilth and husbandry.
>
> (1.4.40–44)[9]

Contrary to the laws of Vienna, Lucio implies that human repro-duction is a positive event whether it occurs inside or outside the bonds of matrimony. Therefore, as Alexander Welsh points out, "Lucio implicitly argues . . . that the state's interpretation of biology is merely political, because Vienna can be populated just as readily without marriage as with it" (1978, 27).[10] Despite Angelo's attempts to defend the law against fornication as a means to eradicate sin,[11] the state's condemnation of procre-ation outside of marriage also remains a political maneuver designed to protect the government from the economic conse-quences of rampant illegitimacy.

The governors of Vienna must cope with the failure of fathers to assume financial accountability for their bastard children because, in the absence of other means of support, the care and maintenance of illegitimate children rests with the state. Mari-lyn L. Williamson summarizes how the economic problem of bastardy in Vienna reflects a similar crisis in Shakespeare's England, where the illegitimacy rate had peaked in 1604, the same year that *Measure* was written (1986, 81–91). She notes that historians of the period attribute this growth to two factors: first, the existence of "a 'bastardy-prone sub-society,'[12] made up of prostitutes, libertines, and the hard-core poor" and second, an increase in "circumstances where an intended marriage by socially acceptable citizens was delayed by economic condi-tions" (81–82). These factors are represented in the play by the birth of bastard children fathered by Lucio and Claudio respec-tively. In Lucio's case, Mistress Overdone has sustained Kate Keep-down's baby, but her incarceration removes the infant's only means of support; unless Lucio can be constrained to take financial responsibility for the infant, the Duke, as the personi-fication of the state of Vienna, will be forced to provide for its subsistence. Lucio prompts the disguised Duke to recall this duty when he attributes to his absent ruler a casual approach toward illegitimacy: "Ere he would have hanged a man for the getting a hundred bastards, he would have paid for the nursing a thousand" (3.2.113–15).[13] In the following act, the Duke meditates on the susceptibility of princes to such slanderous comments:

> O place and greatness! Millions of false eyes
> Are stuck upon thee: volumes of report
> Run with these false, and most contrarious quest
> Upon thy doings: thousand escapes of wit
> Make thee the father of their idle dream
> And rack thee in their fancies.
>
> (4.1.60–65)

Having listened to Lucio disparage him as being willing to nurse "a thousand" bastards, the Duke depicts this calumnious remark metaphorically as a form of specious paternity: in the same way that bastards unfairly force the state to become their foster parent, a "thousand escapes of wit" falsely make him "the father of their idle dream." Constable Elbow blames the high incidence of illegitimate births in the city on the prevalence of the sex trade; as he tells Pompey, "Nay, if there be no remedy for it, but that you will needs buy and sell men and women like beasts, we shall have all the world drink brown and white bastard" (3.2.1–4). Widespread illegitimacy, stemming from irresponsible sexual behavior, poses a serious financial danger to the state of Vienna.

The monetary angle of Angelo's strict enforcement of the law against fornication is evident in his intent to deter those who would "coin heaven's image / In stamps that are forbid" (2.4.45–46). Yet his own vulnerability to lecherous impulses becomes manifest once Lucio brings the deputy into contact with Isabella. Claudio has advised Lucio to encourage the young novice to use her "prone and speechless dialect" (1.2.173) to move Angelo to pity, yet it is precisely her speech that touches the Duke's substitute and prompts him to conceive a lustful passion for the condemned man's sister. As Angelo admits in an aside, "She speaks, and 'tis such sense / That my sense breeds with it" (2.2.142–43). Two scenes later, Angelo tries to compass the object of his desire by blackmailing her into bartering her chastity for her brother's life, but Isabella rebukes him vehemently: "I will proclaim thee, Angelo, look for't. / Sign me a present pardon for my brother, / Or with an outstretched throat I'll tell the world aloud / What man thou art" (2.4.150–53). Not only does Isabella's refusal take the form of a sharp verbal retort, but her speech itself also contains an ultimatum threatening to employ her "outstretched throat" to ruin Angelo's spotless reputation. After the bed trick, Angelo betrays a persistent anxiety over the hazard presented by the possibility that Isabella will use her voice to defame him: "But that her tender shame / Will not proclaim against her maiden loss, / How might she tongue me! (4.4.21–23). Isabella's vocal resistance to Angelo's proposal casts her in the role of the Shrew, the woman whose voice intimidates and yet arouses men.[14] Her scolding reaches its apex during her dialogue with Claudio in prison, when she brutally denounces his desire to live at the expense of her virginity: "Take my defiance, / Die, perish! . . . / I'll pray a thousand prayers for thy death; / No word to save thee" (3.1.142–46). As in her exchange with Angelo, Isabella vocally refuses a man's attempt to bargain away her chastity and vows to use her own voice to commence a counteroffensive against him. Thus, in consecutive scenes, Isabella squares off verbally against the two Forgiven Comic Heroes of *Measure* and repels the threat to her virginity that both men represent.

Overhearing Isabella's tirade against her brother, the Duke emerges and assumes his role as the matchmaking Authority figure. To protect Isabella, as well as to promote the institution of marriage as a safeguard against costly illegitimate births, Vincentio must prevent Angelo's violation of the novice's virginity and redirect his sexual urges toward a willing, socially acceptable target. Shakespeare, therefore, suddenly introduces Mariana, who was at one time betrothed to Angelo and still maintains her first affection for him. Unlike Claudio and Juliet's espousal *de praesenti*, which is at once legally binding, Angelo and Mariana's betrothal was apparently of the type known as *de futuro*, which depends upon the performance of certain future conditions, such as the delivery of a dowry, in order to attain legal standing (Lever 1965, liii–liv).[15] Angelo's termination of this contract upon Mariana's failure to hold up her end of the bargain, though cold-hearted, is entirely within the law as Shakespeare's audience would have understood it.[16] The mercenary quality of Angelo's behavior is also callous and yet, from an early modern perspective, understandable, since marriage is, by necessity, a financial arrangement even for those couples whose mutual desire originally brings them together. Claudio and Juliet, for example, clearly maintain a reciprocal affection that prompts them to plight their troth to one another and consummate their alliance, but even so, they indefinitely postpone their marriage ceremony "for propagation of a dower / Remaining in the coffer of her friends" (1.2.139–40). Angelo's similar premium on Mariana's dowry, and the lack of textual evidence for any other motivation to marry on his part, supports only an economic, and not a romantic, basis for his original decision to wed her.[17]

Although Angelo's scrupulous adherence to the letter of his contract does not damage his integrity per se, the Duke pinpoints the truly reprehensible aspect of the deputy's conduct toward his betrothed bride when he reveals that Angelo "swallowed his vows whole, pretending in her discoveries of dishonour" (3.1.226–27). Angelo's slandering of Mariana's chastity, designed to camouflage his own mercenary behavior, amounts to a serious crime against her, yet Mariana, like a true Griselda, carries a torch for her former fiancé that no amount of adamant disinterest on his part can extinguish. As the Duke puts it, Angelo's "unjust unkindness, that in all reason should have quenched her love, hath, like an impediment in the current, made it more violent and unruly" (3.1.240–43).[18] No false reports of Mariana's death follow her renouncement by her "husband" (as they do for Julia, Hero, and Helena), but Isabella does exclaim, upon hearing Mariana's story, "What a merit were it in death to take this poor maid from the world!" (3.1.231–32). In fact, Mariana has withdrawn from society to live at the "moated grange" of Saint Luke's (3.1.265), and as Angelo thinks, "since which time of five years / I never spake with her, saw her, nor heard from her" (5.1.221–22).[19] Until the final scene of the play, Mariana remains dead to the world of Vienna, particularly to her former suitor.

The bed trick not only protects Isabella's virginity and prevents her conception of an illegitimate child, but it also draws Mariana out of seclusion to play her own part in the peopling of the world. Isabella, explaining to the Duke her reasons for refusing Angelo's proposal, declares, "I had rather my brother die by the law, than my son should be unlawfully born" (3.1.188–90). The novice assumes that, if she pays Angelo's monstrous ransom, their single coupling will result in the birth of an illegitimate, and specifically male, child. Indeed, Helena's one-time sexual encounter with Bertram in *All's Well*, like similar bed tricks in the folklore tradition, does make her pregnant, but there is no irrefutable evidence in *Measure* that Mariana's visit to Angelo's garden house results in a pregnancy. The time scheme of *Measure* (in contrast to that of *All's Well*, which allows for the passage of several months at the beginning of act 5), places the Duke's return to Vienna within two days of the bed trick; thus, the final scene of the play comes too early to confirm whether Angelo's sexual act with Mariana has impregnated her. However, the Duke, when he formulates the bed trick, predicts that Mariana's assignation with Angelo may result in a pregnancy: "If the encounter acknowledge itself hereafter, it may compel him to her recompense" (3.1.251–53). N. W. Bawcutt (1991, 162n) glosses the phrase "acknowledge itself" as "reveal itself, become publicly known (perhaps by Mariana becoming pregnant)." The Duke seems to expect Angelo and Mariana's encounter in "the heavy middle of the night" (4.1.35) to become evident in the same way that Claudio's act of fornication, with "character too gross," is "writ on Juliet" by her pregnancy (1.2.144).[20] Thus, the Duke contrives to wrest Mariana from her barren isolation, whereupon he compels Angelo to marry her, which both restores her honor and makes Angelo economically responsible for any child who may potentially spring from their union.

As the bed trick in *All's Well* must exploit Bertram's lust for Diana to consummate Helena's marriage to the Count, so the Duke's bait-and-switch operation in *Measure* must rely on Angelo's illicit passion for Isabella as the means to lure him into a sexual act that will turn his espousal *de futuro* into a legally binding alliance. Angelo sometimes refers his feelings for the young novice as "love"; for example, in his first soliloquy, he exclaims, "What, do I love her, / That I desire to hear her speak again?" (2.2.177–78). However, the perverted nature of this "love" differs widely from the healthy erotic impulses associated with that emotion in romantic comedy. In contrast to the deputy figure in some of Shakespeare's sources, Angelo never considers his initial attraction to Isabella as a prompt toward courtship and sexuality within marriage.[21] For him, "Celibacy and fornication seem to be the only alternatives" (Jaffa 1981, 182). Therefore, he perceives his arousal as a sin that he blames first on Isabella, then on himself: "Is this her fault, or mine? / The tempter, or the tempted, who sins most, ha?" (2.2.163–64). Angelo realizes that his temptation arises from the novice's "modesty" and takes the form of a desire to pollute the holiness of her chaste body: "Having waste ground enough, / Shall we desire to raze the sanctuary / And pitch our evils there?" (2.2.170–72). As Janet Adelman notes, Angelo's urge to desecrate Isabella resembles Bertram's hunger to flesh his will in the spoil of Diana's honor:

> Bertram and Angelo are both presented as psychological virgins
> about to undergo their first sexual experience. In the course of their
> plays, we find that both can desire only when they imagine their
> sexuality as an illegitimate contamination of a pure woman, the con-
> version in effect of one kind of nun into the other. (1989, 151–52)

The similarity between Angelo's appetite and Bertram's sexual
service is also apparent in Angelo's martial vocabulary: "the
words *raze* and *pitch* . . . indicate the military character of the
imagery. Angelo . . . compares himself to a conquering and
destroying army; women in general to invaded land, and Isabella to a besieged sanctuary, about to be desecrated and turned
to military use by the soldiery" (Suhamy 1979, 59). In the midst
of his crackdown on one form of service, prostitution, Angelo
engages in another by trying to take Isabella's virginity and
abandon her to her own desecration. Through the Duke's
deception, Angelo's corrupt passion may unknowingly be spent
upon Mariana, but such an encounter hardly lays the ground-
work for a salutary marriage between them.[22]

Although Claudio and Juliet's reciprocal attraction more
closely resembles an ideal romantic union, the play insistently
links their "mutual entertainment" (1.2.143) to Angelo's unsa-
vory passion and its illusory fulfillment through the bed trick.
As Angelo declares upon discovering in himself the same "foul"
impulses that led Isabella's sibling to his condemnation, "O, let
her brother live! / Thieves for their robbery have authority, /
When judges steal themselves" (2.2.175–77). Angelo equates
Claudio's crime with his own illicit desire, admitting that his
transgression grants authority to Claudio's parallel fault. The
Duke later echoes Angelo's comparison between the two unlaw-
ful liaisons as he anticipates the arrival of Claudio's reprieve:
"This is his pardon, purchas'd by such sin / For which the pardoner himself is in" (4.2.106–7). Despite the Duke's assurances
to Mariana in the previous scene that her pre-contract with
Angelo removes all taint of vice from the bed trick—"To bring
you thus together 'tis no sin" (4.1.73)—in soliloquy, he acknowledges that their coupling before a marriage ceremony is indeed
a sinful act. According to both the Duke and his substitute, the
pardoner and the pardoned have committed equally immoral
sexual offenses emanating from the same foul vice of lechery.

Ultimately, the Duke blames the spread of lechery throughout
his dukedom on his own failure to enforce the state's existing
laws against fornication. As he admits to Friar Thomas,

We have strict statutes and most biting laws,
The needful bits and curbs to headstrong jades,
Which for this fourteen years we have let slip;
Even like an o'er-grown lion in a cave
That goes not out to prey.

                                        (1.3.19–23)

This speech transforms the image of the hungry lion linked to the aggressive sexuality of the Forgiven Comic Hero in the earlier comedies of forgiveness by applying it to *Measure*'s Authority figure, who, like a lion grown too old to hunt, ventures out no more in search of sexual prey. In jest, Lucio alleges that the Duke, though once a proponent of service, is "now past it" (3.2.176), and Vincentio himself confirms that, at his age, he is no longer interested in liaisons with women. In response to the suggestion that he has withdrawn from the city to pursue a romantic tryst, the Duke answers Friar Thomas, "No. Holy father, throw away that thought; / "Believe not that the dribbling dart of love / Can pierce a complete bosom" (1.3.1–3). At this early point in the play, the Duke portrays himself and his purposes as "grave and wrinkled," immune to the attractions of love and sex, the "aims and ends / Of burning youth" (1.3.5–6). Like the King of France and Lafew in *All's Well*, the Duke of Vienna faces his own declining sexuality and a concomitant impetus to correct the abuse of sexual potency exhibited by his young male subjects.

In place of the ravenous lion, *Measure* substitutes the willful horse as its primary symbol of the youthful male propensity toward licentious sexuality. The Duke refers his "most biting laws" against extramarital sex as "the needful bits and curbs to headstrong jades,"[23] which he has, for fourteen years, "let slip," like reins released by a careless rider, allowing the citizens of Vienna to pursue their lecherous impulses without restraint. Angelo repeats this image when he unleashes the full extent of his lustful passion for Isabella: "I have begun, / And now I give my sensual race the rein" (2.4.158–59). By relating the unruly sexual desires of the Forgiven Comic Hero to an obstinate horse, *Measure* elaborates a prominent metaphor from *All's Well*: Bertram as "a wayward young animal being tamed into his social role"; specifically, "a colt being broken" (Snyder 1993, 29).[24] This figure follows in turn from *Much Ado*'s equation of "Benedick, the married man" with "good horse to hire," and the presentation of the virile bachelor as the "savage bull" who must be constrained to "bear the yoke" of marriage (1.1.241–45). In the comedies of forgiveness, the intractable sex drives of young men are metaphorically embodied as beasts—lions and horses and bulls—which must be domesticated within the confines of matrimony to preserve current social standards for procreation and childrearing.

The Duke brings this domestication of masculine lust to its culmination through his elaborate staging of his "return" to Vienna. In a sequence reminiscent of the final scene of *Much Ado*, Mariana enters veiled, like Hero in the guise of Leonato's niece, and stands unrecognized before the man to whom she was once betrothed. As Claudio, in the earlier play, appeals, "Sweet, let me see your face" (5.4.55), so Angelo, puzzled by the masked woman's riddles, also asks her to remove her veil: "Let's see thy face" (5.1. 204). However, the revelation of the Griselda in *Measure* does not function as a miraculous climax like its corresponding segment in *Much Ado*, since Mariana has not been reported as literally dead. Rather, the character in this play who fits the resurrection motif exemplified in the other three comedies by Julia, Hero, and Helena is Claudio, whose unmuffling serves as the wondrous return from death that paves the way for the series of marriages that terminate the action.

The other crucial disclosure of identity in *Measure*'s final scene is the unhooding of the Duke, which leads to Angelo's confession of his wrongdoings. More fully than any other Forgiven Comic Hero, the Duke's deputy accepts the blame for his crimes, without excuse, and calls, at the end of his eight lines, for the most severe punishment the Duke can inflict upon him: "Immediate sentence, then, and sequent death / Is all the grace I beg" (5.1.364–72). In terms of its sheer discursive space, this speech, along with a similar passage in which Angelo calls again for his own execution (5.1.472–75), represents the most extensive repentance allotted to any of the Forgiven Comic Heroes. In spite of this relative length, critics of the play are split on the question of its sincerity and its ability to move spectators toward Angelo's forgiveness.[25] The text provides no reason to doubt the genuineness of Angelo's remorse, and his request for the death sentence supplies the acknowledgement of due punishment that early adapters felt was missing from Proteus's speech of penitence, which they furnished through the interpolated phrase, "I merit death." As Lawrence J. Ross proposes, by begging for his own beheading, Angelo, in effect, "preempts our desire to see him get what he deserves" (1997, 128) and thereby lessens an audience's resistance to his eventual pardon by the Duke.

After securing Angelo's admission that he was once contracted to Mariana, the Duke sends him off to "marry her instantly" (5.1.375). This compelled union provides a father for any children conceived during the bed trick and forces on Angelo the outlet for his sexual urges that he did not consider when first confronted with his passion for Isabella: legitimate conjugal relations. Over the course of the play, Angelo evolves from an ascetic, who "scarce confesses / That his blood flows" (1.3.51–52), to a man who can admit privately, "Blood, thou art blood" (2.4.15). Still, he cannot conceive of a middle ground between celibacy and fornication as a means for dealing with his sexual impulses. The Duke therefore imposes upon Angelo the institution of marriage, "which constitutes the mean between sexual asceticism and sexual license" (Lowenthal 1997, 256). As a by-product of this union, Angelo's alliance with Mariana, whom the Duke refers to as "gentle daughter" during his sojourn as her fatherly protector (4.1.71), ultimately reinforces Angelo's male tie to his ruling prince.

Observing that the deputy is married off to a beautiful and virtuous woman who loves him, then generously pardoned, one might object that "Angelo has been rewarded, not punished" for his transgressions (Levin 1982, 268). This extramerciful treatment has occasioned centuries of critical disapproval, the nature of which may be summed up in the words of Susan Jacoby: "*Measure for Measure* is a perennially disturbing and unsatisfying play precisely because no real retribution is exacted for acts that are—by the standards of our own day as well as Shakespeare's—truly evil" (1983, 46). Several critics counter that Angelo does receive painful punishment for his wrongdoing by having his reputation for virtue, in which he takes so much pride, destroyed through a public disclosure of his misdeeds. As James Black asserts,

No-one who feels that Angelo is treated too leniently has fully taken into account the city-gate setting and the public humiliation there endured (to Shakespeare's contemporaries it was a recognised factor in punishment). The exposure of so essentially withdrawn a man and the breaking through of his *persona* is in itself a punishment which if it does not exactly fit the crime certainly fits the offender. To Angelo execution would be preferable, entailing as it does the

concealment of prison and the oblivion of death: it is the public ses-
sion he wants curtailed. (1973, 127)[26]

Given Angelo's preference for execution, some scholars argue
that Vincentio's pardon ironically consigns his deputy to a fate
worse than death: "For Angelo the Duke's indulgent benevolence does not confer felicity; rather, it perpetuates his
anguish. . . . The play leaves him in a state of torture, mitigated
only by the fact that Claudio is not, after all, dead. . . . [Angelo]
longs to discharge his debt, to rest his burden. The Duke makes
sure that he carries it to the end" (Nuttall 1969, 247). In spite of
these arguments, other critics maintain that embarrassment
and lingering guilt are not penalty enough to expiate Angelo's
criminal violation of the public trust. As David Thatcher contends, "surely Angelo deserves (in addition to the suffering he
feels) some formal punishment for his corrupt abuse of authority" (1995, 35).

This debate over the fitness of Angelo's pardon assumes that
a proper balance between justice and mercy is the standard by
which to judge the Duke's behavior in this case. I would argue,
however, that the Duke is not concerned with justice or mercy
at this point; rather, he chooses to follow the course of action
that will "keep the procreative machine running" under the
control of the state, whether that path leads to the chastisement
or the indulgence of sins past. He forgives Angelo, not because
Angelo deserves mercy, but because pardoning him into a marriage to a woman with whom he may have conceived a child
makes the most sense for Vienna. The Duke must walk a thin
line between allowing too much sexual license, which leads to
illegitimacy and its inherent economic burdens, and strict
enforcement of the death penalty for fornication, which will
"unpeople the province with continency" (3.2.168–69).[27] As
Pompey predicts, "If you head and hang all that offend that way
but for ten year together, you'll be glad to give out a commission
for more heads" (2.1.235–37). Angelo himself offends "that way"
by having sex with Mariana before they are married, and this
"violation / Of sacred chastity" (5.1.402–3) is one of the two
crimes for which he is sentenced to death. The Duke ultimately
stays Angelo's beheading, along with Claudio's, so that the Forgiven Comic Heroes who have threatened the state with their
sexual offenses may continue to contribute to the procreation of
the world and the sustenance of their offspring. As the Provost
describes Claudio to the Duke earlier in the play, he is "a young

man / More fit to do another such offence, / Than die for this"
(2.3.13–15).

The Duke's forgiveness of Claudio has been overshadowed by
Vincentio's more outrageous leniency toward Angelo, but the
play clearly reminds us that the just-unmuffled prisoner has
also committed a serious crime for which the Duke chooses to
absolve him. Significantly, the Duke links this pardon to his first
proposal to Isabella and mentions explicitly the relationship
that a marriage between them will forge between himself and
her sibling: "If he be like your brother, for his sake / Is he pardon'd; and for your lovely sake / Give me your hand and say you
will be mine. / He is my brother too" (5.1.488–491). The Duke's
unusual phrasing makes his pardon of Claudio appear to be
contingent upon Isabella's response to the Duke's request for
her hand in marriage. The prisoner's forgiveness depends on
his relationship to Isabella (he will be pardoned if he is like her
brother), and the Duke's attitude toward Isabella will undoubtedly be colored by her reaction to his proposal. Vincentio also
specifies that Isabella's acceptance of his proposition will make
Claudio into the Duke's brother, forming a second alliance
between the Authority figure and the other Forgiven Comic
Hero. As in the three previous comedies of forgiveness, marriage in *Measure* serves, among other purposes, to unite the
male relatives or father figures of the Shrew and Griselda to the
women's future mates.

Though Angelo is still guilty of breaking his promise to spare
Claudio's life (the other violation for which he is condemned to
death), the Duke refrains from further disciplinary action
against his deputy and notes the relief on Angelo's face:
"Methinks I see a quickening in his eye. / Well, Angelo, your evil
quits you well. / Look that you love your wife: her worth, worth
yours" (5.1.493–95). According to Vincentio, Claudio's resurrection prompts a parallel "quickening" in Angelo's eye; despite his
two earlier requests for death, Angelo's spirits have revived, and
he now desires to live. If the Duke is correct, Angelo's evil has
indeed requited him well, for the restoration of Claudio removes
one of the deputy's main sources of punishment, his lingering
remorse over Claudio's execution. Some critics also discover in
Angelo's revival a sense of gratitude toward Mariana that may
form the basis for a successful marriage. For example, Carol
Thomas Neely comments that the quickening in Angelo's eye
"may imply that Mariana, by delivering him from guilt and punishment, has conferred on him new life" (1985, 102). No evi-

dence indicates, however, that Angelo attributes his deliverance to his wife. In fact, Vincentio must enjoin Angelo to love Mariana, not only here, but again in the play's final speech: "Joy to you, Mariana; love her, Angelo. / I have confess'd her, and I know her virtue" (5.1.523–24). The Duke assumes, in opposition to the usual pattern of romantic comedy, that love, based on an appreciation of virtue, will follow marriage rather than precede it. The phrase "her worth, worth yours" glances back to Mariana's lost dowry: her intrinsic, rather than economic, worth now makes the match appropriate for Angelo (Ross 1997, 140). Similarly, Vincentio also forces marriage on Claudio without regard for Juliet's dowry, the reason for their postponement of wedlock: "She, Claudio, that you wrong'd, look you restore" (5.1.522). In both cases, the Duke constrains the Forgiven Comic Hero to relinquish individual monetary motives for marriage in favor of matrimonial practices that best serve the financial interests of the state.

Angelo does not respond verbally to the Duke's interpretation of his facial expression or his ruler's repeated injunction that he love his spouse. This restraint renders his future attitude toward Mariana entirely ambiguous; as Philip C. McGuire observes, "The more often the Duke calls and the more persistently Angelo stays silent, the less certain we can be that Angelo feels the love which in a comedy we expect a newly married husband and wife to share" (1985a, 246). Of course, Angelo may develop affection for Mariana over time, but Terrell L. Tebbetts doubts that a successful marriage between the two can be expected: "Angelo has been tricked and then forced into a disadvantageous marriage with Mariana, one that Renaissance law held that he had every right to repudiate. What kind of relationship is he likely to have with the woman who connived in the trick and consented to his public disgrace?" (1985, 133). Despite Mariana's love for her husband, one may suspect that such a match will not necessarily bring happiness to her either. Hal Gelb writes, "Knowing Angelo does not want to marry Mariana, remembering his recent anger with her, and knowing Angelo's character, we feel that the Duke has created a marriage for Mariana in which hell is the other person" (1971, 32). The Duke, by mandating this union, shows that he cares less about the couple's prospects for wedded bliss than he does about maintaining control over the way in which his world is peopled.

The Duke's determination to regulate the procreative machine becomes most evident in his harsh treatment of Lucio, the scapegoat for the lecherous acts of the Forgiven Comic Heroes. After acquitting Claudio and Angelo of their sins, Vincentio locates his slanderer, the "one in place [he] cannot pardon" (5.1.497), and again wields marriage as a tool to enforce paternal duty:

> Proclaim it, Provost, round about the city,
> If any woman wrong'd by this lewd fellow,
> —As I have heard him swear himself there's one
> Whom he begot with child—let her appear,
> And he shall marry her. The nuptial finish'd,
> Let him be whipped and hang'd.
>
> (5.1.506–11)

To give Kate Keep-down's child a father, the Duke ordains a wedding between Lucio and the prostitute he has wronged. Although Vincentio later "forgives" Lucio's slanders and suspends his other more severe penalties, the Duke will not revoke his marital decree: he will not nurse Lucio's bastard, much less a thousand, if he can employ his power to prevent it. Moreover, as Lucio points out, "Marrying a punk . . . is pressing to death, / Whipping, and hanging" (5.1.520–21), a punishment far worse than matrimony with a gentle loving wife, as experienced by Claudio and Angelo. The vindictiveness with which the Duke turns upon his antagonist suggests that he is taking out upon him a desire for vengeance against the Forgiven Comic Heroes that he knows he must repress for the good of Vienna. As Anthony Caputi explains, Lucio "is something of a scapegoat in the sense that, though he deserves his punishment, it seems in part contrived to relieve feelings of righteous indignation aroused in other quarters" (1961, 433).[28] Through the castigation of Lucio, spectators see at least one lecherous man receive severe discipline, but, since he is not directly responsible for the sins of Angelo or Claudio, the scapegoating of Lucio merely demonizes the vice of lechery; it does not excuse the Forgiven Comic Heroes.

Marriage forces Lucio, like his counterpart Benedick, to confront the threat of cuckoldry: "I beseech your Highness, do not marry me to a whore. Your Highness said even now, I made you a duke; good my lord, do not recompense me in making me a cuckold" (5.1.512–15). Because cuckoldry does not appear to pose as immediate a danger to Vienna as does the widespread production of bastards, the Duke compels men as individuals to

marry and endure the potential hazards of matrimony to protect the state from the repercussions of illicit sexual gratifica-
tion. Watson outlines the communal basis for this decision:

> The essence of the Duke's final triumph . . . is marriage—not as indi-
> vidual fulfillment but as a practical, worldly, even legalistic solution
> to the problem of maintaining the size of the Viennese population,
> and to the no-more-romantic problem of controlling illegitimacy . . .
> among the city's many wayward citizens. (1990, 417–18)

Structurally, *Measure* may end like a romantic comedy, with as
many as four marriages sealed or on the horizon, but the element of compulsion present in each of the matches hampers an
audience's ability to endorse marriage as a solution to Vienna's
problems. Thus, orthodox productions that seek to recast *Measure* as a traditional comedy must labor to reconcile viewers to
the forgiveness of Angelo and to suggest that his union with his
wife rests on a romantic foundation. Alternatively, a feminist
production of the play may attempt to clarify the state's efforts
to oversee procreation, with or without loving marriages, as a
basis for the Duke's actions in the final scene.

*   *   *

As with *Two Gentlemen*, the early post-Restoration stage history of *Measure* is dominated by two adaptations that significantly alter the play's presentation of the Forgiven Comic Hero.
William Davenant's *The Law against Lovers* (1662) introduces
into the plot of *Measure* the characters Beatrice and Benedick
from *Much Ado*, while simultaneously eliminating Mariana and
almost all of the underworld figures except Lucio. In 1700
Charles Gildon produced his own stage version, entitled *Measure for Measure, or Beauty the Best Advocate*. Strongly influenced by Davenant, Gildon also omits the low characters, but he
restores Mariana and removes all of the material imported from
Much Ado, adding instead four operatic interludes drawn from
Henry Purcell's *The Loves of Dido and Aeneas*.[29] By various
means, both of these adaptations also transform the characters
Angelo and Claudio, rendering them less blameworthy for their
actions and, in the case of Angelo, less difficult for an audience
to forgive.

Comparing Davenant's comedy to Shakespeare's, the "chief
dramatic change is . . . in the conception of Angelo, who, instead
of being a scoundrel who meets with a better fate than he

deserves, is made, as the hero of the play, a model of virtue"
(Kilbourne 1906, 49). The deletion of Mariana accomplishes part
of this transfiguration, for it removes from Angelo's past the
taint of his contemptible behavior toward her. However, her
absence also leaves Angelo without a marriage partner at the
end of the play, so Davenant further restructures the plot so that
Isabella is free to marry Angelo. Davenant's Duke does not propose to the novice; rather, he resigns his throne to the young
couple and hints that he will retire to a monastery.[30] This pairing of Angelo and Isabella also requires the adapter to modify
Shakespeare's representation of the deputy's feelings and conduct toward the novice. For instance, Davenant retains the soliloquy in which Angelo reveals his attraction to Isabella, but
Davenant's revisions transform the nature of that emotion. In
response to Isabella's parting words—"Save your honour"—
Angelo replies,

> From all, but from thy virtue, Maid!
> I love her virtue. But, temptation! O!
> Thou false and cunning guide! who in disguise
> Of virtue's shape lead'st us through heaven to hell.
> No vicious beauty could with practised art,
> Subdue, like virgin-innocence, my heart.
>
> (1874, 142)

In both versions of this speech, Isabella's purity provokes Angelo's desire, but whereas Shakespeare characterizes this passion
as a compulsion to pollute the sacred sanctuary of Isabella's virtue, Davenant recasts Angelo's lustful attraction as a romantic
appreciation of the novice's "virgin-innocence" that leads him
to love her from the heart.

In fact, the affection of Davenant's Angelo for Isabella precedes their initial interview and is the cause, rather than an
unintended effect, of his strict enforcement of the law against
fornication. As the Duke's substitute later reveals to Isabella in
a wholly interpolated third meeting,

> I loved you ere your precious beauties were
> In your probation shaded at Saint Clare:
> And, when with sacred sisterhood confin'd,
> A double enterprise perplext my mind;
> By Claudio's danger to provoke you forth
> From that blest shade, and then to try your worth.
>
> (1874, 189)

In Davenant's version, Angelo's prosecution of Isabella's brother stems, not from the deputy's own rigid, puritanical adherence to the statutes, but from his desperate desire to prevent the woman he loves from entering the convent. Having drawn Isabella out of the sisterhood, Angelo claims that his monstrous ransom demand was a mere contrivance designed to test the mettle of her virtue:

> I'll now, at once, cast off my whole disguise.
> Keep still your virtue, which is dignified,
> And has new value got by being tried.
> Claudio shall longer live than I can do,
> Who was his judge, but am condemn'd by you.
> The martial of the guards keeps secretly
> His pardon seal'd; nor meant I he should die.

(1874, 188)

Here, Davenant reverses Angelo's attempt to soil the purity of a chaste maid by turning his proposal into a trial of Isabella's virtue, which gains enhanced value by surviving such a test. Now that Isabella has passed her examination, Davenant's Angelo announces, "submissively I woo / To be your lover and your husband too" (188–89). This proposal directly contrasts with the original character's failure even to consider courtship and marriage as an alternative to aggressive sexual coercion. With Mariana, and consequently the bed trick, out of the play, Angelo has no opportunity to commit his most heinous crime: breaking his promise to release Claudio in exchange for Isabella's virginity. Nevertheless, Davenant goes one step further in his whitewashing of Angelo and has the deputy divulge that he has always intended to pardon Claudio, regardless of Isabella's response to his proposition. Despite Angelo's excuses, this abrupt change in his behavior fails to convince Isabella of his sincerity.

At the end of Davenant's revision, the Duke, in off-stage action, removes his disguise and puts Angelo in prison, where the entire final act takes place. Angelo, clearly repentant, suffers the official punishment that Shakespeare omits, but as in the original comedy, the reappearance of Claudio leads to the Duke's forgiveness of his substitute. Vincentio then asks for Isabella's hand, not for himself, but for the man who once tested her honor: "Lend me, / Chaste Isabella, your fair hand; which with / Your heart, I dedicate to Angelo" (1874, 210). In contrast to her silent reaction to the Duke's marriage proposals in *Mea-*

sure, the Isabella of *The Law against Lovers* explicitly agrees to the Duke's command that she dedicate her heart to Angelo in holy matrimony: "I am taught not to suspect / Much happiness will still attend / Th' obedience which does yield / To your command" (210–11). The deputy, who speaks no words at all in response to his union with Mariana in the original, here delivers an unequivocal expression of joy at the prospect of marriage to Isabella, whom he has loved from the beginning: "I fear my joys are grown too great to last" (211). Overall, Davenant reduces and justifies Angelo's offenses while increasing his punishment and repentance, which renders the character's pardon and his marriage easier for viewers to endorse. Thus, Davenant refashions the conclusion of the play along the lines of romantic comedy rather than the comedy of forgiveness.

Also, Davenant's addition of Benedick to the play considerably diminishes the role of Lucio, who becomes little more than an echo of his antimatrimonial counterpart. The interchangeability of the two characters is evident in the reassignment to Lucio of a version of Benedick's remark from *Much Ado*: "If I ever marry, let mine eyes be / Pickt out with the pen of a balladmaker, / And hang me up at the door of a brothel, / For the sign of blind cupid" (1874, 134). In passages authored completely by Davenant, Lucio resembles Benedick most closely in this professed opposition to marriage. Hearing that Benedick has gone to seek Beatrice, Lucio observes, "We shall never out-face the world with our / Invectives against marriage, for I find / Sexes will meet, though mountains and rough seas / Make a long space between them" (144–45). In Davenant's revision, marriage, rather than illicit sexuality, appears as the inevitable consequence of human sexual desire. Lucio no longer functions as a spokesman for the value of procreation outside matrimony, for his tribute to the natural fruitfulness of Claudio's union with Juliet has been cut. In Lucio's place, Davenant's Benedick disparages Angelo for his hostility toward extramarital sex:

> As ill as he governs, if my
> Design thrive against the fetters of marriage,
> As his does against the liberty of lovers,
> His rule may last till the end of the world;
> For there will be no next generation.
>
> (150)

The Law against Lovers, to some degree, preserves Shakespeare's focus on procreation, noting that either marriage or illicit sexuality is necessary to the perpetuation of the species, but the play does not follow this concern all the way to child-rearing, as *Measure* does. Lucio attributes to the Duke, not the willingness to nurse a thousand bastards, but the founding of "a charitable foundation . . . for poor / Diseas'd lovers" (172). The play also omits any reference to Kate Keep-down or her baby, which removes the most prominent instance of a bastard child in need of the state's economic support. With the elimination of Lucio's parental irresponsibility, Vincentio need not punish his slanderer with marriage; in fact, the Duke foregoes any vengeance at all: "Your slanders, Lucio, cannot do me harm. / Be sorrowful and be forgiven" (210). Davenant's rehabilitation of Angelo's character does away with the demand for a scapegoat to bear the brunt of the Duke's anger, and Lucio escapes scot free.

The Law against Lovers also partially recuperates Claudio, the other Forgiven Comic Hero in Shakespeare's play, by effacing his understandable yet desperate plea to Isabella to sacrifice her virginity for his life. Although Davenant's Claudio expresses an intense fear of death, he concludes, "Sweet Sister! I would live, / Were not the ransom of my life much more / Than all your honour and your virtue too, / . . . can ever pay, / Without undoing both" (1874, 161). Similarly, Charles Gildon's Isabella, in *Beauty the Best Advocate*, suspects that her brother will beg her to comply with Angelo's request; Claudio replies, "No,—my Sister,— / I have no thoughts of living on your Ruin. / My Honour's not so shrunk with my low Fortune" (1987, 120). Gildon goes beyond Davenant in his purgation of Claudio's sins, however, by transforming his lecherous crime of fornication into a blameless act of conjugal relations. In Gildon's version, Claudio and Juliet are not merely betrothed, but secretly married by a priest who has returned to France and therefore cannot bear witness to their nuptials. Gildon maintains Shakespeare's parallel between the two couples by introducing a second secret marriage between Angelo and Mariana. The Duke tells Isabella that, while Mariana's brother Frederick, who opposed the match, was away at sea, the deputy married Mariana in private, but when news arrived of Frederick's demise with his sister's dowry, Angelo concealed all evidence of the marriage and deserted his bride (122–23). Angelo's treatment of Mariana in Gildon's version is no less shameful than his behavior in Shakespeare's play, but the conversion of both betrothals into legal marriages alters the significance of the couplings at the end of the play. Here, the

Duke need not enforce matrimony upon his subjects: since neither Claudio and Juliet's child nor Angelo and Mariana's potential offspring would be a fatherless bastard, the question of the
state's duty to care for such a dependent does not arise. With
Lucio, the other sire of a misbegotten child, excised from all but
the first scene of Gildon's version, the issue of childrearing simply disappears.

Lucio's near-absence from Gildon's adaptation leaves a void
at the figure of the Vice/scapegoat, which the author attempts to
fill by introducing a new, off-stage character, Juliet's uncle
Pedro. The *dramatis personae* lists Juliet as "A Lady of Considerable Fortune; but left in the hands of a Covetous Uncle
[Pedro], who is a Hypocrite, and will give Consent to none, that
he may not part with it."[31] Pedro also functions as "the Deputy's
Privado, his Right-hand" (1987, 111), through whose influence
Angelo elects to persecute Claudio. In reference to this pressure
from Juliet's relatives, Escalus reminds Angelo, "They wou'd
not press you thus, / Did they not hope, by *Claudio's* Death, to
save / *Julietta's* Wealthy Fortune for themselves" (79). As an evil
counselor to the Duke's substitute, Pedro hearkens back to Phallax, the Vice figure in Whetstone's *Promos*, and serves to deflect
some of the blame away from Angelo for his harsh treatment of
Claudio. However, Pedro plays no part in Angelo's reprehensible conduct toward Isabella; indeed, Gildon intensifies the
"actively sadistic and lecherous" aspect of Angelo's characterization to the point that he becomes "reminiscent of a villain of
melodrama" (Miles 1976, 103). By simplifying Shakespeare's
psychologically complex portrayal of the deputy, Gildon fore-
stalls objections to the plausibility of Angelo's reformation and
thereby lessens an audience's resistance to the enforcement of
his marriage to Mariana.

During the eighteenth and nineteenth centuries, the tendency to rewrite Shakespeare's *Measure* gives way to a gradual
return to the original text in a condensed form. Performances
continue to excise large amounts of material, dealing primarily
with the lowlife characters and their sexual frankness, but long
speeches by major figures are often trimmed as well. The most
unexpected of these "puzzling omissions" are deep cuts in
Angelo's soliloquies in 2.2 and 2.4, since Angelo clearly "need[s]
the sympathy which these speeches bid for" (Miles 1976, 108).[32]
Shakespeare gives his two young counts, *Much Ado's* Claudio
and *All's Well's* Bertram, no introspective soliloquies in which
to demonstrate a struggle with their consciences before commit-

ting their reproachable acts; consequently, they tend to appear closed off to viewers and evoke at best slight empathy for their dilemmas. However, when Shakespeare creates his other Forgiven Comic Heroes, Proteus and Angelo, who commit the more serious crimes of attempted rape and sexual extortion, he balances their portrayals by giving them substantial opportunities to reveal directly to viewers the intensity of their moral predicaments and earn a measure of understanding, if not approval, for their actions.

Focusing on Angelo, Rosalind Miles asserts that the "amazement, disgust, and grief expressed in the soliloquies of II. ii. and II. iv. almost invariably elicit an unconditionally sympathetic response from the audience" (1976, 199). Yet by failing to take into account the range of responses an actor might provoke through the delivery of Angelo's soliloquies, Miles overgeneralizes about their effect on spectators. A greater awareness of the importance of performance choices to the impact of the lines appears in the remarks of Anthony B. Dawson:

> How sympathetic his obsession is likely to make Angelo is very much up to the actor. . . . But for me this scene [2.2], and even more the next scene with Isabella [2.4], can bring Angelo very close to an audience by focusing on a horrifying self-awareness, a revelation of himself to himself. Brian Bedford, in the 1975 production at Stratford, Ontario [directed by Robin Phillips], experienced his passion "like an attack of fever"; he sipped water; he tried "to examine his malady."[33] A strange combination of cerebration and violent emotion makes the character fascinating, if not exactly sympathetic, and the actor who can catch both should succeed in bringing Angelo uncomfortably close. (1988, 71)

Richard Paul Knowles records that, at the line "O, let her brother live!" (2.2.175), Bedford as Angelo sat down and

> began to write (a pardon?), but stopped himself abruptly, slapping his desk in self disgust. At the end of the scene he was left at the desk as ominous music played, and the lights faded to a back-lit tableau in which the shadows of the set's metal grille-work closed like prison bars over the desk and the deputy. (1989, 42)

In this production, Angelo's compassionate impulse to draft Claudio's pardon momentarily eases a viewer's disapproval of the deputy's severe prosecution of sexual offenses, but Angelo's failure to follow through on this sudden resolve emphasizes that he cannot fully abandon his rigid self-righteousness. Phillips's music and lighting effects after the soliloquy combine to encourage spectators to commiserate with Angelo as a fallible human being, susceptible to illicit desires, yet imprisoned within his own saintly self-estimation.

Among the people, Angelo maintains a reputation for monastic repression of instinctive human desires. As Lucio informs Isabella, the deputy is "one who never feels / The stings and motions of the sense; / But doth rebate and blunt his natural edge / With profits of the mind, study and fast" (1.4.58–61). Carolyn E. Brown, taking the verb "rebate" to mean "beat out," asserts that this passage suggests "self-abusive practices, much like the self-flagellating techniques commonly practiced by religious devotees." Therefore, Brown claims, Lucio "intimates that Angelo subjects himself to rigorous mortification to kill his desires" (1986, 143). Perhaps taking their cue from this allusion, several contemporary productions have dramatized Angelo's mortification of the flesh by having the actor scourge himself before or during his soliloquies in 2.2 or 2.4. In director John Blatchley's 1962 RSC production, Angelo gave the lash of his knout a "resounding crack and whistle" as it "whipped through the air when he was at his devotions" (Brahms 1962, 15). Seven years later, in David Giles' production at Stratford, Ontario, actor Leonato Ciceri was "given the difficult task . . . of punctuating a speech of self-recrimination by lashing himself into a bloody mess" (Pettigrew 1970, 6). In 1977, under the direction of Richard Sewall, Angelo demonstrated "a religiosity at once trite and perverse by scourging himself before a crucifix that had hung quietly in an alcove during Isabella's interview" (Weil 1978, 227). Most recently, in Robert Cohen's 1998 production for the Colorado Shakespeare Festival, at the end of 2.2, "Angelo begins his soliloquy . . . by tearing away his shirt to flagellate himself with a whip" (Harrawood 1998, 35).[34]

The literalizing of Angelo's verbal self-flagellation on the stage may strike spectators merely as a perverse manifestation of his zeal to eradicate his own passions, but such a choice also, to some degree, satisfies in advance an audience's otherwise unrequited desire to see Angelo receive formal discipline for his misdeeds. In Vienna, the most common public punishment for crime is whipping: the Duke refers to his "biting laws" against fornication metaphorically as "twigs of birch" designed to deter the children who are his subjects (1.3.19, 24); Angelo, Escalus, and the Provost each threaten Pompey with a whipping for being a bawd (2.1.136, 2.1.247, 4.2.1–12); and the Duke orders Lucio to be "whipp'd and hanged" at the conclusion of the play (5.1. 511). Like Angelo's request for a death sentence, which "preempts our desire to see him get what he deserves," the deputy's self-inflicted scourging fills the place of the official punishment that the Duke elects not to impose; therefore, the audience at such a performance may never feel dissatisfied at the thought that Angelo has avoided appropriate chastisement for his offenses.

Angelo's final soliloquy occurs after the audience discovers that he has failed to keep his promise to release Isabella's brother. According to Dawson, until Angelo's treachery, "we are very much *with* him. It is only when he becomes viciously cruel, when he orders Claudio killed and his head brought up for inspection, that our sympathies are repulsed. But even this action can be mitigated if we realize what Angelo is going through—the guilt and the fear of being detected" (1978, 116). To assuage spectators' indignation, some twentieth-century productions have italicized Angelo's remorse over his "execution" of Claudio by interpolating a silent appearance for the Provost during Angelo's soliloquy. Wondering whether Isabella might proclaim his abuse of power, Angelo reassures himself that his immaculate reputation will protect him: "Yet reason dares her no, / For my authority bears so credent bulk / That no particular scandal once can touch, / But it confounds the breather. He should have liv'd" (4.4.23–26). In the last line of this passage, there is a curious break: Angelo considers the threat posed to his good name by Isabella, but then shifts without transition to his regret over the death of Claudio, using the pronoun "He" without a referent. The promptbook for W. Bridges-Adams's Stratford-upon-Avon production provides the missing transition through stage business: "Enter Provost R with head in cloth. Angelo looks at it and motions him off R" (1931, 63). In this performance, the Provost's appearance redirects Angelo's train of thought, and the ostensible head of Claudio serves to identify the man who "should have liv'd." Graham Nicholls's response to John Barton's repetition of this business in his 1970 RSC production confirms Dawson's assessment of the soliloquy's potential to help recuperate Angelo:

Following instructions, [the Provost] carried a basket containing, Angelo supposed, Claudio's head. Confronted with this physical reminder of what he had done, [actor Ian] Richardson broke down and wept like a child at his desk. Despite his pride and cruelty, Richardson's Angelo, because of [his] childishness, inspired a good deal of pathos. . . . This lack of evil grandeur . . . meant that his release from adult punishment did not seem inappropriate. (1986, 81)

Thus, the usual cumulative effect of the performance of these three soliloquies is to bring the audience emotionally closer to Angelo's temptation, horrifying self-awareness, and guilt, thereby prompting viewers to concur in the justice of his ultimate forgiveness.

As intense as Angelo's private suffering may be, it pales in comparison to the anguish he experiences once his crimes are made manifest. Does Angelo's ordeal reform him as a judge and as a husband, or does it leave him essentially unchanged? Certainly, his attitude toward his own crimes maintains the rigid adherence to the letter of the law that the deputy has consistently advocated. Calling for his own death, he condemns himself to a punishment as stringent as the sentence he intended to impose upon Claudio. In the theater, however, most traditional renditions of *Measure* have employed nonverbal elements of performance to suggest that Angelo has been altered by his tribulations and will now value mercy and the virtues of Mariana more highly. Peter Brook, for instance, in his 1950 Stratford-upon-Avon revival, had John Gielgud react audibly to Isabella's plea for Angelo's forgiveness: "Her words came quiet and level, and as their full import of mercy reached Angelo, a sob broke from him. It was perfectly calculated and perfectly timed; and the whole perilous manoeuvre had been triumphantly brought off" (David 1951, 137). When Angelo openly breaks down at the merciful generosity of Isabella's request, he exhibits a depth of feeling that no one in Vienna could hitherto have thought him capable. This crack in Angelo's impassive demeanor hints at a loosening of his accustomed sternness and a new appreciation for the quality of mercy.

Brook's production, along with several others in the second half of this century, also implied through stage business that Angelo will submit to the Duke's behest that he love Mariana. A publicity still from 5.1 of Brook's stage version shows Angelo kneeling contritely at the feet of Mariana with his head cast down in shame, desperately grasping her hand with both of his (see Figure 5). A second photograph, depicting Angelo still on his knees with Mariana, both of them gazing toward Vincentio (see Figure 6), is accompanied in Kittredge's *Complete Works* by

Figure 5—Angelo (Sir John Gielgud) kneels contritely at the feet of Mariana (Maxine Audley) in Peter Brook's 1950 production of *Measure for Measure* at the Shakespeare Memorial Theatre. Photo courtesy of the Shakespeare Birthplace Trust, Stratford-upon-Avon.

Figure 6—Later in Brook's production, a reconciled Angelo and Mariana gaze toward the Duke (Harry Andrews). Photo courtesy of the Shakespeare Birthplace Trust, Stratford-upon-Avon.

a caption: "Through the efforts of the duke, Mariana and Angelo are reconciled" (1958, 108–9). At the end of David Thacker's BBC television production (1994), Angelo listens to the Duke's injunction—"Joy to you, Mariana; love her, Angelo"—and completes a similar motion of clasping his wife's hand in his two, representing his affection for his new spouse. Thacker prepares for the romantic import of this gesture through his presentation of the Duke's early portrait of his substitute: "Lord Angelo is precise; / Stands at a guard with Envy; scarce confesses / That his blood flows; or that his appetite / Is more to bread than stone" (1.3.50–53). As the Duke speaks, Thacker jumps to a shot of Angelo working at his desk. After the word "stone," Angelo sets down his pen and pulls a snapshot out of a drawer; the camera angle shifts to a close-up on this photograph of the deputy and a seated woman smiling and holding hands as the Duke continues in voice-over: "Hence shall we see / If power change purpose, what our seemers be" (1.3.53–54). Angelo puts the photo back in the drawer, and the camera cuts to a view of the same woman through the window of a house, her sad eyes gazing outside into the rain. The woman turns out to be Mariana,

whose undying love for Angelo parallels his own secretive nos-
talgia for the happier days of their betrothal. Here Angelo is a
"seemer" in more ways than one, for not only does his virtuous
exterior mask his viciousness, but his superficial disinterest in
Mariana hides a fondness for her that he has, perhaps unwillingly, concealed since the loss of her dowry.[35] When the Duke
forces Angelo to wed Mariana at the end of Thacker's teleplay,
we realize that Angelo is ironically reestablishing the same loving relationship that he has yearned for all these years.

   In contrast to Thacker's strategy, recent performances of
Measure have limited their efforts to suggest a reciprocal relationship between Angelo and Mariana to the play's last scene.
The conclusion to Trevor Nunn's 1991 RSC production at the
Other Place provoked some disagreement among reviewers
over the couple's prospects for shared happiness. Robert Smallwood observes that Angelo "seemed mesmerized by shame, a
posture he sustained until the latest moments of the final scene,
when he submitted to an embrace from Mariana" (1992, 355).
Although this description suggests that Angelo did not respond
warmly to his wife's touch, a photo captures this embrace,
which appears mutually affectionate (see Figure 7). Angelo's
right arm almost completely encircles Mariana's waist, pulling
her close to his body as they press their foreheads together. This
gesture coincides with the production's "conclusively happy
ending, with Claudio and Angelo shaking hands, Isabella
accepting the Duke's proposal, and all dancing offstage" (Holland 1992, 139). A paired exit for Angelo and Mariana also contributed to the optimistic finale of Michael Kahn's production at
the Shakespeare Theatre the following year. The deputy "exited
slowly with Mariana in agonized dejection; but when Mariana,
who had been looking back wistfully at the Duke and Isabella,
reached tentatively for Angelo's hand, he slowly put his arm
around her, and they walked off. There was hope, after all, for
his redemption" (Johnson-Haddad 1992, 465). Both productions, by portraying Angelo's changed attitude toward Mariana,
strive to convince an audience to second the wisdom of the
Duke's pardon of the Forgiven Comic Hero.

   In an especially earnest attempt to secure Angelo's pardon
from viewers, director Keith Hack's 1974 RSC production combined stage business with textual alterations to indicate Angelo's transformation. McGuire's analysis of this production points
out that Hack took Angelo's final speech, in which he calls a second time for his own execution, and moved it forward almost

Figure 7—Angelo (David Haig) and Mariana (Kelly Hunter) embrace stage right at the conclusion of Trevor Nunn's 1991 RSC production of *Measure for Measure* at The Other Place. Photo courtesy of the Performing Arts Library, London.

one hundred lines, so that it preceded Mariana's petition for a reprieve. This rearrangement "meant that the Angelo of Hack's production did not—as he does in Shakespeare's playtext—continue to call for death even after he is married to Mariana and after both she (as his wife) and Isabella plead for his life." Instead of choosing death over matrimony, Hack's Angelo displayed his assent to his new marriage, which was evident in the fact that Angelo and Mariana

> embrace[d] one another, crying and on their knees, as the Duke, speaking lines that were significantly different from Shakespeare's, called in the same breath for Angelo to be both married to Mariana and executed with dispatch. . . . Thus, the Duke in Hack's production called for the death of an Angelo whose gestures forcefully and unequivocally conveyed both his acceptance of Mariana and his desire to live. (1985b, 72)

Immediately after this sequence, Mariana broke away from Angelo to plead for his life, but after Claudio's resurrection, Mariana approached her husband "and they remained side by side, holding hands. When the Duke spoke his last words to them . . . they came forward together, as a couple, to accept the applause of an audience who had seen in their gestures evidence that Angelo's silence expressed his full acceptance of Mariana as the wife-to-be with whom he would live out a life that he now intensely wanted" (73). Hack's onstage audience commends Angelo and Mariana's relationship, which in turn encourages theatrical spectators to endorse the match with their own applause. Like several other directors who seek to justify the forgiveness of Angelo, Hack converts the character's ambiguous attitude toward matrimony in Shakespeare's text to a definitively positive one in the spirit of romantic comedy.

Since the mid-1970s, a trend toward emphasizing Angelo's passive resistance to his marriage has arisen to counter the romanticization of his relationship with Mariana. Robin Phillips's 1975 production, which drew some sympathy to Angelo through Brian Bedford's performance, refused to grant him an opportunity to express affection for Mariana through gestures or other stage action:

> The Angelo of Phillips' production stayed apart from Mariana even after Claudio was revealed. The Duke's twice-repeated call for him to "love" his wife was addressed to a man whom the audience never saw paired with her except when . . . they were taken off to be married and then brought back. Phillips also used the play's final exits to establish the distance between Mariana and Angelo that his silence toward her can imply. (McGuire 1985b, 74–75)

Keeping Mariana separate from her new husband, Phillips adopts a strategy for suggesting a lack of affinity between the two that differs from the more subtle approach taken by Desmond Davis, the director of the 1978 BBC-TV video. Davis allows Angelo to stand near Mariana throughout the end of the final scene and even grants them two paired exits, but as McGuire describes, Angelo's posture and expression still communicate his discomfort with his bride:

> At the Duke's command, the couple left to be married and walked through the crowd holding hands in a formal manner—arms held chest-high, her hand atop his without their fingers interlocking. They returned in the same way, and never once did the audience

see Angelo smile, nor did they witness between the newlyweds any physical contact such as an embrace or a touch that was any less stiff or more intimate than their hand-holding. (74)

Comparably, Michael Langham's revival at Stratford, Ontario, in 1992 made use of Angelo's impassivity to convey his dissatisfaction. Angelo, "apparently more deeply embittered by his exposure, never cracked a smile—not in the finale, not when the cast took its bows. As a result, Mariana's warmth was no match for her husband's chilly disposition" (McGee 1993, 479). Although, on the stage, Angelo may acquiesce to the Duke's mandate that he wed Mariana, a lack of tender physical contact between the two of them will likely be interpreted by viewers as a prefiguration of disharmony within their marital bond.

Several recent productions have amplified Angelo's self-contained opposition to his enforced marriage into active and overt expressions of displeasure. Nicholas Hytner, directing for the RSC in 1987, allows the deputy to display his resentment by creating, in the final scene, a stage picture that "isolates an angry and reproved Angelo" (Tatspaugh 1988, 10). Steven Pimlott also underlines the deputy's hostility at the end of his 1994 RSC production by having Angelo sink to the ground "in tears of rage and shame" (Stokes 1994, 21). This anger Angelo expends upon his wife, humiliating Mariana by departing for the final time "without so much as a glance at her, and she has to run after him" (Geckle 1995, 14). Russell Jackson takes this action as evidence that Angelo's trials have not changed him: "His absurd zest for efficiency, which made him so prompt to punish, showed even when the Duke forced him to marry: he stalked off, leaving Mariana to rush after him. There was no suggestion that he had reached some sort of enlightenment" (1995, 356). Pimlott's Angelo is "irredeemable" (Geckle, 14), an epithet that might also be applied to the Duke's substitute in Barbara Gaines's Chicago Shakespeare Repertory production of the same year. Gaines highlights Angelo's "lack of sincere repentance" and stubborn resistance to his union with Mariana through a similarly disengaged withdrawal for the deputy and his wife at the end of the play: "After his forced marriage to Mariana, the supposedly contrite Angelo starts to stride offstage, then hesitates and pauses for his bride to follow. When she does, he irritably shakes her hand from his arm and, with a scowl, exits ahead of her" (Shaltz 1994a, 25). Gaines's spectators are thereby left with the disturbing impression that, while

Angelo has agreed to enter the bonds of matrimony, his imposed marriage offers little hope of evolving into a mutually affectionate union.

Gaines's revival, the only major performance of *Measure* with a female director since Margaret Webster's 1957 effort at the Old Vic, could be considered a feminist production in that it stresses the ways in which the male characters degrade and exploit women for self-serving purposes.[36] Even the Duke manipulates Mariana into a one-sided marriage as part of his larger political agenda, which reveals him to be no less an abuser of power than his villainous substitute. By resisting the traditional choice to sentimentalize Angelo and Mariana's legal bond, a feminist director may illuminate the politically expedient aspects of this union and their effects on Mariana's future. Kathleen McLuskie suggests that "through acting, costume and style," a feminist production of the play could also:

> deny the lively energy of the pimps and the bawds, foregrounding their exploitation of female sexuality.[37] It might celebrate Isabella's chastity as a feminist resistance, making her plea for Angelo's life a gesture of solidarity to a heterosexual sister and a recognition of the difficulty of breaking the bonds of family relations and conventional sexual arrangements. (1985, 94)

In addition to these strategies, performance criticism has generally focused on Isabella's reaction to the Duke's two proposals of marriage as the key to a feminist rendition of the play.[38] While I agree that these aspects of *Measure* may be coopted to attain feminist objectives, I would like to concentrate here on a different current in the play's stage history that has not received much attention in performance criticism: the tendency for Angelo's second interview with Isabella to be performed as a violent assault bordering on rape.

In the middle of the twentieth century, directors begin to supplement Angelo's verbal attack on Isabella in 2.4 with relatively tame physical overtures springing from his newly unleashed sexual desires. Bridges-Adams has Angelo take Isabella in his arms on "I give my sensual race the rein" and hold her; finally, she breaks away from him and falls to the ground, where she remains until her soliloquy at the end of the scene (1931, 33). In 1950 Peter Brook also directs Angelo to grasp Isabella by the arms—at "My words express my purpose" (2.4.147)—and hold her against a table. Six years later, also at the Shakespeare

Memorial Theatre, Anthony Quayle's deputy, according to the promptbook, threatens Claudio with "lingering sufferance" (2.4.166), then kisses Isabella violently (1956, 50). These assaults, while clearly brutal and deplorable, cannot match the graphically sexual viciousness often enacted during this scene since the 1970s. John Barton's production heightens Isabella's distress by having Angelo butt her with his groin across the room (Nicholls 1986, 81; Wardle 1970, 12a), where he seizes her hair "to pull her down onto the judgement table and stroke her body from breast to groin" (Thomson 1971, 124).[39] In Kahn's 1992 production, during Angelo's confrontation with Isabella, he "ripped off her wimple and veil and flung her across his desk while he leaned over her, pinning her arms as if immediately to overcome her" (Johnson-Haddad 1992, 465). The same year, Michael Langham also choreographed this episode to include Angelo's forcible removal of part of the novice's habit: "At 'and now I give my sensual race the rein' (2.4.161), he pounced on Isabella, tearing off her wimple. Covering her mouth with his hand to stifle her outcries, he dragged her to the couch; then, as she stared in powerless horror, he sensuously rubbed his hand over her close-cropped hair" (Watermaier 1992, 21). Langham plainly intends to link Angelo's proposition to contemporary sexual harassment cases, for a note in the program "explicitly refer[s] to the Anita Hill scandal, tellingly observing that 'the characters seem more real than symbolic today, and the story itself seems disturbingly plausible rather than allegorical' " (Steele 1992, 17).[40]

However, this connection was not clear-cut for all reviewers of Langham's production. Kenneth Steele, noting Angelo's "surprisingly violent attempted rape of Isabella," asserts that the "audience witnessed not an innuendo-laden moment of sexual harassment but a very real physical brutalization" (1992, 17). Steele's characterization of Angelo's conduct as an "attempted rape" coincides with the eyewitness accounts of several stage versions of the scene performed over the last two decades. In addition to the Hytner (1987), Nunn (1991), and Cohen (1998) revivals already discussed, productions directed by Michael Rudman for the New York Shakespeare Festival in 1993 and Declan Donnellan for Cheek by Jowl in 1994 also prompted reviewers to compare Angelo's physical aggression to a rape attempt (see Figure 8).[41] Moreover, at least two major productions have performed the scene in such a way that, in a sense, the rape is not merely attempted but completed. The Angelo of

Figure 8—Angelo (Sean Baker) attempts to rape Isabella (Josette Simon) in Nicholas Hytner's 1987 RSC production of *Measure for Measure*. Photo courtesy of the Performing Arts Library, London.

Michael Bogdanov's 1985 stage version of *Measure* at the Canadian Stratford "thrust himself against [Isabella], wedging her against the desk until he mimed an orgasm" (Weil 1986, 246–47). Likewise, Gaines's Angelo also carries his brutal advances through to their conclusion:

> When he assaults Isabella . . . it is with repugnantly complete physical domination. Bending over her from behind, he paws her arms, her breasts, and her loins and even reaches inside her wimple to stoke her hair. He ceases only when he reaches a sexual climax. Angelo leaves the hunched Isabella in a state of shock, physically and emotionally violated. (Shaltz 1994a, 25)

Performing Angelo's offer as part of an attempted rape has become so universal that reviewers consider the absence of such business noteworthy. Recounting Pimlott's *Measure* of 1994, Michael Coveney submits that Angelo "never touches Isabella in the interview scenes" (1994, 13), and Jackson adds that the deputy "spoke with an urgency and brutality that made any use of physical violence against Isabella unnecessary" (1995, 356). Evidently, a sexual assault is not required to make sense of the scene itself; however, I would argue that some directors insert such an attack to render more acceptable to modern spectators Isabella's notorious declaration "More than our brother is our chastity" (2.4.184) at the end of her soliloquy following this segment.

Due to the declining premium placed on virginity in the modern world, any contemporary director of *Measure* faces the possibility of a negative audience reaction to Isabella's resolution to preserve her chastity at the expense of Claudio's life. Most directors attempting a feminist rendition, like David McCandless, wish to avoid making Isabella appear unattractive in her devotion to her own honor, and staging Angelo's proposition as a rape attempt, he argues, helps viewers to endorse the novice's decision:

> Isabella's choice of chastity over her brother's life becomes much more sympathetic when viewed as a defense against sexual violence. Such chastity expresses not an exaltation of virginity but an abhorrence of rape, of a "pollution" not imagined but threateningly real. Audiences could therefore be expected to grasp that Isabella stands to lose something far more than virginity if she gives in to Angelo. While "chastity" would not normally seem the correct word for this precious, irreplaceable "something," it can, in the context of an attempted rape, take on that meaning. (1997, 109)

While I agree that staging 2.4 as a rape attempt may forestall a contemporary audience's objections to Isabella's preference for her chastity, such a choice also risks oversimplifying the intricate moral dilemma that she faces by making the alternative to Claudio's death seem absolutely intolerable. Part of the wrenching effect of Isabella's next scene with Claudio depends upon our recognition that Isabella *could* decide, as her counterpart does in Shakespeare's sources, to sacrifice her virginity to the judge. But if the option of submitting to Angelo appears unthinkable because of the deputy's violent assault in the previous scene, Isabella can make her decision to protect her chastity from him at any cost without vexatious deliberation. As Jean Peterson observes of Isabella after the sexual assault in Rudman's production, "the equation so hard on twentieth-century ears—"more than our brother is our chastity" . . . —is wrung from her as an hysterical response to near-rape rather than a considered moral choice. While this may be more palatable to contemporary sexual mores, it considerably diminishes Isabella's and the play's complexity" (1994, 10).

Turning Angelo into an attempted rapist also has repercussions for the presentation of the Forgiven Comic Hero and his reunion with the Griselda at the end of the play. First, the act of rape distorts the nature of the perverted sexuality of Angelo, whose arousal flows from the thought of contaminating the purity of Isabella, not from a desire to exert power over her or to experience the pleasure of the sexual act itself. Angelo does not wish to violate Isabella sexually against her will; rather, he lusts to befoul her immaculate spirit by convincing her to give up her virginity voluntarily in order to obtain her suit.[42] While rape implies a lack of consent, Angelo bids Isabella, "Fit thy consent to my sharp appetite; / Lay by all niceties and prolixious blushes / That banish what they sue for" (2.4.160–62). Angelo wants Isabella to consent willingly to her own defilement by yielding to his desire, but an element of coercion comes into play when the deputy vows to torture Claudio unless Isabella agrees to the bargain: "Or else he must not only die the death, / But thy unkindness shall his death draw out / To ling'ring sufferance" (2.4. 164–66). As a general rule, consent may not be obtained by force or threats, but the legal issue is complicated by the fact that Angelo's threat is not directed at his ostensible victim, but at her brother, whose life is forfeit to the law already. It is perhaps fair to say that, while some modern readers may consider Angelo's proposition a form of rape, for others, a term like "sexual blackmail," without connotations of physical force, may seem more accurate. However, performing the scene as an attempted rape, complete with graphic sexual advances, settles this question more simply than the text presents it.

Moreover, making Angelo a would-be rapist skews his portrayal so far to the side of evil that his marriage to Mariana at the end of the play becomes problematic for a feminist interpretation. Some productions of *Two Gentlemen* that enact Proteus's "rude uncivil touch" as an episode of extreme sexual violence also elect to suggest that Julia, who witnesses the attack, is later unwilling to marry him. By contrast, Mariana's desire to wed Angelo pervades the conclusion of *Measure* so thoroughly that it can hardly be eliminated from a performance of Shakespeare's play. Thus, those productions of *Measure* that dramatize an equivalent attack by Angelo on Isabella cannot later avoid showing Mariana's undying love for this abusive man, which tends to paint female sexual desire as a form of masochism. Actor Ian Richardson, who played both Proteus and Angelo as sexually violent offenders for the RSC in 1970, recalls the

effect that this conception of Angelo had on the portrayal of
Mariana in Barton's production: "I found his sexuality sinister,
perhaps a kind of sadist who has met a masochist, and this
rubbed off again on Sarah Kestleman who played Mariana, who
felt that if this was so then, as she had been in love with Angelo,
then she must play the part as someone who really rather goes
in for that kind of thing" (Cook 1983, 99). A performance that
shows Mariana electing to marry and plead for a man who
abuses power may still accomplish some aspects of a feminist
agenda, especially if, through her influence, he shows promise
of becoming "much more the better / For being a little bad"
(5.4.438–39). However, a production that depicts Angelo as a
man who abuses women physically and Mariana as "someone
who really rather goes in for that kind of thing" sends a message
about sexual dynamics that runs counter to the designs of feminism. Therefore, although the depiction of Angelo's proposition
in 2.4 as a sexual assault may achieve a feminist goal by evoking
sympathy for Isabella's devotion to her chastity, such a choice
may also have repercussions later in the play that operate
against feminist objectives.

As an alternative, I will suggest a staging of the final scene of
Measure that may contribute to a feminist production of the
play as a comedy of forgiveness that foregrounds the Duke's
struggle to maintain control of Vienna's procreative machine.
Two minor female characters, Juliet and Kate Keep-down, represent the key to such an enactment, for they both become pregnant and bear illegitimate children whose fathers are, for the
time being, unwilling or unable to support them. After Juliet's
pregnant appearance in 1.2, we next hear of her imminent delivery from the Provost, who inquires of Angelo, "What shall be
done, sir, with the groaning Juliet? / She's very near her hour"
(2.2.15–16). Juliet's "groaning" indicates that she has already
gone into labor; in fact, Thacker's televised performance set her
interview with the Duke in 2.3 in a prison hospital room, with
her agonized cries punctuating the dialogue. When Juliet
emerges in the final scene, at least one and a half days later, she
has probably completed her delivery and therefore "may
appear holding the new baby" (Schleiner 1982, 234). Along with
Thacker's teleplay, several other productions have elected to
bring Juliet on stage with her child in 5.4, including Davis's
BBC-TV version: "Babe in arms, Juliet entered from the rear of
the crowd and proceeded on her own down the lane they
formed for her. As she approached the foot of the slightly raised

platform on which the Duke sat, Claudio stepped toward her and they embraced" (McGuire 1985b, 76).[43] Davis's family reunion seems to be staged for purely sentimental purposes, but in a feminist production, Juliet's entrance with her child may also call attention to Claudio's responsibilities as the father of this infant. If Juliet hands the bastard child over to her

Figure 9—At the end of Hytner's production, Claudio (Hakim Kae-Kazim) and Juliet (Kate Littlewood) cradle their newborn infant, framed by the Duke (Roger Allam) and Isabella. Photo courtesy of the Shakespeare Birthplace Trust, Stratford-upon-Avon.

betrothed husband as the Duke orders the young lovers to follow through on their marriage—"She, Claudio, that you wrong'd, look you restore"—spectators may perceive more clearly the burden of parental duty Claudio must assume should he accede to the Duke's command.

The play's other unwed mother, Kate Keep-down, mentioned in the text but allotted no lines, has nonetheless been introduced into at least three productions during the 1990s. Holland's account of Nunn's conclusion remarks on "the grotesque arrival onstage of a fat prostitute, presumably Kate Keepdown, to claim Lucio" (1992, 139). Thacker's TV version swells Kate's part considerably, assigning her lines cobbled together from the conversation between the First Gentleman and Lucio at the beginning of 1.2. Interrupting the Duke's transfer of power at Angelo's arrival, Thacker cuts to a shot of Mistress Overdone at her establishment carrying a young child. Moments later, we see Lucio in conference with one of the prostitutes, who screams at him, "Thou art always figuring diseases in me; but thou art full of error; I am sound" (1.2.49–50). After the Duke's departure, the scene returns to the brothel, where the punk, on a staircase landing, shouts at Lucio, "thou . . . art a wicked villain" and bites his finger, adding, "Do I speak feelingly now?" (1.2.25–26, 33). She then continues down the stairs and takes the child from a seated Mistress Overdone, who glares at Lucio accusingly. These segments establish the prostitute as Kate Keep-down and the baby as her child, which has been under her bawd's care. In the final scene, Thacker brings Kate on stage alone to drag Lucio off to marriage; by contrast, Kahn's stage production introduces her along with her illegitimate child: "In an amusing piece of business, Lucio's punk, Kate Keep-down, appeared at the end of the play, with babe in arms, and she shrieked with delight when the Duke ordered Lucio to marry her" (Johnson-Haddad 1992, 467).

Although these last two performances both embody Kate's bastard offspring, in neither staging is the child the focus of attention, as it would be in the type of feminist production I have been describing. In such a rendition, when the Duke announces that Lucio will be compelled to wed the woman "Whom he begot with child," Kate Keep-down bursts from the crowd of onlookers and happily presents the ragged toddler to its father. The repetition of this action by Juliet and Claudio a few lines later emphasizes for spectators the way in which the enforced marriages imposed by Vincentio at the end of the final

scene are designed to transfer the financial support of these
children away from the state to their rightful fathers. If, for the
play's final stage image, Angelo and Mariana are grouped
together with the other two couples and their children, whom
Mariana eyes longingly, this blocking may designate a similar
duty for Angelo should any offspring issue from the bed trick.

The only marriage mentioned at the end of *Measure* that does
not provide a father for a living or potential child is the union
Vincentio proposes between himself and Isabella. In performance, one way to approach this offer as an element of the comedy of forgiveness is to underscore the male bond between the
Duke and Claudio that such a marriage would create. Some
modern directors, like Margaret Webster in her 1957 production
at the Old Vic, have chosen to highlight the creation of this link
through the enactment of the Duke's first proposal to Isabella.
As Joseph H. Summers remembers, Webster's Duke addressed
most of his speech to the novice, but one crucial line to her sibling:

> [*To Isabella.*] If he be like your brother, for his sake
>   Is he pardon'd; and for your lovely sake—
> [*To Claudio.*] Give me your hand and say you will be mine—
> [*To Isabella.*] He is my brother too.
>
> (1984, 119)

Even though such a delivery does imply a developing bond
between the two men, the redirection of "Give me your hand"
to Claudio turns a marriage proposal to Isabella into a request
for a handshake from her brother, obscuring the fact that it is
the marriage itself that creates the male tie.[44] A more effective
expression of the familial consequences of the Duke's offer
occurs in Barry Kyle's 1978 RSC production. McGuire records
that Vincentio knelt to address his speech to Isabella, with the
following result:

> When the Duke finished speaking . . . Isabella crossed past him to
> Claudio and caressed her brother's face for a moment before
> recrossing to the Duke and raising him from his knees. The gestures
> and blocking in Kyle's production emphasized Isabella's status as
> the person who has the power to make Claudio and the Duke broth-
> ers, to make true the words with which the Duke concludes his pro-
> posal of marriage: "He is my brother too." In the specific context of
> that production, the silence that Isabella maintained established the
> possibility of reconciling fraternal and marital bonds—of merging

the family into which she was born with the new family that the Duke asks her to help bring into being. (1985b, 81)

Alternatively, if a director elects to have Isabella react immediately in the affirmative to the Duke's offer, perhaps by extending her hand or embracing him after "say you will be mine," the Duke's observation, "He is my brother too" may be spoken as a declaration stemming directly from her acceptance of his proposal. If her acceptance comes later, after Vincentio's statement, "What's mine is yours, and what is yours is mine" (5.4.534), the Duke may place an arm around Claudio as he speaks this line in order to designate Isabella's brother as one of her "possessions" that will also become his through their union. Of course, it might also be argued that a feminist production of *Measure* should suggest that Isabella declines the Duke's offer as an act of resistance to his exploitative manipulation of women throughout the play. This argument I hope to address in greater detail in my upcoming final chapter.

Chapter 6
The Taming of the Shrews

> Perhaps Innogen represents the sort of silent, submissive wife that Elizabethan culture officially recommended, and that much of its social surveillance was aiming to reinforce. Yet her dumb, watching presence in [*Much Ado*], and its power here to promote an undermining hilarity or to indicate a smouldering resentment, also offers a challenge to that doctrine far more effective than Beatrice's volubility which, despite its noise and wit, eventually succumbs to the apparent inevitability—and inevitable silencing—of marriage.
>
> (Hawkes 1994, 205)

RECALLING LEONATO'S ADMONITION TO BEATRICE, "THOU WILT never get thee a husband, if thou be so shrewd of thy tongue" (2.1.16–17), Terence Hawkes envisions the possible response of the "ghost" character Innogen, who appears as Leonato's wife in the opening stage directions for 1.1 and 2.1 of *Much Ado* but has no speeches assigned to her. Although editors usually relegate Innogen to a footnote, Hawkes observes that, in performance, her nonspeaking presence on stage can help to shape the significance of this moment. If Innogen smiles and nods in agreement with her husband, her assent reinforces the cultural expectation of wifely silence and submission, but if she makes her "smouldering resentment" to Leonato's reprimand visually evident, her opposition questions that assumption and perhaps provokes the same type of questioning in the minds of modern spectators. Despite Innogen's silence, the character's potential challenge to the doctrine of wifely obedience is paradoxically greater than that of the "shrewd" Beatrice, whose mouth is stopped at the end of the play as she herself agrees to become a wife. In fact, the other three female figures whom I have designated Shrews according to the model narrative of the comedy of forgiveness also endure a period of silence that coincides with their possible marriage at the play's conclusion.[1] Silvia of *Two Gentlemen*, after undergoing Proteus's rape attempt, does not say another word as her father and suitors bicker over who will claim her hand. Diana of *All's Well* extends no verbal response to the King of France's offer to provide her dowry if she, like Helena earlier in the comedy, will choose her own husband. And most notoriously, Isabella of *Measure for Measure* gives no answer to either of the Duke's two proposals of matrimony in the final scene of the play. In each of these cases, as in *Much Ado*, a production's performance choices will determine the degree to which these silences fortify or confront the notion of wifely subservience.

The similar fates of all four Shrews in the comedies of forgiveness suggest that the subgenre incorporates a paradigm for women that corresponds to the channeling of sexual desire experienced by the Comic Hero. For the women, however, the quality that must be harnessed and turned to a socially sanctioned function is not their sexual *desire*, but their will toward self-determination, which includes control over their own sexuality. Each of the Shrews, at some point, vows a retreat from the world of love, marriage, and sex into a life of maiden chastity, which she vociferously defends with her sharp tongue. The action of the play then draws the Shrew out of her dedication to virginity and the single life in favor of the state of matrimony, within which she can play her designated role in the legitimate peopling of the world. Her potential acceptance of marriage to an authorized partner coincides with her silence at the end of the play; therefore, her relinquishment of her most effective weapon against male domination, her voice, represents her capitulation to a procreative machine controlled by powerful men, including the husband to whom she surrenders herself and/or the Authority figure who approves of the match.

This paradigm for independent women I will call "the taming pattern," with reference to its similarities to the process of muting and verbal refashioning undergone by Katherine in *The Taming of the Shrew*. Near the beginning of that play, we hear that Baptista Minola has two daughters, Kate and Bianca, "The one as famous for a scolding tongue / As is the other for beauteous modesty" (1.2.252–53). While Bianca's modest manner of speaking causes several suitors to consider her an attractive candidate for marriage, the men of Padua shun her elder sister because Kate's unruly voice ostensibly indicates her unsuitability for the submissive role of a wife. However, Petruchio under-

takes to woo Katherine by contesting her own conception of the
way in which she speaks: "Say that she rail, why then I'll tell
her plain / She sings as sweetly as the nightingale" (2.1.170–71).
Petruchio's first tactic in his taming of Kate is to convert her
aggressive, disagreeable railing to pleasant discourse.[2] Significantly, he does not intend to silence her completely; indeed,
Kate's refusal to speak could indicate her resistance to her wooer's will rather than consent to his advances: "Say she be mute
and will not speak a word, / Then I'll commend her volubility /
And say she uttereth piercing eloquence" (2.1.174–76). Rather,
Petruchio aims at the transfiguration of Kate's scolding into a
form of speech that moves men to pleasure rather than irritation.

If Petruchio ultimately desires a wife who converses mod-
estly, why does he labor to tame a shrew when he could simply
seek the hand of Bianca, a woman who already fits his description of a congenial spouse? The reason appears in Petruchio's
reply to Hortensio's account of the "vile terms" (2.1.158) with
which Katherine has recently misused him: "Now, by the world,
it is a lusty wench! / I love her ten times more than e'er I did. / O,
how I long to have some chat with her! (2.1.160–62). Petruchio
professes to love Kate more than ever, for her sharp tongue
marks her as "a lusty wench," a woman whose sexual appeal
derives largely from her lively, spirited nature. Petruchio longs
to engage in verbal intercourse (some "chat") with Kate, but
when he does so, he does not merely suffer through the abusive
treatment endured by Hortensio; instead, he reconceives her
abrasive disparagement as mild conversation:

> 'Twas told me you were rough, and coy, and sullen,
> And now I find report a very liar,
> For thou art pleasant, gamesome, passing courteous,
> But slow in speech, yet sweet as springtime flowers.
> Thou canst not frown, thou canst not look askance,
> Nor bite the lip, as angry wenches will,
> Nor hast thou pleasure to be cross in talk;
> But thou with mildness entertain'st thy wooers,
> With gentle conference, soft and affable.
>
> (2.1.240–48)

Despite the pointed insults with which Katherine has greeted
him, Petruchio denies her habit to be "cross in talk" and commends the "gentle conference" with which she has entertained
him as her wooer. Unlike Lucentio, who desires a spouse like
Bianca, already "pleasant, gamesome, [and] passing courte-

ous," Petruchio seeks to create his own custom-made version of such a wife, complete with the controlled spirit of a lusty wench, by taming a notable shrew.

Petruchio's preference for a made-to-order wife obligates him to put his new partner through a coercive training period after their wedding. His description of this indoctrination introduces the central metaphor of the taming pattern, which compares the shrew to a hawk broken to her keeper's hand:

> My falcon now is sharp and passing empty,
> And till she stoop she must not be full-gorged,
> For then she never looks upon her lure.
> Another way I have to man my haggard,
> To make her come and know her keeper's call:
> That is, to watch her, as we watch these kites
> That bate and beat and will not be obedient.
>
> (4.1.178–84)

Like a falconer domesticating his kite through starvation and sleep-deprivation techniques, Petruchio intends to "man [his] haggard," to prove his masculinity by bending his recalcitrant wife to his will. A haggard, significantly, is a female hawk captured after reaching adulthood in the wild.[3] Although much more difficult to train, a haggard is highly prized because it is "fiercer-spirited than a hawk trained from its nestling stage for hunting" (Humphreys 1981, 145n). By choosing for his wife a woman who has been allowed to run wild by her indulgent father, Petruchio has taken on the more arduous challenge of taming her, under the expectation that his efforts will be rewarded with a spouse whose fiercer spirit, under his management, will render their match all the more passionate and pleasurable, at least for him.[4]

Petruchio's program of coercion succeeds in making Katherine desperate for food and rest, but she resists the surrender of her self-determination as embodied by her freedom of speech. After her husband swears that she shall not possess the Haberdasher's cap until she becomes more gentle, Kate replies,

> Why, sir, I trust I may have leave to speak,
> And speak I will. I am no child, no babe.
> Your betters have endured me say my mind,
> And if you cannot, best you stop your ears.
> My tongue will tell the anger of my heart,
> Or else my heart, concealing it, will break.

And rather than it shall, I will be free
Even to the uttermost, as I please, in words.

(4.3.73–80)

Katherine's declaration of her absolute intention to speak her
mind, despite the likely offense to her husband's ears, demonstrates that she remains, for the time being, an untamed shrew.
Indeed, Kate does not capitulate to Petruchio's verbal domination until he halts their return to Padua and insists that she call
the sun the moon. Kate's eventual agreement to speak in a way
that pleases her husband, no matter how ludicrous her comments may seem, marks the point at which she becomes offi-
cially tamed:

> *Kath.*   Forward, I pray, since we have come so far,
> And be it moon, or sun, or what you please;
> An if you please to call it a rush candle,
> Henceforth I vow it shall be so for me.
> *Pet.*   I say it is the moon.
> *Kath.*   I know it is the moon.
> *Pet.*   Nay, then you lie. It is the blessèd sun.
> *Kath.*   Then, God be blessed, it is the blessèd sun.
> But sun it is not, when you say it is not,
> And the moon changes even as your mind.
> What you will have it named, even that it is,
> And so it shall be so for Katherine.
> *Hort.*   Petruchio, go thy ways. The field is won.

(4.5.12–23)

Petruchio wins the field when Kate consents to say what her
husband wishes to hear, in the manner that he wishes to hear it.
Katherine outwardly acquiesces to Petruchio's whims, but her
lively wordplay ("God be blessed, it is the blessèd sun") suggests
the persistence of her exuberant spirit in a playful, domesticated form.[5] Ultimately, Petruchio mans his haggard and, at the
end of the play, sends her into an obedience competition with
Bianca and the Widow, where she crowns her husband's victory
with her infamous speech on the duties that wives owe to their
husbands. Having traded the "chattering tongue" (4.2.59) of a
shrew for the energetic, yet gentle voice of a modest wife, Katherine heads offstage "to bed" with Petruchio (5.2.188) to assume
the woman's part in the legitimate peopling of the world.

Among the four verbally aggressive women in the comedies
of forgiveness, the journey of Beatrice from the beginning to the

end of *Much Ado* resembles most closely the experience of Katherine Minola. Like her Paduan counterpart, Beatrice initially derides her suitors as a form of opposition to the subordination of women required by the institution of matrimony. This antagonism is evident in Beatrice's response to Leonato's announced desire to see her "fitted with a husband": "Not till God make men of some other metal than earth. Would it not grieve a woman to be overmastered with a piece of valiant dust, to make an account of her life to a clod of wayward marl? No, uncle, I'll none" (2.1.53–59). Although Beatrice may yearn for the positive aspects of marriage, she would rather remain single than place herself under the command of her spouse. Therefore, when confronted with potential husbands, who represent a threat to her autonomy, Beatrice invariably "mocks all her wooers out of suit" (2.1.327–28). As Hero details her cousin's attitude, "I never yet saw man, / How wise, how noble, young, how rarely featur'd, / But she would spell him backward" (3.1.59–61). Beatrice defends the independence of her single life through a form of spoken conjuration: by spelling her suitors backwards, she turns "every man the wrong side out" (3.1.68), transforming his virtues into shortcomings that justify her reluctance to accept a proposal. This perpetual scorn earns for Beatrice Benedick's mock title, "my dear Lady Disdain" (1.1.109).

Verbal disdain for men emerges as the foremost action for which Hero and Ursula, under the tutelage of the matchmaking Authority figure Don Pedro, censure Beatrice. During the second gulling scene, while Beatrice eavesdrops, Hero attributes her cousin's treatment of wooers, not to a desire for self-determination, but to proud self-love: "Disdain and scorn ride sparkling in her eyes, / Misprising what they look on, and her wit / Values itself so highly that to her / All matter else seems weak" (3.1.51–54). According to Hero, Beatrice prizes her witty ability to cut her suitors to shreds with her sharp tongue above all other things. Being so selfishly in love with her own scornful attitude, Beatrice, Hero argues, cannot possibly return Benedick's affection: "No, truly, Ursula, she is too disdainful; / I know her spirits are as coy and wild / As haggards of the rock" (3.1.34–36). Hero's reference to her cousin's spirits as "haggards" recalls the central metaphor of the taming pattern, the comparison of the Shrew to a hawk broken to her keeper's will. The difference is that, in *Much Ado*, the falcon is not manned by her eventual master; rather, she domesticates herself in response to social pressure:

> What fire is in mine ears? Can this be true?
> Stand I condemn'd for pride and scorn so much?
>   Contempt, farewell, and maiden pride, adieu!
> No glory lives behind the back of such.
>   And, Benedick, love on, I will requite thee,
> Taming my wild heart to thy loving hand.
>   If thou dost love, my kindness shall incite thee
> To bind our loves up in a holy band. . . .

(3.1.107–14)

Hearing other women condemn her pride and scorn, Beatrice vows to abandon such contempt and join with Benedick in holy matrimony, placing her own wild heart under her husband's control like a haggard tamed to the hand of her keeper. In this fashion, Don Pedro works through Hero to induce Beatrice to accept the wifely role, despite the subjection it involves, as her proper station in life.

Benedick, though he takes no direct role in the taming of Beatrice, gives every indication that he approves of this transformation. Near the beginning of the first gulling scene, he imagines a hypothetical paragon of womanliness who might deserve his love: "Rich she shall be, that's certain; wise, or I'll none; virtuous, or I'll never cheapen her; fair, or I'll never look on her; mild, or come not near me" (2.3.30–32). As the Governor's ward, Beatrice likely commands a rich dowry, and as Benedick himself admits after hearing the Prince and his confederates depict her love-sick suffering, she also fulfills his next three qualifications for an ideal bride: "They say the lady is fair—'tis a truth, I can bear them witness; and virtuous—'tis so, I cannot reprove it; and wise, but for loving me" (2.3.222–24). No one, however, claims that Beatrice is *mild*. Until she tames her heart to Benedick's hand at the end of the next scene, such an epithet describes her no more accurately than Petruchio's declaration—"Nor hast thou pleasure to be cross in talk; / But thou with mildness entertain'st thy wooers"—befits Kate.[6] In both cases (Petruchio in his wooing and Benedick in his fantasy), the man depicts the Shrew, not as she is, but as he wishes her to be: a lusty, spirited wench who has learned an appropriately mild manner in which to speak to her future husband.

Although Petruchio must accomplish Kate's transfiguration from a shrew to a demure wife on his own, Benedick receives help from Don Pedro and his accomplices, whose efforts produce a sea change in Beatrice's disposition toward her former sparring partner. After Benedick challenges Claudio, he returns to Leonato's house and sends Margaret to fetch Beatrice, who shortly appears:

> Bene. Sweet Beatrice, wouldst thou come when I call'd thee?
> Beat. Yea, signior, and depart when you bid me.
> Bene. O, stay but till then!
> Beat. "Then" is spoken; fare you well now.
>
> (5.2.41–45)

Sheldon Zitner compares Beatrice's dutiful response to Benedick's summons to the end of *Shrew*, when the "public proof of the 'taming' of Kate is Petruccio's hundred-crown bet that she, of all the wives present, will come soonest at her husband's call" (1993, 58). While Beatrice also literally obeys Benedick's command, her residual linguistic prowess, evidenced by her wordplay on "then," allows her to redirect Benedick's orders for her own purposes. This acquiescent yet playful manner of speaking recalls Katherine's vigorous puns in the sun/moon sequence and reveals the tenacious disposition submerged but not extinguished beneath the external complaisance of both women. Benedick, after several more exchanges of witty banter with Beatrice, celebrates the verbally contentious nature of their courtship: "Thou and I are too wise to woo peaceably" (5.2.67). As long as his haggard ultimately submits to his authority, Benedick, like Petruchio, tolerates, and perhaps even enjoys, a certain amount of mischievous resistance as evidence of his lover's passionate spirit.

On the other hand, Beatrice's feelings about her entry into the married state are not so clear, since none of her remaining lines comment on the limitations that she faces within matrimony. Her final speech, however, does glance wryly at the social pressures that have pushed her to agree to marry Benedick:

> Beat. I would not deny you; but, by this good day, I yield upon great persuasion, and partly to save your life, for I was told you were in a consumption.
> Bene. Peace! I will stop your mouth. [*Kisses her.*]
> D. Pedro. How dost thou, "Benedick, the married man"?
> (5.4.91–98)

Finally agreeing in public to be overmastered by a man, Beatrice yields to the "great persuasion" applied by the Prince through her cousin Hero. From this perspective, the play's climactic moment occurs when Benedick stops his lover's mouth with a kiss.[7] In one fell swoop, he both silences her for the remainder of the play and makes himself into a "married man." The coincidence of these two actions suggests that Beatrice's relinquishment of her voice to Benedick's control renders her a married woman, her husband's subordinate partner in his duty to people the world.[8] Marrying the man she calls "the Prince's jester," Beatrice may, as she prophesies, "prove the mother of fools" (2.1.127, 268).

In contrast to the sociable Beatrice, Isabella begins *Measure* as an unlikely candidate for participation in the procreative machine. As a novice in the reclusive sisterhood of Saint Clare, she will not only be expected, when she enters the society permanently, to take a vow of chastity, but other aspects of her contact with men will also be governed by the restrictive code of the convent. As Sister Francisca explains,

> When you have vow'd, you must not speak with men
> But in the presence of the prioress;
> Then, if you speak, you must not show your face;
> Or if you show your face, you must not speak.
>
> (1.4.10–13)

Since these stipulations apply only when a nun interacts with a man, they are presumably intended to inhibit the stimulation of male sexual desire, which may be easily excited by the combination of a woman's voice and beauty. As Barbara J. Baines points out, "The law of the convent thus anticipates the danger to chastity inherent in man's gaze and in women's speech that will become apparent when Isabella and Angelo meet" (288). After the deputy's first encounter with Isabella, his soliloquy confirms that the confluence of her speech and radiance have aroused his unexpected passion: "What, do I love her, / That I desire to hear her speak again? / And feast upon her eyes?" (2.2.177–79). However, when Angelo attempts to extort Isabella's maidenhood from her, her captivating speech modulates into the scolding, abrasive voice of the Shrew (see chapter 5), which she brandishes as a defense against this attack upon her virginity.

Angelo's effort to convince Isabella to exchange her chastity for her brother's life relies in part upon the argument that women are fated by their own weak nature to succumb to sexual desire and its consequences. Hearing Isabella confess that women are "ten times frail" (2.4.127), the deputy seizes upon her admission and exhorts her to resist being a woman no longer: "If you be one—as you are well express'd / By all external warrants—show it now, / By putting on the destin'd livery" (2.4.135–37). Isabella's "external warrants" (her beauty and clothing) indicate that she is indeed a woman, susceptible to carnal passions like the rest of her sex. Therefore, Angelo encourages her to put on "the destin'd livery": to shed her novice's habit (and the chastity it implies) in favor of the natural sexual destiny of all frail women.[9] Behind this argument lies the assumption that a retreat from the world of male/female intercourse into the convent represents a holy but unnatural lifestyle choice for a woman. As Theseus in *A Midsummer Night's Dream* counsels Hermia, faced with the choice between marrying Demetrius or entering the nunnery,

> Know of your youth, examine well your blood,
> Whether, if you yield not to your father's choice,
> You can endure the livery of a nun,
> For aye to be in shady cloister mewed,
> To live a barren sister all your life,
> Chanting faint hymns to the cold fruitless moon.
> Thrice-blessèd they that master so their blood
> To undergo such maiden pilgrimage;
> But earthlier happy is the rose distilled
> Than that which, withering on the virgin thorn,
> Grows, lives, and dies in single blessedness.
>
> (1.1.68–78)

While Theseus concedes that a woman who overcomes the sexual desire in her blood and adopts "the livery of a nun" is therefore blessed, he stresses that the "single" sister also lives a "barren" and "fruitless" life, less "earthlier happy" because she has declined to participate in the natural process of procreation. With similar logic, Angelo urges Isabella to embrace her destiny of active sexuality, but he ignores the fact that his proposition calls upon Isabella to engage in fornication rather than the lawful conjugal relations of marriage. Such an argument cannot succeed with a woman who would prefer her brother to die by the law than her son to be unlawfully born (3.1.188–90). To rescue Isabella from the sterile nunnery, the play must ultimately provide her with a partner for legitimate procreation in the figure of the Duke.

Vincentio demonstrates his fitness to be Isabella's husband through his effective management of her speech. Disguised as the Friar, he intervenes into Isabella's dilemma and recommends the bed trick, which will require her to pretend to accept the deputy's proposal: "Go you to Angelo; answer his requiring with a plausible obedience; agree with his demands to the point" (3.1.243–45). Although the Duke expects Mariana to fulfill Angelo's sexual demands on the novice's behalf, the success of the scheme hinges upon Isabella's readiness to follow the Duke's advice to abandon her shrewish tone with Angelo and to respond to him in an obedient voice. Although Isabella's compliant answer does succeed in deceiving the Duke's substitute, the bed trick fails to achieve its main objective, for Angelo breaks his promise to release Claudio. Therefore, the Duke must once again employ Isabella's voice in a deceptive fashion, this time by having her charge Angelo at the city gates with the violation of her virginity. "To speak so indirectly I am loth," Isabella admits (4.6.1), but she levels the charge anyway. As Marcia Riefer notes, "Whatever autonomy Isabella possessed in the beginning of the play . . . disintegrates once she agrees to serve in the Duke's plan. As soon as this 'friar' takes over, Isabella becomes an actress whose words are no longer her own" (1984, 165). Thus, before the Duke ever proposes marriage to Isabella, he assumes the prerogative of a husband by taking control of his future wife's speech.

Mariana acknowledges a comparable verbal subordination to her own spouse when she appears in the final act to rebut Isabella's testimony against Angelo. As the witness approaches the Duke, he orders her to remove her veil:

> Duke.   First, let her show her face, and after, speak.
> Mariana. Pardon, my lord; I will not show my face
>   Until my husband bids me.
>
> (5.1.170–72)

Mariana's hesitation to speak with her face visible to the Duke recalls the rules of the nunnery,[10] but here, the husband replaces the prioress as the authority who may suspend the code limiting dialogue between a woman and a man. This interchange thereby demonstrates the parallel between the convent and marriage as institutions that regulate female voices, but matrimony, unlike the nunnery, establishes the mastery of women's speech as a male privilege. To recapture Isabella for the male-supervised procreative machine, the play must wrest control of her speech from celibate female hands and induce her to trade the vituperation of the Shrew for the obedient voice of a wife. Alone among the comedies of forgiveness, *Measure* fuses, in the figure of the Duke, the matchmaking Authority who oversees the perpetuation of the species and the husband to whom the Shrew is asked to grant sovereignty at the end of the play.

The taming pattern of *All's Well* differs from that of *Measure* in that the play does not pair the Shrew Diana up with any particular mate; it seems to suffice that she take a husband, any husband, rather than fulfill her oath to retain her maidenhood. After Helena arrives in Florence, the Widow explains to the disguised pilgrim that Diana, as the object of Bertram's desire, represents a threat to the Count's wife: "This young maid might do her / A shrewd turn if she pleas'd" (3.5.67–68). This remark hints at the role Diana will play in 4.2, where she initially repels Bertram's adulterous suit with shrewish words that both aggravate his conscience and inflame his desire for her (see chapter 4). Eventually, however, Diana prefigures Isabella's reversal by modulating her voice at the end of the seduction scene and extending to Bertram a spurious invitation to join her in her bed, where Helena will be waiting. In *Measure*, Shakespeare elects not to dramatize the scene in which Isabella returns to Angelo and agrees to his monstrous ransom "with a plausible obedience," but in *All's Well*, the playwright concludes 4.2 with the Shrew's apparent capitulation to the illicit desire of the Comic Hero. After Bertram triumphantly exits, Diana reveals that the Widow's prior knowledge of the dishonesty of men prepared her daughter to counterfeit trust in the Count's false promises: "My mother told me just how he would woo / As if she sat in's heart; she says all men / Have the like oaths" (4.2.69–71). When Bertram perfectly exemplifies her mother's negative stereotype, Diana becomes convinced that men are deceptive, and she pledges to reject all future suitors for her hand: "Since Frenchmen are so braid, / Marry that will, I live and die a maid" (4.2.69–74).

To keep this vow, however, Diana must overcome the social expectation that she will eventually marry and produce legitimate offspring. In order to secure the Widow's cooperation in the bed trick, Helena has already given her a "purse of gold" and committed herself to provide Diana's wedding portion: "To marry her I'll add three thousand crowns / To what is pass'd already" (3.7.14, 35–36). Helena later assures the Widow that this bargain has divine sanction: "Doubt not but heaven / Hath brought me up to be your daughter's dower, / As it hath fated

her to be my motive / And helper to a husband" (4.4.18–21). Like
Hero in *Much Ado*, who drags her cousin Beatrice with her
towards matrimony, Helena carries out what she views as God's
plan to reunite her with Bertram and marry off Diana. In the
final scene of *All's Well*, the Authority figure, the King of France,
echoes Helena's provision of a dowry for Diana by offering to
finance an alliance for the Widow's child: "If thou beest yet a
fresh uncropped flower / Choose thou thy husband and I'll pay
thy dower" (5.3.321–22). As long as Diana's virginity, and therefore her ability to guarantee legitimate heirs, is still intact, the
King will exercise his full power to persuade her to renounce
her shrewish vow of eternal maidenhood and begin a fruitful
marriage.

Finally, among the four vocal women in the comedies of forgiveness, Silvia in *Two Gentlemen* bears the faintest resemblance to Katherine the Shrew, but the major outlines of the
taming pattern are still visible in her experience. Because Silvia
also functions as the heroine of a romantic comedy plot, she initially exhibits no reluctance to love or marry; in fact, she treats
both of her suitors, Valentine and Thurio, with the utmost kindness. Only after Valentine's banishment does Silvia display a
verbal antipathy toward her wooer Proteus, to whom she
swears, "I despise thee for thy wrongful suit" (4.2.99). Proteus
furthers his inappropriate advances by claiming that "Valentine
is dead," but Silvia replies, "And so suppose am I; for in his
grave, / Assure thyself my love is buried" (4.2.109–11). Silvia
does not necessarily believe the unreliable Proteus, but she
does assert that, if the news of her lover's demise is true, she will
withdraw entirely from the world of romantic ties. In this vow
to bury her love forever in remembrance of the "dead" Valentine, she emulates her friend Sir Eglamour, whom she admires
for his dedication to his own deceased paramour: "I have heard
thee say / No grief did ever come so near thy heart / As when thy
lady and thy true love died, / Upon whose grave thou vow'dst
pure chastity" (4.3.18–21). If Silvia cannot join with her true
love, she, like Sir Eglamour, will retreat into a life of pure, but
barren, chastity.

To determine Valentine's condition, Silvia leaves Milan for
the forests of Mantua, where Proteus saves her from the Outlaws. Suffering her disdain for his efforts, Proteus laments that
"the gentle spirit of moving words" cannot change the shrewish
object of his affections "to a milder form," so he will be forced
to woo her "like a soldier" (5.4.55–57). Just as Petruchio and

Benedick seek to convert their vociferous ladies to a mild demeanor, Proteus hopes to evoke a similar response in Silvia through his wooing, but when she persists in her defense of her chaste devotion to Valentine, Proteus aims to satisfy his desire by force. Since this rape attempt cannot lead to lawful procreation, the play immediately produces Valentine to intervene in Proteus's attack and serve as a viable marriage partner for Silvia. Earlier in the play, Valentine proves his capacity for this role by becoming the "spokesman from Madam Silvia" (2.1.138), writing a letter to Silvia's "beloved" on her behalf. As Jonathan Goldberg observes, "Silvia can only speak to her lover if he speaks for her. Already she has no voice" (72). Silvia's demonstrated willingness to turn her voice over to Valentine suggests that her silence throughout the conclusion of the final scene may represent the play's method for indicating that she has assumed, from now on, the verbally subdued role of Valentine's wife.

Thus, all four Shrews in the comedies of forgiveness progress through a taming pattern that more or less corresponds to the experience of Kate Minola; however, Shakespeare does not assign to any of these women a verbal declaration of obedience to her spouse that matches Katherine's homily on the duty of wives to their husbands. Instead, Shakespeare concludes each of these plays with the Shrew facing the prospect of an imminent marriage, to which she responds with an ambiguous silence. According to the old legal adage, silence implies consent, but as Petruchio anticipates, a woman who is "mute and will not speak a word" conversely may be expressing her defiance of male attempts to deprive her of her autonomy. As a third option, stage productions may highlight the local ambiguity of the text by electing to leave the question of the Shrew's response to her approaching marriage entirely open. For example, Roger Allam, the Duke in Nicholas Hytner's 1987 RSC production of *Measure*, remembers the reaction of Isabella (played by Josette Simon) to his second marriage proposal:

> Josette gave me a long appraising stare, and still did not consent. The play stops rather than ends, leaving many possibilities in the air. . . . [W]e tried to show this open, unresolved ending by putting a wordless coda after the text has finished. . . . [T]he huge city gates had been drawn up to reveal a kind of idyllic pastoral never-never land beyond . . . . Isabella goes towards the pastoral scene at the back, stops, and turns back towards the city and the Duke as the

lights go down. People often used to ask me whether they married or not, annoyed at our denying them a happy ending, or suspicious at our being over-optimistic. (1993, 39–40)

No conclusion to a play like *Measure* will satisfy all spectators, but as Allam's recollection exhibits, a performance that leaves Isabella's reply unspecified risks annoying *both* those who favor a wedding and those who would prefer to see the novice return to the convent. Other viewers may simply be puzzled by a lack of resolution. Therefore, most directors have decided that the maximum theatrical impact of the endings to these comedies flows from a clear choice between the Shrew's acceptance or denial of matrimony.

For the majority of the plays' production histories, there has been no question that the Shrew consents to her upcoming nuptials. In the case of *Two Gentlemen*, for example, a critic like Edward Dowden notes the puzzling nature of Silvia's silence, but instead of finding a thematic significance in this failure to speak out, he attributes the anomaly to a textual corruption:

> The *dénouement* in Act V., if written by Shakspere [sic] in the form we now have it, is a very crude piece of work. Proteus' sudden repentance, Valentine's sudden abandonment to him of Silvia . . . and Silvia's silence and passiveness whilst disposed of from lover to lover, are, even for the fifth act of a comedy, strangely unreal and ill-contrived. Can it be that this fifth act has reached us in an imperfect form, and that some of the speeches between Silvia and Valentine have dropped out? (1877, 68–69)

During the eighteenth and nineteenth century, Benjamin Victor and J. P. Kemble, perhaps thinking along the same lines as Dowden, interject speeches for Silvia into act 5 of their productions (see chapter 2), but this additional dialogue does not reveal Silvia's attitude toward her marriage with Valentine. Until the latter half of the twentieth century, producers primarily employ stage business to suggest Silvia's delight at the prospect of her wedding. For instance, after the Duke of Milan hands Silvia over to Valentine, he replies, "I thank your grace; the gift hath made me happy" (5.4.146). At this point, Kemble's Valentine opens his arms, Silvia runs to him, and they embrace (Becks 1890s, 59).[11] In productions of the other three plays, stagings have featured some sort of nonverbal confirmation, such as a nod, a handclasp, or a kiss, to indicate that the Shrew has become reconciled to entering the married state.[12]

Since the early 1970s, however, many performances of *Measure*, and some versions of the other plays except *Much Ado*,[13] have implied that the Shrew's silence manifests her rejection of matrimony and subjection to her spouse. This interpretation corresponds with the arguments of feminist critics like Baines, who comments on *Measure*: "Isabella does not lose, but only holds, her tongue; she is not silenced but, instead, chooses silence as a form of resistance to the patriarchal authority and to the male discourse within which this authority operates" (1990, 299).[14] Ralph Berry remarks that the trend toward embodying this reading on the stage begins with John Barton's 1970 RSC production, in which Isabella remains "alone on stage, unresponsive to the Duke's overtures, silently resistant." Berry calls this choice "a revolutionary departure in *Measure for Measure*'s stage history" (1977, 242), which he attributes partly to the coincidental revolution in attitudes toward the social position of women:

> In the past, it has always seemed natural and virtually inevitable for Isabella to accept the Duke's proposal. . . . But today, a climate of opinion exists in which these assumptions no longer hold. It appears impossible to the actress playing Isabella, and to the director who must advise her, that the truth of the part entails a serene acquiescence. . . . Simply, a contemporary actress will not perceive marriage as the automatic close to the play; and neither will the audience. (243–44)

Not long after something other than "serene acquiescence" becomes possible for Isabella at the end of *Measure*, similar choices open up for the Shrews in both *Two Gentlemen* and *All's Well*. As discussed in chapter 2, performances directed by Daniel Sullivan in 1978 and Calvin MacLean in 1994 suggest that Silvia rejects her alliance with Valentine. The conclusion to Dolores Ringer's 1989 production implies a similar rebuff by focusing attention on a symbolic prop, Silvia's shiny gold cape, which symbolizes her objectification as a prize:

> [T]he actress stood silent, shocked, in the center of the activity—no one acknowledged her, and she did not acknowledge them. Valentine gave the cape, the gold loving cup, to Proteus. Thurio entered and grabbed the cape away from Proteus, then the Duke grabbed it from him. The Duke teased Valentine a bit with it, then gave the cape to him, the true victor. Everyone was happy and they all marched off to the weddings. But the actress who had played Sylvia

was left, standing alone on the stage. As the lights dimmed she took
the most ostentatious items of her costume off and threw them at
the others. (1990, 4)

Silvia's rebellious actions at the end of this enactment strongly
suggest her renouncement of the values of her society, in which
a woman is the possession of her father or husband. Her isolation from the other characters also implies her refusal to participate in a wedding that would merely transfer this ownership
from one man to another. As for Diana in *All's Well*, Rita Giomi's
1992 Colorado Shakespeare Festival production offers a final
instance of the Shrew's silence interpreted as a disinclination to
marry: "In the final scene . . . Helena and the Countess
embraced, and the king extended his arm to offer Diana the
man of her choice. Diana turned and left the court and the stage,
asserting her independence and refusing to take part in the
fairy tale" (Beck 1993, 122).

Although equating the Shrew's lack of verbal activity with
resistance is possible within the limited context of the final
scene of these plays, such a reading does not necessarily coin-
cide with the entire work's treatment of feminine discourse. In
Measure, for example, female silence denotes submission to
authority (the prioress or the husband) while resistance always
takes the form of virulent speech. Moreover, a comedy of forgiveness proceeds ultimately toward lawful procreation, which
cannot occur if Isabella abstains from matrimony. As Philip C.
McGuire notes, "Such a refusal would suspend rather than confirm the values of comedy, particularly if in refusing Isabella
makes clear her resolve to return to the convent, to a realm that
excludes the sexual energies by which human life continues"
(1985a, 250). Therefore, a stage version of any of these four plays
as a comedy of forgiveness would suggest that the Shrew will
marry, but such a directive does not rule out a performance that
opposes the subordination of wives to husbands. Through careful performance choices, a feminist production may manipulate
an audience's response to the Shrew's fate in such a way that
spectators both perceive and regret the sacrifice of her self-
determination for the sake of the biological imperative.

In a satirical work like *Two Gentlemen*, this type of audience
reaction may be elicited through a humorous emphasis on the
male characters' obliviousness to Silvia's failure, or inability, to
speak during the final 112 lines of 5.4.[15] In the three nonsatirical
plays, however, the preservation of a comic tone becomes more

difficult if a production explicitly problematizes both the For-given Comic Hero's marriage to the Griselda and the Shrew's alliance to her partner. Ultimately, the performance of a comedy of forgiveness will never equal the unalloyed delight evoked at the end of a romantic comedy, but neither must it inevitably carry the demonization of marriage to the extreme achieved by Di Trevis's 1988 RSC *Much Ado*, in which "black petals or bits of black confetti" floated down on the two pairs of lovers in a "macabre or ironic comment on the hollowness of the relation-ships being presented" (Smallwood 1989, 84). Even an inequita-ble marriage may exhibit some redeeming characteristics; therefore, a feminist production might balance comedy and ide-ology by tempering the potentially positive aspects of such a union with a heightened attention to the freedom the Shrew must forfeit once she becomes a wife. In *Much Ado*, this increased perception may be accomplished through an on-stage association of Beatrice with Innogen, the play's paragon of the chaste, silent, and obedient wife.[16] Performances of *Measure* may likewise make evident the verbal limitations imposed on Isabella through marriage by exploiting the text's comparison between the wimples worn by nuns in conversation with men and the veil employed by Mariana to cover her face in the play's final scene.[17] In both cases, such an enactment may qualify, but not obliterate, the contentment often experienced vicariously by spectators in response to the marriages at the end of a comedy.

To illustrate further, I will propose stagings of crucial moments from 2.3 and 5.3 of *All's Well* designed to indicate that the Shrew Diana accepts the marriage thrust upon her by the King of France at the end of the play, but also to protest her silencing and subordination as she enters the married state. This enactment relies upon the observation that, when the King gives Diana the chance to choose her own husband, a privilege he earlier offers to Helena, the play is, in a sense, threatening to start up all over again (Snyder 1992, 29). The parallel between these two royal deeds sets the stage for a further connection between Helena's act of choosing Bertram and Diana's poten-tially analogous response to the King's invitation. As Helena selects Bertram for her mate, she says to him, "I dare not say I take you, but I give / Me and my service, ever whilst I live, / Into your guiding power" (2.3.102–4). At the pinnacle of her marital quest, Helena transforms the aggressive action of picking her own spouse into the subservient act of placing herself under her husband's power. In two recent RSC productions (Trevor Nunn's

in 1981 and Barry Kyle's in 1989), Helena began this speech by
kneeling at Bertram's feet in a gesture of submission (Rutter
1991, 136). Such an action embodies the Griselda's devotion to
her husband and her dedication to the passive role of a wife.

By creating an analogous gesture for Diana at the appropriate
point in 5.3, a director may portray the unfortunate conversion
of her independent spirit to the obedient humor of a married
woman, as well as the social pressure that contributes to this
taming. In this staging of the play's final sequence, the young
wards from whose ranks Helena selected Bertram stand on the
opposite side of the platform from Diana. As the King offers to
allow her to choose a husband, he approaches Diana and leads
her across the stage to stand before the assembly of gentlemen.
At the end of the King's address, Diana pauses, recalling the les-
sons she has learned about the treachery of men and her own
vow to remain forever a maid. One by one, she looks to the King,
the Widow, and Helena, receiving from each a smile or a nod
encouraging her to seize this opportunity for a fortunate alliance. Finally, she turns back to the row of young wards and
slowly kneels before one of them without even looking at his
face, remaining in that position as the King's optimistic speech
culminates the scene. This echo of Helena's previous gesture of
subservience may indicate Diana's agreement, at the behest of
her monarch, her mother, and her friend, to adopt the submissive woman's part within marriage, but her evident hesitation
to embrace this role may provoke viewers to contemplate the
coercive element in this match and to deplore the consequent
sacrifice of her self-governance. Additionally, when Diana fails
to identify the man to whom she silently surrenders her autonomy, an audience may comprehend more fully her society's will
to see her married, to any eligible man, rather than to fulfill her
pledge to remain a barren virgin. Such an enactment would, I
believe, drive home a feminist point about the power relations
between men and women within matrimony without necessarily suspending what McGuire calls "the values of comedy."[18]

Diana's intention to live single for the rest of her life, which is
overruled by the King's sudden resolution to see her married,
prefigures the final destiny of Paulina in The Winter's Tale, in
which Leontes first contradicts the lady's plan to lament the loss
of her husband Antigonus until her own death and then unex-
pectedly matches her with Camillo, his trusted counselor. Paulina's failure to reply to this proposed alliance resembles the
silence exhibited by all four Shrews faced with marriage at the

end of the comedies of forgiveness. Indeed, as I hope to show, Paulina functions as the Shrew of *The Winter's Tale*, which, in many respects, adapts the conventions of the comedy of forgiveness to the distinct genre of romance. Leontes, who corresponds to the Forgiven Comic Hero, begins the play in the company of his Friend, Polixenes, but this relationship suffers when he suspects the Griselda, Hermione, of joining with his companion to cuckold him. Leontes slanders Hermione with baseless suspicions, and she appears to die, but like Griselda, she remains loyal to her lover despite her humiliation and the loss of her children. She endures sixteen years of seclusion, but eventually she emerges to forgive her spouse for his outrages against her. Leontes' reunion with his wife coincides with the renewal of his friendship with Polixenes, whose son Florizel will marry Leontes' daughter Perdita to seal the male bond between the fathers. This late play differs from the comedies of forgiveness primarily in that Shakespeare's text provides Leontes with more than enough opportunities to express his contrition and to demonstrate that his repentance is sincere. Consequently, the forgiveness of the Comic Hero does not appear to be undeserved (to the same degree as the pardons of Proteus, Claudio, Bertram, and Angelo), and theatrical productions have not felt the need to alter the text specifically to make such forgiveness possible.[19] Shakespeare adapts Paulina's role as the Shrew to the reconciliatory agenda of romance by amplifying the part she plays in the punishment and absolution of the erring Leontes, but, like her talkative sisters, she is nevertheless silenced through marriage at the play's conclusion.

The Winter's Tale introduces us to the Comic Hero at a later stage in life than is usual in the comedies of forgiveness: Leontes has already married and produced a son, Mamillius, and he has ascended to the throne to become the Authority figure in his society. Yet the play begins with a nostalgic look backward to a time of exclusively male comradeship, when Leontes and Polixenes were "Two lads that thought there was no more behind / But such a day tomorrow as today, / And to be boy eternal" (1.1.63–65). The King of Bohemia portrays his childhood friendship with Leontes as perfectly prelapserian: "We were as twinned lambs that did frisk i' the sun / And bleat the one at th' other. What we changed / Was innocence for innocence; we knew not / The doctrine of ill-doing" (1.1.67–70). The two boys, Polixenes tells Hermione, remained free from the taint of sexual desire ("stronger blood") until their Edenic male world was invaded by their future spouses: "Temptations have since then been born to 's, for / In those unfledged days was my wife a girl; / Your precious self had then not crossed the eyes / Of my young playfellow" (1.2.73, 77–80). The beginning of the play reenacts this female intrusion when the sexual jealousy provoked by Hermione's entertainment of Polixenes comes between the two male friends, and Leontes attempts to arrange the murder of his boyhood companion.[20] Like Proteus, whose zeal toward Valentine and Julia turns cold of his own accord, Leontes does not betray his friend and the Griselda due to another's influence. As Camillo explains to Polixenes, Sicilia's own observations have confirmed his suspicions: "He thinks, nay, with all confidence he swears, / As he had seen 't or been an instrument / To vice you to't, that you have touched his queen / Forbiddenly" (1.2.413–16). Although Leontes may be as sure of Polixenes' crime as if he had "viced" his friend into adultery himself, he has actually played the Vice to lead *himself* into suspicion of his wife's fidelity, which initiates the shameful behavior characteristic of the Forgiven Comic Hero.

Leontes' jealousy stems from the same mistrust of women's honesty that initially plagues Claudio and the rest of the male characters in *Much Ado*. At the end of that play, the men joyfully accept that their potential cuckoldry binds them together into a fraternity of horns; similarly, Leontes receives a modicum of solace from the knowledge that he is not alone in his predicament:

> There have been,
> Or I am much deceived, cuckolds ere now;
> And many a man there is, even at this present,
> Now while I speak this, holds his wife by th' arm
> That little thinks she has been sluiced in's absence
> And his pond fished by his next neighbor, by
> Sir Smile, his neighbor. Nay, there's comfort in't
> Whiles other men have gates and those gates opened,
> As mine, against their will. Should all despair
> That hath revolted wives, the tenth of mankind
> Would hang themselves.
>
> (1.2.190–200)

Leontes' mistrust of Hermione arises in part from his general lack of faith in womankind; he assumes that at least ten percent of all married men are cuckolds like himself, and although he finds some comfort in this "fact," his inability to prevent himself from joining their number drives him toward despair. As he

proclaims, there is no "barricado for a belly" (1.2.204), no absolute method for preventing a woman from cuckolding her husband if she chooses. Therefore, a husband may only achieve
peace of mind through faith in his wife's chastity. Before his
happy marriage can be restored, Leontes must abandon his
mistrust of women as a group and embrace a stronger belief in
female honor.

Trying to convince Leontes of his wife's loyalty, Paulina
brings the Queen's newborn baby girl to court to display her
resemblance to her father. The King, however, refuses to note
the likeness or to acknowledge his child: "This brat is none of
mine; / It is the issue of Polixenes. / Hence with it, and together
with the dam / Commit them to the fire!" (2.3.93–96). Hermione's legitimate child, denied by its true father, is actually in a
worse situation than the illegitimate children of Juliet and Kate
Keep-down in *Measure*, for in that play, the state of Vienna, as
represented by the Duke, is charged with the responsibility to
nurse and maintain bastards. In *The Winter's Tale*, the irresponsible father also happens to be the head of state, so his rejection
of his child commits the infant to a death sentence.[21] Like Claudio (and Lucio) in *Measure*, the Forgiven Comic Hero of *The
Winter's Tale* must publicly recognize his child as his own flesh
and blood before he can be completely forgiven.

For her impudence in criticizing Leontes' conduct, the King
denounces Paulina as a "callet / Of boundless tongue, who late
hath beat her husband, / And now baits me! (2.3.91–93). Leontes'
outburst attributes to Paulina the scolding voice of the Shrew,
but the King adds to this portrayal the accusation that Paulina
beats her husband, which differentiates her from the Shrews of
the comedies of forgiveness in that Paulina has apparently married without passing through the taming process.[22] When Paulina first lays the King's child before his feet, Leontes upbraids
Antigonus with his failure to control his wife:

> *Leon.* Thou dotard, thou art woman-tired, unroosted
> By thy Dame Partlet here. Take up the bastard!
> Take't up, I say. Give't to thy crone.
> *Paul.*   Forever
> Unvenerable be thy hands if thou
> Tak'st up the Princess by that forcèd baseness
> Which he has put upon't!
> *Leon.*   He dreads his wife.
> *Paul.* So I would you did. Then 'twere past all doubt
> You'd call your children yours.

>   (2.3.75–82)

Later, Leontes reviles Antigonus again for allowing Paulina to speak unchecked: "lozel, thou art worthy to be hanged, / That will not stay her tongue" (2.3. 109–10). Because Antigonus fails to curb his wife's sharp tongue, Paulina continues to abuse the ears of men, particularly Leontes, with her reminder that he has neglected his duty to his wife by refusing to acknowledge his own child.

Hermione, unlike Paulina, demonstrates that she under-stands the limitations on her speech traditionally required by marriage. Her first lines in the play, spoken at Leontes' urging to convince Polixenes to remain in Sicilia, exemplify the verbal deference that wives supposedly owe to husbands:

> *Leon.*   Tongue-tied, our Queen? Speak you.
> *Her.*   I had thought, sir, to have held my peace until
>   You had drawn oaths from him not to stay.
>
> (1.2.27–29)

While Paulina's tongue is "boundless," Hermione's is "tied"; she obediently holds her peace until her husband orders her to plead his case. After Leontes mistreats his wife, however, she gradually begins to rebel against her verbal restraints and warns him that he will later regret his groundless charges:

>   How will this grieve you,
>   When you shall come to clearer knowledge, that
>   You thus have published me! Gentle my lord,
>   You scarce can right me throughly then to say
>   You did mistake.
>
> (2.1.97–101)

Hermione's prediction that Leontes will repent his false accusa-tions and face difficulty in making recompense for his offenses foreshadows the typical plight of the Forgiven Comic Hero, but in *The Winter's Tale*, Shakespeare raises the stakes by incorpo-rating permanent repercussions for Leontes' actions and increasing the amount of penance he must perform before he can be excused and his losses partly recovered. In the comedies of forgiveness, all of the deaths of major characters (such as Hero, Helena, and Claudio of *Measure*) are, at the ends of the plays, revealed to be illusions. In the later romance, however, the King's son, Mamillius, truly dies as a result of his father's tyranny, and the play does not let Leontes off the hook for his misdeeds with only a brief display of contrition like the short speeches allotted to the younger Forgiven Comic Heroes. Instead, Leontes must endure an extended period of atonement supervised by the Shrew Paulina to pay the full reckoning for his sins.

When Leontes recognizes the extent of his offenses against his wife, his friend, and the gods, he delivers a penitent speech, which begins, "Apollo, pardon / My great profaneness 'gainst thine oracle! / I'll reconcile me to Polixenes, / New woo my queen" (3.2.153–56). But unlike the other Forgiven Comic Heroes, Leontes' forgiveness will not come so easily; Polixenes resides at a great distance, and the Queen, as we hear shortly, has followed her son into eternal rest. Paulina therefore argues that no amount of penance can earn Leontes a pardon for his offenses:

Paul.	Do not repent these things, for they are heavier
	Than all thy woes can stir. Therefore betake thee
	To nothing but despair. A thousand knees
	Ten thousand years together, naked, fasting,
	Upon a barren mountain, and still winter
	In storm perpetual, could not move the gods
	To look that way thou wert.
Leon.	Go on, go on.
	Thou canst not speak too much. I have deserv'd
	All tongues to talk their bitt'rest.
A Lord.	Say no more;
	Howe'er the business goes, you have made fault
	I' the boldness of your speech.

(3.2.208–18)

Leontes accepts that he deserves the condemnation of bitter tongues, specifically the shrewish vituperation of Paulina, but the attendant Lord assays to silence her, faulting Paulina for the "boldness" of her speech. This exchange reveals a tension that persists for the rest of the play: the conflict between Paulina's function as the verbal "scourge of Leontes" (Dash 1980, 276), and her concurrent duty, as a woman, to moderate her voice in the presence of men. This tension will eventually be resolved when Leontes quiets Paulina by marrying her off in the final scene, but in the meantime, the Shrew fulfills her duty to lash the offender unmercifully with her sharp tongue.

In the comedies of forgiveness, the Shrew sometimes expresses a desire to take personal vengeance upon the Forgiven Comic Hero in a shockingly violent fashion. Beatrice swears that, if she were a man, she would "eat [Claudio's] heart in the market-place" (4.1.305–6); Isabella likewise declares, after hearing of her brother's execution by Angelo, "O, I will to him and pluck out his eyes!" (4.3.119).[23] Shakespeare allows neither Beatrice nor Isabella to carry out her revenge, but in *The Winter's Tale*, he does permit Paulina to retaliate against Leontes by speaking poniards for the duration of Perdita's absence. In act 5, we receive a vivid sense of the psychological torture that Paulina has inflicted upon Leontes for the past sixteen years. Although the King has "performed / A saintlike sorrow" and "paid down / More penitence than done trespass" (5.1.1–4), Paulina challenges Cleomenes' contention that Leontes should forgive himself and endeavor to beget an heir by taking a new wife:

> Paul.   If one by one you wedded all the world,
>   Or from the all that are took something good
>   To make a perfect woman, she you killed
>   Would be unparalleled.
> Leon.   I think so. Killed?
>   She I killed? I did so, but thou strik'st me
>   Sorely to say I did. It is as bitter
>   Upon thy tongue as in my thought. Now, good now,
>   Say so but seldom.
> Cleo.   Not at all, good lady.
>   You might have spoken a thousand things that would
>   Have done the time more benefit and graced
>   Your kindness better.
>
>   (5.1.13–23)

Even though Leontes agrees that he has "killed" his matchless wife, he pleads with Paulina to "Say so but seldom," which hints that this is not the first time she has tormented him with this remembrance. The impatience of Cleomenes, who implores her not to speak such venom, also implies that Paulina has unleashed her bitter tongue upon the King without a pause since the "death" of Hermione, and this incessant reiteration of his guilt has punished Leontes far beyond the level of retribution usually endured by the Forgiven Comic Hero. After such penitence and protracted suffering at the hands of the Shrew, Leontes is more likely to be pardoned by an audience without significant theatrical intervention than are his counterparts in the comedies of forgiveness, which typifies the generic distinction between this romance and the earlier plays.

Paulina discovers another opportunity to afflict Leontes with guilt upon the arrival of Florizel, who, as Paulina recalls, was very close in age to the dead Mamillius: "Had our prince, / Jewel of children, seen this hour, he had paired / Well with this lord. There was not full a month / Between their births" (5.1.115–18). In reply, Leontes begs Paulina to cease her relentless recollection of the victims of his suspicion, for he fears that, when he encounters Florizel, his remorse over the death of his own son will drive him to madness. However, the meeting between the King and the Prince of Bohemia ironically delivers to Leontes two beneficial effects:

> Your mother was most true to wedlock, Prince,
> For she did print your royal father off,
> Conceiving you. Were I but twenty-one,
> Your father's image is so hit in you,
> His very air, that I should call you brother,
> As I did him, and speak of something wildly
> By us performed before.
>
> (5.1.124–30)

First, Florizel's strong resemblance to his father guarantees, in Leontes' mind, that the Prince's "mother was most true to wedlock." This willingness to credit the married chastity of a woman marks a significant departure from the King's earlier mistrust, which implies that the ordeal of mistakenly doubting and losing his wife has taught him the belief in female honesty necessary for a successful marriage. As Paulina later instructs Leontes before reviving Hermione, "It is required / You do awake your faith" (5.3.94–95). By awakening his faith in womankind, Leontes merits his chaste wife back again. Second, because the Prince resembles Polixenes so closely, it is as if Leontes' "brother" himself has been restored to the remorseful king. In fact, Florizel has been pursued by his father, whose arrival in Sicilia with evidence of Perdita's true identity leads to the off-stage reunion of the two monarchs. As the third Sicilian gentleman reports, "Our king, being ready to leap out of himself for joy of his found daughter, as if that joy were now become a loss, cries, "O, thy mother, thy mother!" then asks Bohemia forgiveness" (5.2.40–53). The reappearance of Perdita ushers in the restoration of the male bond between Leontes and Polixenes, the Forgiven Comic Hero and his Friend, which is sealed by Bohemia's pardon and the marriage of their two children. Yet even in the midst of his immeasurable joy, Leontes cannot escape his guilt over the death of Hermione, for whose irreparable loss he apologizes to his daughter. Leontes cannot fully forgive himself and recover his peace of mind until the miraculous resurrection of his wife, engineered by Paulina, relieves him of his distress.

When the statue of Hermione comes to life, the text sets up a parallel to her first appearance in the play by emphasizing that, like a good wife, she is slow to speak in the company of men. Instead of voicing her forgiveness of her husband, she silently expresses her pardon with an embrace. As Camillo notes, "She hangs about his neck. / If she pertain to life, let her speak too" (5.3. 112–13). Paulina responds, "That she is living, / Were it but told you, should be hooted at / Like an old tale; but it appears she lives, / Though yet she speak not" (5.3.116–19). Despite her afflictions, Hermione emulates Griselda by reaccepting her husband, child, and former life without a word of recrimination for the man who deprived her of them for sixteen years. Paulina, who provided such verbal censure on Hermione's behalf, now withdraws from this role and announces her intention to spend the rest of her life mourning her dead husband: "I, an old turtle, / Will wing me to some withered bough and there / My mate, that's never to be found again, / Lament till I am lost" (5.3.134–37). Even though Paulina has always assumed that Antigonus perished with the infant Perdita (5.1.42–44), no proof of his death exists until the Clown's testimony confirms his demise (5.2.60–67). Now that her status as a widow is clear, she imagines the rest of her life as a condition of perpetual verbal activity, lamenting her lost mate like a turtledove forever singing a mournful dirge.

Leontes, however, has other plans for his counselor. Since Paulina is now eligible to marry, the King exercises his prerogative as the matchmaking Authority figure and, like his predecessors in the comedies of forgiveness, impels the Shrew toward marriage and its implied limitations on female speech: "O, peace, Paulina! / Thou shouldst a husband take by my consent, / As I by thine a wife . . / . . Come, Camillo, / And take her by the hand" (5.3.137–39, 145–46). Leontes negates Paulina's plans for a lonely but verbally independent retirement from the institution of matrimony by imposing upon her a husband to manage her tongue. Like Beatrice before her, quieted by the command "Peace! I will stop your mouth," the former wife of Antigonus hears "O, peace, Paulina!" and does not speak a word in response to Leontes' subsequent proclamation of her match with Camillo. The fact that nothing in the text before this moment prepares us for this pairing reveals the cultural imperative that the Shrew must not be allowed to speak unbridled for the rest of her days.[24] Camillo has already demonstrated a flair for manipulating difficult people, which bodes well for his ability to govern Paulina in a way that Antigonus was never able to accomplish. Thus, in *The Winter's Tale*, the Shrew diverges from the path followed by the talkative woman in the comedies of forgiveness, but her final destination remains the same, the verbal subordination of marriage.

While the comedies of forgiveness create a glaring discrepancy between the crimes of the Forgiven Comic Hero and his punishment, Shakespeare employs the Shrew Paulina's vindictive tongue to remove this incongruity from his romance *The Winter's Tale*. Such an alteration to the model narrative shifts the focus of attention away from the social powers that manage the procreative machine to the providential forces in the universe that operate through accidents and coincidences to dispense poetic justice, as well as to reconcile and reunite broken families. As in the earlier plays, however, the late romance takes the Forgiven Comic Hero through two of the major phases in the channeling process of male sexual desire: the overthrow of the fear of cuckoldry and the acceptance of the duty to acknowledge children born of any sexual encounter. At the end of *The Winter's Tale*, the King awakes his faith in female chastity and finally recognizes his daughter, who has been dressed for most of the play as Flora, the goddess of fertility. The recovery of Perdita restores fruitfulness to Sicilia by assuring that the King now has an heir to whom he may bequeath his responsibility to beget legitimate offspring and to maintain them. The Forgiven Comic Hero himself may never reproduce again, but through the next generation, the peopling of the world will continue.

Notes

CHAPTER 1: PERFORMANCE CRITICISM

1. John F. Cox carries out this task in his article "The Stage Representation of the 'Kill Claudio' Sequence in *Much Ado About Nothing*" (1979).

2. David Bevington examines *All's Well that Ends Well* as colored by his service as a "dramatic consultant" to Nicholas Rudall's 1989 production at the Court Theatre in Chicago (1995, 162), but his article is primarily concerned with the insights into the play that he gained thereby rather than the spectator's theatrical experience of witnessing this specific stage version.

3. As if to underscore the interchangeability of these four characters, Barton's estimation of Claudio echoes one of the earliest and best-known condemnations of Bertram, offered by Dr. Johnson in 1765:

> I cannot reconcile my heart to Bertram; a man noble without generosity, and young without truth; who marries Helena as a coward, and leaves her as a profligate: when she is dead by his unkindness, sneaks home to a second marriage, is accused by a woman whom he has wronged, defends himself by falsehood, and is dismissed to happiness. (1968, 404)

David Haley argues that "Johnson's remark that Bertram is 'dismissed to happiness' better fits Angelo" (1993, 219); likewise, William Witherle Lawrence includes Proteus, along with Angelo and Bertram, in a group of erring male figures who "are 'dismissed to happiness,' despite their earlier cruelties" (1931, 117).

4. Jean E. Howard and Marion F. O'Connor, influenced by Louis Althusser, write,

> There is, in short, no way to place drama outside of ideological contestation, ideology being understood as that inescapable network of beliefs and practices by which variously positioned and historically constituted subjects imagine their relationship to the real and through which they render intelligible the world around them. Ideology can never be "disinterested" because it functions to render "obvious" and "natural" constructions of reality which, often in oblique and highly mediated ways, serve the interests of particular races, genders, and classes within the social formation. (1987, 3)

5. Osborne coins the term "performance scholarship" to refer to a combined focus on "kinetic performances as they have actually occurred" and "the potential for performing the dramatic text independent of any actual historical performance" (1996b, 124). Within performance scholarship, "the commitment to archival historical detail coincides with the critical aim of understanding the potentialities of theatrical enactment" (125).

6. Within her discussion of the literary history of "garrulous, determined

and ingenious women," Lisa Jardine notes that "there is a disturbing consensus . . . as to the unacceptable, emasculating, and yet curiously seductive nature of such female attributes. If the definition of the virtuous wife is as chaste, obedient, dutiful and silent, then the definition of the wife without virtue is as lusty, headstrong and talkative. These qualities make her both provocative and threatening" (1989, 104).

7. Influenced by Gayle Rubin's theories concerning the exogamous traffic in women, Eve Kosofsky Sedgwick locates in Shakespeare's sonnets "the presence of male heterosexual desire, in the form of a desire to consolidate partnership with authoritative males in and through the bodies of females" (1985, 38). This sort of homosocial bonding occurs, I would argue, in the comedies of forgiveness as well.

8. As Linda Anderson asserts, "The absence of revenge in *The Two Gentlemen of Verona* and its general condemnation by modern critics largely for that reason foreshadows similar critical dissatisfaction with *All's Well that Ends Well* and *Measure for Measure*" (1987, 25). M. R. Ridley calls Shakespeare's handling of Claudio in *Much Ado* "the one blot on the play" (1938, 106).

9. Hunter uses the phrase "romantic comedies of forgiveness" to refer to four plays, *Much Ado, All's Well, Cymbeline,* and *The Winter's Tale,* in which "the *humanum genus* figure offends the woman who loves him and is forgiven by her." He regards *Two Gentlemen* as an early "misguided" experiment along these lines, for by "setting up the theme of friendship alongside that of romantic love and by making his *humanum genus* figure an offender against both ideals, Shakespeare has dissipated the emotional force of his climax" (1965, 87). Hunter also devotes a chapter to *Measure for Measure*, but he excludes that play from the ranks of the romantic comedies of forgiveness because in it, "the offense of the *humanum genus* is against, not love, but law" (204). I adapt Hunter's term to "comedies of forgiveness" for two reasons: first, I mean to refer only to the four earlier plays, which I believe fit perfectly well under that heading, and to differentiate these plays from the romances, where, as I will argue in my discussion of *The Winter's Tale* in chapter 6, Shakespeare does encourage an audience to accede in the pardon of the Forgiven Comic Hero. Second, I wish to distinguish between the model narrative associated with the comedies of forgiveness and that which underlies romantic comedies, although, as *Two Gentlemen* demonstrates, both may operate in the same play.

10. For example, Bertram also claims that he could not love Helena earlier because his heart was set on Maudlin, the daughter of Lafew, but neither Bertram nor any other character mentions the existence of Maudlin until 4.5, and Bertram specifically states that his objections to marrying Helena are based on the fact that she is "A poor physician's daughter" (2.3.115).

11. For the difference between spousals *de futuro* and *de praesenti* and an explanation of how a sexual encounter turns the former into the latter, see Lever (1965, liii–liv).

12. Penny Gay also seizes upon this passage to highlight the way in which society appropriates and turns to its own uses the unruly desires of nonconformists:

None can finally escape the powerful coercion of our social system: "The world must be peopled!" (II.3). Despite Benedick's apparent libertarian bravado here, what he means and what the play means is a world peopled via the ceremony of Christian marriage only. The play's triumph is to make the audience assent to its vision of a community always to be revitalised from within, by the incorporation of rebellious energy, not its expulsion. (1994, 143)

13. As Anne Barton observes, "Long before the appearance of feminism, the outrage of Shakespeare's Beatrice over the way Claudio waits to expose her cousin Hero until the church ceremony itself . . . was something audiences and readers, male and female alike, needed no prompting to endorse" (1993, 11).

14. Oliver Taplin writes, "Generally . . . a degree of shared response, even in retrospect, is part of the pleasure of a successful play. And the shared experience can include an awareness that a controversial work is calculated to provoke discordant responses" (1995, 114).

15. Many theatrical companies now routinely videotape their performances as well, but an archival videotape of a production directed for the stage can also distort the nature of the theatrical experience. In particular, a videotape may use closeups or midrange shots to channel the viewer's field of vision in such a way that elements of the enactment visible and meaningful to the theatrical spectator are, perhaps unintentionally, eliminated.

16. I owe a huge debt to the members of the 1997 Shakespeare Association of America Conference seminar "Writing about Performances," whose papers contributed a great deal to my understanding of the issues surrounding the use of evidence from stage productions in performance criticism. For a broad overview of these questions, see editor Edward Pechter's collection of essays (1996), some of which were written by members of the SAA seminar.

17. For an important recent discussion of the status of performance editions as evidence, see Osborne (1996a).

18. Compare Barbara Hodgdon's response to both Postlewait's and Kennedy's attitudes toward the employment of photographs as evidence (1996, 184–86).

Chapter 2. "Were man but constant"

1. John D. Cox calls Proteus "Shakespeare's first attempt to adapt the Vice to a contemporary social context" (1989, 78).

2. The adaptations of *Two Gentlemen* published by Benjamin Victor in 1763 and John Philip Kemble in 1808 both interpolate scenes for Launce in the forest in act 5. In these scripts, Launce and Crab are captured by the outlaws, but in Victor's version, the disguised Speed exacts revenge on Launce by helping to convince him that either he or his dog will be executed:

> Speed.   Come, let us be contented with one of their lives—let them
>   draw lots which shall suffer.
> 1Out.   Agreed.
> Speed.   Come—draw—the longest straw lives.
> Launce.   Ah, dear sir,—I cannot die—nor can I live, if you kill my poor Crab.
>   [*The company burst into a laughter;* Launce *seems amaz'd.*]

After Speed removes his disguise, Launce cries, "I am disgrac'd! I am undone" (1763, 54). This scene of surrogate retribution, enacted by Valentine's servant upon Proteus's man, substitutes for the punishment of Proteus by Valentine absent from the original text.

3. John Cutts, noting Proteus's "own bestiality desecrating the object it was supposed to adore," writes, "this, I think, is the significance of Launce's long description of his dog heaving up his leg and making water against Silvia's farthingale" (1968, 41).

4. See Leech (1969, 116–17n) for a rundown of the efforts of commentators to explain away these lines, as well as for parallel passages from the story of Titus and Gisippus in Sir Thomas Elyot's *The Boke named the Governour* and *A Midsummer Night's Dream.*

5. Girard argues that, by offering Silvia to Proteus, a "repentant Valentine is trying to atone for his sin" of enticing his friend to love his own mistress (1988, 241). However, I discover no textual evidence of Valentine's awareness of his own role in evoking Proteus's love for Julia, nor any indication of this specific motivation for Valentine's gesture.

6. Quotations from Kemble's promptbooks refer to Shattuck's facsimile edition (1974).

7. Ostwald's own description of this moment from his production differs from his spectator's recollection of the staging in that he claims that Proteus releases Silvia *after* Valentine appears: "When Valentine revealed himself, Proteus, stunned, pulled back while Valentine bent over the prostrate Silvia who had fainted" (1982, 132). This discrepancy may indicate either a misperception on the part of the reviewer or the failure of the staging to convey the director's own conception.

8. Productions in which Proteus falls to his knees during these lines include those by William Charles Macready (1841, 255), Charles Kean (Sprague 1944, 73), W. Bridges-Adams (1925, 84), B. Iden Payne (1938, 291), and Ostwald (1981, 132).

9. In addition to Victor and Kemble, directors who have chosen to cut Valentine's offer include B. Iden Payne (1938, 292), Denis Carey (Schlueter 1990, 39), and Janet Farrow, who used the 1808 Kemble text (Keyishian 1984–85, 27). John Russell Brown asserts that, in Peter Hall's 1960 production at Stratford-upon-Avon, "Valentine's embarrassing, impossible, generous 'All that was mine in Silvia I give thee,' was spoken so that it was hardly noticed" (1961, 132).

10. Kemble, at several opportunities, attempts to remedy Shakespeare's neglect of Silvia by granting her a larger verbal role in the final scene.

11. Keyishian's review of the BBC *Two Gentlemen* infers that director Don Taylor "calculated, probably correctly, that he had better play the scene straight and not reveal Silvia's reaction to her lover's extraordinary gesture or convey just what Proteus would have done had Julia's presence not fortuitously been revealed" (1984, 6).

12. Such a reaction actually occurs in one of Shakespeare's major sources for *Two Gentlemen.* In Elyot's retelling of the story of Titus and Gisippus, Gisippus renounces his bride Sophronia to his friend Titus, who accepts the proposal and sleeps with her after the wedding ceremony (Leech 1969, xxxvi–xxxvii).

13. Kemble alters the diction of Proteus's apology to Julia to change Shakespeare's rhymed verse to blank verse, perhaps to render the language of the speech less artificial. He also inserts two of his own lines that depict Proteus's love for Silvia as a "magick spell" (9:68) that irresistibly drew him to his friend's mistress. Silvia, in this enactment, joins only the hands of Proteus and Julia, not those of the two men, but she does encourage Valentine to abandon

his enmity for Proteus and forgive his friend. Kemble then allots Proteus a few more lines of penitence derived from an earlier point in the original text, and Valentine eventually elects to pardon his erring companion with an embrace. On the whole, the sequence appears calculated to achieve the same effects as Victor's version through slightly different means.

14. I do not perceive any textual encouragement for interpreting Proteus's repentance as insincere or Julia's forgiveness of his offenses as unwilling. The text does not forbid such ironic readings of 5.4.73–77 and 5.4.119, but I prefer to assume that characters mean what they say unless there is specific evidence to suggest otherwise.

15. For example, Ringer writes, "The rape and its easy dismissal were completely dehumanizing to Sylvia—what has happened to her was of no concern to anyone else" (1990, 4).

16. One notable exception to this generalization occurs in the musical adaptation of *Two Gentlemen* produced by Joseph Papp in the early seventies. According to Benedict Nightingale, "Julia pursues Proteus from Verona less as a 'true-devoted pilgrim' than because she is pregnant" (1973, 667).

CHAPTER 3: "GET THEE A WIFE"

1. Claudio has been vigorously denounced as, among other things, "a pitiful fellow" (Swinburne 1880, 152); a "most hateful young cub" (Lang 1891, 498); "a worm" (Chambers 1925, 134); a "miserable specimen of humanity" (Ridley 1938, 106); and "the least amiable lover in Shakespeare" (Harbage 1947, 192).

2. In addition to Schoff, Claudio's apologists include Charles T. Prouty (1950), Kerby Neill (1952), Lodwick Hartley (1965), and David Cook (1981).

3. David Cook writes, "In stage presentation it is not surprising if spectators often find [Claudio] callow and uninteresting: actor and producer have a hard task to restore the portrait that seems to be intended" (1981, 36).

4. Alison Findlay notes the danger of the soldiers' retreat from marriage into the male camaraderie of war: "their desire to preserve the all-male community represents a significant threat to the perpetuation of a society based on a conventional family model. . . . [A] widespread withdrawal of consent from marriage would mean either extinction or a community of bastards" (1994, 105).

5. On Don John as a descendant of the Vice, see Spivack (1958, 408–13).

6. For an analogue to this passage, Humpreys quotes Randall Cotgrave's *A Dictionarie of the French and English Tongues* (1611): "*Mangeur de charrettes ferrées*: A notable kill-cow, monstrous huff-snuff, terrible swaggerer: one that will kill all he meets, and eat all he kills" (1981, 91n). Matthew Warchus underscores Benedick's descent from the *miles gloriosus* in the first scene of his 1993 Queen's Theatre production by having Benedick enter with a "heavily bandaged head," only to fling "the bandage aside to reveal no trace of a wound" after Leonato's family exits the stage (Holland 1997, 157–58).

7. Kahn points out that in Cesare Ripa's *Iconologia* (1603), "the figure representing Matrimony wears a yoke and a clog." Kahn's translation of the accompanying text reads, in part, "The yoke shows that Matrimony tames the young man and renders him profitable to himself and others" (125–6n). In *All's Well that Ends Well*, Shakespeare returns to the icon of Matrimony when

Bertram notes the approach of Helena, to whom he has been unwillingly married for his own benefit: "Here comes my clog" (2.5.53).

8. For instance, Beatrice laments that there is no one in Messina willing to emulate Hercules' example of masculine fortitude by challenging Claudio: "O that I were a man for his sake, or that I had any friend would be a man for my sake! But manhood is melted into curtsies, valour into compliment, and men are only turned into tongue, and trim ones too: he is now as valiant as Hercules that only tells a lie and swears it" (4.1.316–21).

9. See, for example, the promptbook of T. Agnew Dow (1854, 21).

10. Certainly, the father of a bastard child is no less guilty of transgressive sexuality than the mother, but the masculine double standard of the play world tends to excuse the male partner in an illicit sexual relationship and blame the female partner entirely. For example, Claudio publicly disgraces Hero for her supposed premarital affair with Borachio but takes no action at all against Don John's henchman for his equal participation.

11. Cf. Sonnet 3, "Thou art thy mother's glass, and she in thee / Calls back the lovely April of her prime" (lines 9–10). In *Titus Andronicus*, Aaron the Moor refers to his newborn babe as "the picture of my youth" (4.2.109).

12. Ruth Kelso asserts that, in Renaissance courtesy books, "the reason frankly given for guarding so jealously the virginity of a girl before marriage and exclusive enjoyment of her by her husband afterward was the desire to insure a man heirs of his own body for the continuance of his race. Where estates and titles were in question the legitimacy of heirs easily assumed paramount importance" (1956, 25).

13. In the paragraphs that follow, I owe a debt to Prouty's argument that Claudio and Hero's union is not a romantic love match but a "mariage de convenance" (1950, 46). Prouty's position has been challenged, most notably by Neill (1952), but the antiromantic view has maintained greater critical currency, as evidenced by its repetition in Ranald (1987, 15ff).

14. Listing the qualities of an ideal mate, Benedick proclaims, "Rich she shall be, that's certain" (2.3.30). Likewise, Beatrice tells Leonato that "an excellent man" would have "money enough in his purse" (2.3.6, 13–14).

15. In one of Shakespeare's sources, Bandello's *La Prima Parte de le Novelle, Novella 22* (1554), Sir Timbreo, Claudio's counterpart, breaks off the marriage privately (Humphreys 1981, 8). Claudio's humiliation of Hero in the church is entirely Shakespeare's invention. Marta Straznicky offers a recent example of scepticism about Claudio's contrition when she comments that "there is a notorious sense of dissatisfaction with the conclusion of what is ostensibly the play's main plot. Claudio seems not to have had enough time to consider the weight of his offences, and he gets off rather lightly with the claim . . . '[yet] sinn'd I not / But in mistaking' " (1994, 156). See also Zitner (1993, 27).

16. John F. Cox provides a brief analysis of an eighteenth-century adaptation of *Much Ado* by James Miller entitled *The Universal Passion*, which combines the incidents of Shakespeare work with material from three other plays (1997, 9). Overall, Miller makes his central figure Bellario "a more sincere and sympathetic character than Claudio in *Much Ado*. . . . Bellario is more reluctant than Claudio to believe the slanders against his betrothed, shows sorrow at the broken wedding, and when the plot against Lucilia [Hero's counterpart] is unmasked, is stricken with grief and remorse" (10). To intensify Bellario's appearance of penitence, Miller expands Claudio's five-line apology in 5.1 to sixty-five contrite lines (216).

17. For other discussions of Don John as a scapegoat, see Berger (1982, 311), Findlay (1994, 105–6), Howard (1987, 175), and Richard A. Levin (1985, 109).

18. At the end of Miller's *The Universal Passion*, Lucilia "is reluctant to take Bellario until persuaded by his sincere contrition" (Cox 1997, 10). Shakespeare's Hero is not permitted any such hesitation.

19. As Peter Erickson points out, "an anti-feminist attitude, whether manifested as overt debasement or understated co-option, is routinely incorporated into male bonds" (1985, 7).

20. For example, when Leonato asks Claudio in the final scene if he is still determined to marry the old man's "niece," Claudio responds, "I'll hold my mind were she an Ethiope" (5.4.38). Humphreys offers the annotation, "Claudio's response sounds jaunty, but it is meant to express entire submission and should be spoken soberly, though cheerfully" (1981, 214n). Conversely, Zitner, the Oxford editor, asks about the performer playing Claudio, "How is the actor to speak and behave in 4.1 and 5.1? How make his eagerness to wed even an Ethiope contrition rather than only care for his honour, which marriage into Leonato's family will clear?" (1993, 27).

21. Quotations from Kemble's edition refer to Shattuck's facsimile of Kemble's promptbooks (1974).

22. The first recorded instance of this interpolation occurs in Augustin Daly's 1897 production at the Hollis Street Theatre in Boston, which, according to Henry Austin Clapp's review in *The Boston Advertiser* (4 May 1897), included "a view of the conspirator Borachio, under Hero's window, and an apparition of Margaret above, while Claudio and Don Pedro writhed in anguish, and Don John with fiendish joy [remained] in the background" (Sprague and Trewin 1970, 52). John F. Cox furnishes a complete rundown of several major and minor productions that have included such a sequence (1997, 156).

23. Mares notes the possibility that Langham's decision to interpolate the window scene was directly prompted by Quiller-Couch's introduction (1988, 28).

24. Most recently, in 3.2 of Declan Donnellan's 1998 Cheek by Jowl production, "the upper right balcony was used to provide a brief view of Hero at her 'window,' then a glimpse of Margaret's impersonation (so the playgoers saw a version of the supposed missing scene postulated by some scholars)" (Dessen 1999, 6). The inclusion of this "restored" balcony scene has become so common in stage performances that its absence has been considered an alteration to the play. Justin Shaltz's review of Robert E. Leonard's production for the Illinois Shakespeare Festival in 1998 detects that "Leonard *eliminates* any visual of 'Hero' being seduced by Borachio and instead retains only his confession of the deception" (1998, 25, emphasis mine).

25. Richard A. Levin writes, "The few words that Don Pedro and Claudio exchange between themselves lack a convincing indication of sorrow" (1985, 112). Paul A. Orr adds that the scene "does not seem to have inherent dramatic qualities sufficient to help rather than hinder the play," and he describes audience reaction to it as "indifference, quickly shading into boredom" (1985, 68).

26. Wells and Taylor, in the Oxford *Complete Works*, generally follow Capell's and Rowe's reasoning and emendations, but they allow for the slim chance that the heading is not corrupt. In their *Textual Companion*, they assert, "Q's reading may simply be a variant prefix for Claudio, though it is

just possible that an attendant lord is acting as his spokesman" (1987, 373). The Riverside (1997), Norton (1997), and Bevington (1997) editions essentially concur with Capell and Rowe without providing justification for the changes.

27. Horace Howard Furness, the editor of the *New Variorum*, also employs rhetoric that naturalizes the ideological component of these editorial interventions: "It is hardly worth while to call attention to the obvious error of giving this speech [F's l. 21], which so clearly belongs to Claudio, to one of the Lords in waiting" ([1899] 1964, 276n). Zitner, editing the Oxford individual edition, bases his decision on instinct, but also holds out the possibility that Q could be correct: "Q has no speech-heading for Claudio here, but Capell's assignment of this speech to him *seems right* despite the warm tone; however, epitaphs of this sort were routinely commissioned" (1993, 194n, emphasis mine).

28. Augustin Daly, Charles Kean, T. Agnew Dow, and William Macready all opted to omit 5.3. See Jackson (1979, 18), Odell ([1920] 1963, 2:297), the Dow promptbook (1854), and the Macready promptbook transcribed for Kean (c. 1840s?).

29. In 1993 director Robert Hupp employed a strikingly similar staging of 5.3 in his production for New York's Jean Cocteau Repertory. According to Pamela Brown, "In the tomb scene, when Claudio and Don Pedro act as mourners before the supposed tomb of Hero, a crowd of eight or so mourners in hooded black gowns, with faces covered, surrounds them in a solemn tableau. When the impressive ritual is over, Claudio lingers bent over, sobbing. Don Pedro leads him away. Two mourners remain behind and take down their hoods. They are revealed to be Leonato and Hero—who looks after Claudio lovingly and forgivingly" (16).

30. Schoff complains, "Having established for us that the Prince is to woo Hero for Claudio, Shakespeare promptly muddles the situation with maddening thoroughness" (1959, 13).

31. See also the Macready promptbook (c. 1840s?, 220) and the promptbook of Junius Brutus Booth Jr. (c. 1875, 17). This alteration stems ultimately from David Garrick's adaptation of the play (Cox 1997, 104).

32. The Bevington (1997), Norton (1997), Oxford (1988), and Riverside (1997) editions concur on the substance and placement of these stage directions.

33. Having Claudio exit the stage before Hero faints has the additional effect of eliminating the possibility that spectators will consider the Count even more callous for his lack of concern for her physical well-being. Alternatively, Bill Alexander, in his 1990 RSC production, used stage business to counteract the negative effects of the QF sequence of events. Smallwood recalls that the actor playing Alexander's Claudio

went pathetically out of control in the church scene, blurting out his accusations between his tears, hardly able to resist kissing Hero as he called her "most foul, most fair," and rushing towards her fainting figure when he should have been making a morally self-righteous exit with Don Pedro and Don John, who had to drag him out. If the thrust of the story demands an ultimately forgivable Claudio, John McAndrew was determined to find ways of supplying in action what Shakespeare neglected to supply in words. (1991, 346)

34. Anne Barton also comments on Branagh's extended (and in her eyes, not entirely successful) efforts to redraw Claudio as a romantic lover: "Although a variety of separate excuses can be offered for Claudio's actions— not the least the fact that Don Pedro also credits his brother's lie—he still does

not add up to anything like Romeo. Indeed, it takes an extensive and strategic cutting of Shakespeare's text, together with surging violins in Doyle's musical score, to bring Hero's lover even within hailing distance of Juliet's" (1993, 11).

35. Comparable techniques have been used for the same purpose in several modern performances. Alan Armstrong observes that, in the 1994 Oregon Shakespeare Festival production directed by Kirk Boyd, "The general exit in 1.1 signals the incipient love of Claudio and Hero by giving the pair a brief, silent center-stage conference before a reluctant Hero is pulled away by her cousin Beatrice" (1995, 25). During the first scene of director Michael Boyd's RSC revival, which opened in 1996, "Hero and Claudio . . . briefly held hands and looked for a long moment at each other as she exited" (M. Collins 1998, 21).

36. Anne Barton also notices the effect that the film's omission of 1.2 has on an audience's view of Claudio:

Branagh has not only added and transposed scenes, but smoothed out many of the twists and turns in the comedy, including the initial misapprehension, encouraged by Don John, that Don Pedro intends to marry Hero himself. In the screen version, no one but Claudio ever entertains this idea. . . . The effect is to increase the sense of Claudio's naive gullibility, an overreadiness to jump to conclusions that helps to explain the speed with which, later, he will credit the allegation that Hero is false. (1993, 12)

37. Beatrice's lines, which adapt Shakespeare's text slightly, do not appear in the screenplay but are spoken in the film itself.

38. In *The Universal Passion*, "Miller's omission of Claudio's jesting speeches in the fifth act of *Much Ado* heightened the impression of Bellario's sincerity" (Cox 1997, 10).

39. Timpane reviews this production as it was revived at the Shakespeare Theatre in Princeton, N.J., in 1993.

40. Graham Holderness writes,

In the traditional militaristic ideology of the feudal aristocracy male comradeship is much more important than sexual relations with the female; women are marginalized and tightly circumscribed into the categories of wife and breeder (to be protected), or of whore (to be used and discarded). The qualities required for the successful prosecution of a soldier's career—courage, violence, self-possession—were in the ethical code of this particular class bound up with notions of solidarity based on a masculine fellowship of aristocratic honour. As we will observe in *Much Ado about Nothing*, it can seem far more natural, to the aristocratic warrior, to defend his own honour and that of his male companions, than to invest any real trust and commitment into the keeping of a woman. (1989, 79)

41. Mason (1976, 47, 87, 96–97) records a comparable emphasis at the close of productions directed by Douglas Seale (Stratford-upon-Avon, 1958), Franco Zeffirelli (National Theatre, 1965), and Trevor Nunn (Stratford-upon-Avon, 1968). Peter Roberts notes a similar concluding focus in Terry Hands's 1982 Stratford-upon-Avon revival (1983, 34). In Branagh's screenplay, the description of the final sequence of his film includes the comment, "We note the melancholic, solitary figure of DON PEDRO" (1993, 83). Following this theatrical tradition, Humphreys annotates the passage, "he who has done most to further his younger friends' marriages . . . is left in somewhat touching singleness" (1981, 217n).

42. Shakespeare also uses "sad" to mean "serious" at 1.1.170; 1.3.13, 56; 2.3.213; 3.2.15, 19; and 5.1.277.

43. Don Pedro has participated in the final dance in at least two Stratford productions, partnering with Ursula in Sir John Gielgud's 1949 revival and with Beatrice, briefly, in Barton's 1976 effort (Mason 1976, 22, 138).

CHAPTER 4: "SERVICE IS NO HERITAGE"

1. Jay L. Halio writes, "Where Shakespeare errs is in his failure to dramatize the brighter aspects of Bertram's character: though we hear of his better qualities, we never see them translated into action. . . . Of course, much of what we find wanting in the study may be provided on the stage" (1964, 39).

2. David Ellis states, "To present Parolles as more enterprisingly and, above all, effectively wicked than any lines he is given suggest he should be, makes it easier to turn him into a scapegoat; and if directors often share the same interest as the Countess, Diana, and Lafew in achieving that result it is because it lessens the unattractiveness of . . . Bertram" (1989, 293).

3. Previous explorations of the sexual connotations of "service" in *All's Well* include Adams (1961, 267), Calderwood (1963, 74), Roark (1988, 248–49), and Sacks (1980, 52).

4. Adelman's article is one in a series of studies that explore male desire and sexual anxiety in *All's Well*, including Kirsch (1981, 108–43), Neely (1985, 58–104), Nevo (1987, 26–51), and Wheeler (1981, 34–91).

5. A similar speech occurs after the bed trick when Helena reflects on the "sweet use" that a lustful Bertram has made of the wife he loathes:

> But, O strange men!
> That can such sweet use make of what they hate,
> When saucy trusting of the cozen'd thoughts
> Defiles the pitchy night; so lust doth play
> With what it loathes for that which is away.
> But more of this hereafter.
>
> (4.4.21–26)

6. For further comments on the unsettling quality of this conundrum, see Kirsch (1981, 137) and Hunter (1965, 124–25).

7. Although the play accents Bertram's youth more strongly than that of Parolles, the braggart soldier is constantly associated with fashion, which Bertram's father condemns as an affectation of "younger spirits, whose apprehensive senses / All but new things disdain" (1.2.60–61).

8. As R. B. Parker observes (1984, 110), "After the cure . . . Lafew insists on an erotic element in the King's recovery; 'your dolphin is not lustier,' he claims, and 'Lustique, as the Dutchman says. I'll like a maid the better whilst I have a tooth in my head' " (2.3.26, 41–42).

9. For Bertram's role as the King's sexual surrogate, see Wheeler (1981, 81), Parker (1984, 110), and Asp (1986, 55).

10. Helena is recently compared to Griselda by McCandless (1997, 46), Parker (1992, 374), Williamson (1986, 64–65), and Zitner (1989, 106).

11. As many critics have noticed, Helena's "pilgrimage" carries her far from her ostensible destination to the town where the object of her "idolatrous

fancy" is stationed (1.1.95). Like Julia, who seeks the "divine" Proteus in Milan as a "true devoted pilgrim" (2.7.13, 9), Helena takes a journey that resembles a pilgrimage in a metaphorical, more than a literal, sense (Hall 1995, 147).

12. For a treatment of Parolles as a braggart soldier, see Miola (1993, 29–32).

13. See, most recently, Dessen (1986, 114).

14. The belief that sexuality drains the life out of a man reappears in the Clown's description of "standing to't" as "the loss of men" as well as "the getting of children" (3.2.40–41). Like Parolles, the Clown sees the overlap between military and sexual service. Holding his ground in warfare will compel a soldier to kill or be killed, while rising to the occasion on the sexual battleground also leads paradoxically to both death and the renewal of life.

15. For the war/sex metaphor in *All's Well*, see Parker (1984, 105–9).

16. I agree in principle with Adams's interpretation of this passage, but he bolsters his evidence unjustifiably by reading "barrenness" for "bareness" in line 20 without textual basis.

17. Parolles reminds us that even rape has reproductive consequences. Under interrogation, he says of Captain Dumaine, "he was whipp'd for getting the shrieve's fool with child, a dumb innocent that could not say him nay" (4.3.181–83).

18. This resemblance has been noted by several critics, among them Hunter (1959, 101n), Parker (1984, 106), Taylor (1985, 283), and Welsh (1978, 18–19).

19. As Bertram later accuses Diana, "She knew her distance and did angle for me, / Madding my eagerness with her restraint" (5.3.211–12).

20. Robert Ornstein writes, "After [Bertram] has proved his gallantry, won the esteem of his fellow officers, and possessed the prize of Diana's virginity, he is ready to marry Maudlin, especially when it will redeem him in the eyes of the King, his mother, and Lafew" (1986, 174).

21. McCandless agrees that Bertram's expression of "love" for Helena cannot be taken at face value, since Bertram has falsely professed admiration for Helena once before (2.3.167–73) in order to placate the King (1994, 466).

22. " 'Giletta of Narbona,' The Thirty-eighth Novel of William Painter's *The Palace of Pleasure*" is reprinted in Hunter's Arden edition (1959, 145–52).

23. In Sir Peter Hall's 1992 RSC production, "Helena was helped offstage at the end of 5.1 and was then visibly pregnant in 5.3" (Dessen 1993, 37).

24. An interesting variation on this staging was employed in Jory's revival: "Indeed, in a recent production in which the director was striving for a less culpable Bertram, an exiting Helena blew a kiss to a Bertram who was almost ready to yield only to have Parolles step in front of him, intercept the kiss, and literally brush it away" (Dessen 1986, 114).

25. Nunn's production premiered at Stratford in 1981 with Mike Gwilym as Bertram, then reopened in May of the following year at the Barbican in London with Philip Franks as the Count (Styan 1984, 122).

26. Kemble's original 1794 production ironically featured an actress who was in fact pregnant at the time, but her condition was apparently considered a drawback rather than a feature to be exploited. Charles Shattuck records that "Mrs. Jordan, who played the virginal Helena, was five months gone with child, a circumstance which drew one or two winking comments in the press and rendered further appearances in the role inadvisable" (1974, 1:i).

27. Fraser quotes Smallwood (1972, 60).

28. A different photographer's version of the same scene, with all of the principals smiling, appears in Ansorge (1967, 36).

29. The other three twentieth-century directors who include a kneeling Bertram are B. Iden Payne (1935, 128), Willman (1955), and Hall (Smallwood 1993, 358). Sir Arthur Quiller-Couch and John Dover Wilson also insert the stage direction *"[kneels]"* before the Count's request for pardon in their New Shakespeare edition of the play (1929).

30. As mentioned above, this embrace occurs in the Moshinsky (BBC) and Epps (Old Globe) productions, as well as in the promptbook for Payne's Stratford revival (1935, 128). According to the Guthrie promptbook, Bertram kisses Helena and puts her ring back on her finger *before* speaking the couplet (1959, 127).

31. Warren reviews Nunn's production after it was transferred to the Barbican in 1982, whereas Smallwood records details from the original Stratford version. Although there are differences between these two incarnations of the same production (i.e., Philip Franks replacing Mike Gwilym as Bertram), reviews of both performances are similar enough to justify a qualified discussion of the two versions as a single production. For example, Warren's account of the 1982 revival recalls that Franks, like Gwilym in 1981, "did not soften Bertram's cruel refusal to give Helena the kiss she asks for" (1983, 80).

32. Holland points out that in Kyle's 1989 RSC production, Mariana appeared in 3.5 holding a baby (1991, 160). This directorial decision achieves the same effect as Jones's choice within that segment, but it fails to set up a meaningful visual parallel with Helena's condition in the final scene.

CHAPTER 5: "WE SHALL HAVE ALL THE WORLD"

1. David Lloyd Stevenson surveys the "amazing" number of eighteenth- and nineteenth-century commentators, including Charlotte Lennox, Dr. Johnson, and Coleridge, who would have preferred "eye-for-an-eye justice" to Shakespeare's handling of the story (1966, 77ff).

2. Alwin Thaler disputes Lawrence's claim as it applies to all four Forgiven Comic Heroes: "One may have misgivings as to the outcome of Hero's marriage as well as that of Helena in *All's Well*, in view of the treatment accorded them (before marriage) by young Claudio and Bertram. These two . . . seem as unpromising husbands as Proteus, and Angelo of *Measure for Measure*" (1927, 752).

3. The best analysis of Lucio as an outgrowth of the Vice appears in Winston (1981, 230–40).

4. Other references to Phallax as a Vice figure occur in Gibbons (1991, 11), Hillman (1993, 104), and Winston (1981, 239). The complete text of *Promos and Cassandra* is reprinted in editor Mark Eccles's New Variorum edition of *Measure* (1980, 305–69).

5. Winston also quotes Dessen's observation and later asserts that Lucio might be allegorized "under the name of Liberty" (1981, 234, 240). This attribution is plausible, but I wish to focus on the play's treatment of excessive *sexual* liberty in particular.

6. This technique generally involves associating Lucio with the spread of venereal disease attendant upon unrestrained copulation. See Nagarajan's review of Margaret Webster's 1957 production at the Old Vic (1989, 37) and

McGee's account of Michael Langham's directorial effort at Stratford, Ontario, in 1992 (1993, 477).

7. Cacicedo derives this notion from Freud's arguments about the origins of patriarchal rule in *Civilization and Its Discontents* (1961, 47, 57).

8. R. G. Hunter writes, "The point that, in and of itself, the sexual act is natural and that its results are good is made in this play [*Measure*] in much the same way as in *All's Well*. Just as the disreputable Parolles becomes Nature's spokesman in the earlier play, so Lucio is given the job here" (1965, 209).

9. Richard P. Wheeler compares this passage with lines 5–6 of Sonnet 3: "For where is she so fair whose uneared womb / Disdains the tillage of thy husbandry?" (1981, 152). Melvin Seiden also observes that "Lucio ennobles pregnancy (and, necessarily, sexuality) by associating it with agricultural imagery heightened to the status of pastoral" (1990, 85).

10. For further comments on Lucio's view of the amoral quality of natural reproduction, see Shell (1988, 30) and Trombetta (1976, 68).

11. Angelo tells Isabella, "Those many had not dared to do that evil / If the first that did th'edict infringe / Had answered for his deed" (2.2.92–94).

12. Williamson alludes to the title of Peter Laslett's essay "The Bastardy Prone Sub-society" (1980).

13. This reference to Claudio's situation in the context of the getting of "bastards" shows that the laws of Shakespeare's fictional Vienna do not match those of Shakespeare's own country precisely. In England, "the troth-plight marriage, provided the couple were careful about their tenses, was legally valid. They were not free thereafter to divorce or to marry again and the children were legitimate" (Latham 1975, 134n). The Duke's or Angelo's assumption of the bastardy of Claudio's child might be explained by their lack of knowledge of his handfasting, but Lucio is fully aware of this betrothal (1.2.134–42) and he still refers to the couple's offspring as an illegitimate child.

14. For an earlier analysis of Isabella as a shrew to which I am indebted, see Lyons (1989, 132).

15. Further discussions of the marriage contracts in *Measure* include articles by Birje-Patil (1970), Harding (1950), Hawkins (1974), Nagarajan (1962), Powers (1988), Schanzer (1960), Scott (1982), and Wentersdorf (1979).

16. Critics who note the scrupulous adherence to the letter of the law in Angelo's cancellation of his engagement include Dodds (1946, 254–55), Mikkelsen (1958, 264), Smith (1982, 58), and Tebbetts (1985, 133).

17. The only passage that hints at Angelo's possible romantic affection for Mariana is her declaration, after unmasking in the final scene, "This is that face, thou cruel Angelo, / Which once thou swor'st was worth the looking on" (5.1.206–7). Literally, this statement indicates that Angelo told Mariana she was beautiful, but it does not necessarily establish that he loved her.

18. N. W. Bawcutt (1991, 161n) links this blocked current metaphor to a similar figure of speech employed by Julia to describe her passion for Proteus:

> The current that with gentle murmur glides,
> Thou know'st, being stopp'd impatiently doth rage;
> But when his fair course is not hindered,
> He makes sweet music with th'enamell'd stones,
> Giving a gentle kiss to every sedge
> He overtaketh in his pilgrimage.
>
> (2.7.25–30)

Appearing here in conjunction with the image of the pilgrimage, later associated with Helena's unrequited love for Bertram, the metaphor of the dammed up current seems to epitomize for Shakespeare the intensity of the Griselda's enduring affection for the Forgiven Comic Hero. Significantly, no such image occurs in *Much Ado about Nothing*, where Hero's feelings for Claudio are more ambiguous. For additional comments on Mariana's resemblance to patient Griselda, see Dusinberre (1975, 124) and Smith (1950, 216).

19. Mariana's seclusion recalls the isolation in store for Hero, another Griselda repudiated by her "lover" and slandered with allegations of promiscuity, if the plan to recover her standing with Claudio should fail:

> And if it sort not well, you may conceal her,
> As best befits her wounded reputation[,]
> In some reclusive and religious life,
> Out of all eyes, tongues, minds, and injuries.
>
> (4.1.240–43)

20. In this context, there may be relevance to Pompey's allegation that Constable Elbow's wife, who is now with child, was "respected with him, before he married with her" (2.1.167–68). For the claim that the "natural end of each and every sexual act of intercourse (within or without wedlock) in *Measure for Measure* is procreation," see Shell (1988, 33).

21. In Whetstone's play, Promos admits of Cassandra, "Happie is the man, that inioyes the loue of such a wife, / I do protest, hir modest wordes, hath wrought in me a maze" (Eccles 1980, 315). In a secondary source, Geraldi Cinthio's play *Epitia* (1583), the governor Iuriste, "now enamoured of Epitia, was prepared to marry her and release her brother" (Lever 1965, xxxix).

22. I differ, here, from the position of Arthur C. Kirsch, who claims that the "bed-trick miraculously transforms Angelo's libidinousness, turning it to the consummation of a betrothal he had betrayed" (1975, 100). I can locate no evidence of a transformation in the nature of Angelo's desire.

23. Lever emends F's "weedes" to "jades" to correct the mixed metaphor and cites parallel passages from Marlowe and Shakespeare (1965, 20n). Some editors suggest "steeds" as closer orthographically to "weedes," which also preserves the reference to horsemanship; others leave the passage as it stands in F. For a survey of the editorial treatment of this passage, see Eccles (1980, 43–44n).

24. Snyder (1993, 29n) derives this notion from Karl Elze, whose evidence Snyder summarizes as follows:

Bertram is several times associated with horses: he complains at being "fore-horse to a smock" (2.1.30), is threatened with "the staggers" for disobeying the King (2.3.164), is encouraged in revolt by Parolles' comparison between "jades" who remain in France and "Mars's fiery steed" in Italy (2.3.283–85), is soon made general of the horse for Florence (3.3.1), is to be sold off at market like an unsatisfactory horse when found unworthy of Lafeu's daughter (5.3.148–49), is seen to "boggle" like a horse taking fright when Diana produces the ring (5.3.232).

25. Among those who find Angelo's remorse convincing are Edwards (1968, 115), Miles (1976, 200), and Schleiner (1982, 234); Gelb (1971, 32) and Marsh (1963, 36) find it unpersuasive. Schanzer argues that Angelo's conversion is

supposed to be genuine but that it is "treated so perfunctorily" that "radical dissatisfaction . . . can take root" (1963, 93).

26. Other scholars who emphasize the public humiliation of Angelo as a part of the retribution against him include Caputi (1961, 433), Hillman (1993, 117), and Nicholls (1986, 42).

27. Donald A. Stauffer writes that, in the problem plays, "Lecherers and traitors are of necessity forgiven, else the world would speedily be unpeopled" (1949, 161).

28. Other scholars who recognize Lucio's function as a scapegoat include Levin (1982, 269), Shell (1988, 153), and Trombetta (1976, 69).

29. Factual information about both Davenant's and Gildon's version of *Measure* is available in Miles (1976, 96–106), Odell ([1920] 1963, 1:26–27, 72–75), and Spencer (1927, 137–51, 329–35).

30. The Duke asserts that "many monarchs have their thrones / Forsaken for a cloistral life, and I, / Perhaps, may really that habit take, / Which I have worn but in disguise" (1874, 210).

31. The *dramatis personae* appears in the original quarto version of the play held by the Folger Shakespeare Library (the Betterton promptbook [1704]), but it is not printed in Edward A. Cairns's critical edition (1987).

32. Both the promptbook for Kemble's production (1811–12, 20, 25) and Samuel French's Memorial Theatre edition, based on Macready's 1824 production (Flower 1889?, 27, 29), indicate sizable omissions from these speeches.

33. Dawson quotes Berners W. Jackson's review in the *Hamiliton Spectator*, 5 July 1975.

34. Critic and director David McCandless, who argues for staging the play "in terms of its sadomasochistic dynamics" (1997, 80), records his own similar enactment of the beginning of 2.4: "In my production, the scene opened with the image of Angelo flagellating himself, conveying not simply the ferocity of his guilt but the power of the fantasy engendering it" (100).

35. I am indebted to H. R. Coursen and his review of Thacker's production (1997) for drawing my attention to this segment.

36. Shaltz notes how Gaines's parallel staging of Angelo's assault on Isabella's chastity in 2.4, Claudio's appeal to his sister in 3.1, and the Duke's proposal at the end of the play linked these three male attempts to appropriate female sexuality (1994a, 25).

37. I have examined this particular issue at length elsewhere. See Friedman (1997).

38. See, for example, Williamson (1979, 168–69), Berry (1977, 243–46), McGuire (1985b, 88–93), and Nicholls (1986, 77–80, 89).

39. Ian Richardson, who played Angelo, recalls that this attack was added in the middle of the production's run when the laws regulating potentially offensive stage action were loosened: "about two months after it opened, censorship was withdrawn and it meant that it was possible to do certain things on the stage. So I asked the director, John Barton, if Estelle [Kohler] and I could re-examine what we did in the scene following the proposition scene. He agreed—and we did rather a lot. I physically abused her and pressed my hands firmly up her skirts" (Cook 1983, 98).

40. Johnson-Haddad contends that, hearing Angelo say "Who will believe thee, Isabel" (2.4.153) in Kahn's Washington, D.C., production, spectators associated the line with recent events in that city: "I was certainly not the only

person to be struck by the timeliness of this disturbing scene, which recalled so forcefully the Anita Hill-Clarence Thomas hearings" (1992, 467).

41. Penny Gay relates how, in Hytner's production, Angelo "attempted to rape Isabella, ripping her veil off, hitting her to the ground, then straddling her as she sobbed passionately" (1994, 142). In Nunn's production, Angelo "threw [Isabella] onto the couch, she screaming, her little lace-up shoes kicking in the air, as horribly near a rape as this scene can ever have come" (Smallwood 1992, 355). In Cohen's rendition, "The confrontation scene with Isabella is played almost like a rape, with Angelo at times flinging her around the stage" (Harrawood 1998, 35). Jean Peterson records that Rudman's Angelo flung Isabella onto a piece of stage furniture and "brutally groped" her in a "near-rape" (1994, 10). Finally, according to Benedict Nightingale, the Angelo of Donnellan's stage version "suddenly finds himself grabbing . . . Isabella, goosing her, and very nearly raping her, right there in the prime minister's office" (1994, 37). Strangely, John Simon notes that in Joseph Papp's 1985 New York Shakespeare Festival production, the sexual violence is played as "vulgar farce": "Angelo topples Isabella over a park bench and starts raping her, until she knocks him down on his behind" (1985, 68).

42. Maureen Connolly McFeely writes, "Angelo does not desire simply to rape Isabella; he demands her complicity in her sexual violation. If she were raped, Isabella would remain a virgin, according to Catholic teaching. . . . But acceding to Angelo's demands would mean *voluntarily* giving up her virginity" (1995, 212n).

43. Blatchley's promptbook contains the notation "Claudio takes Isab. up to Juliet U/C on rostrum to show her child" (1962), while a photo from Hytner's revival depicts the Duke's first proposal to Isabella with Claudio and Juliet embracing in the background, cradling their newborn infant (see Figure 9).

44. David Richman also counters that " 'Give me your hand and say you will be mine' is an odd way to greet a prospective brother-in-law, even for a character who does as many odd things as the duke" (1990, 158).

CHAPTER 6: TAMING OF THE SHREWS

1. On the tendency of Shakespeare's heroines to fall silent as they approach marriage at the end of his comedies, see Boose (1987, 719–20), Carlson (1989, 24), Desmet (1986, 51), Neely (1985, 21–22), and Sinfield (1992, 72–74).

2. Cecil C. Seronsy declares, "Petruchio's method is to suppose . . . or assume qualities in Katharina that no one else, possibly even the shrew herself, ever suspects. What he assumes as apparently false turns out to be startlingly true" (1963, 19). Seronsy's account presupposes that these modest qualities are inherent to Kate rather than artificially imposed.

3. For two broad treatments of the use of hawking imagery in *The Taming of the Shrew*, including excerpts from contemporary falconry manuals, see Frances E. Dolan's Texts and Contexts edition of the play (1996, 304–12) and Margaret Loftus Ranald's article "The Manning of the Haggard," where she notes, "The falcon must be taught obedience to her master, but at the same time her wild and soaring nature must be preserved" (1974, 153).

4. Germaine Greer observes, "Petruchio . . . is man enough to know what

he wants and how to get it. He wants her spirit and her energy because he wants a wife worth keeping. He tames her as he might a hawk . . . and she rewards him with strong sexual love and fierce loyalty" (1971, 220–21).

5. Karen Newman perceives how this wordplay continues in the following sequence, during which Katherine mischievously obeys her husband's commands to salute Vincentio alternately as a lovely maid and as a withered old man: "Given Kate's talent for puns, we must understand her line, 'bedazzled with the sun' [4.5.45] as a pun on son and play with Petruchio's line earlier in the scene 'Now by my mother's son, and that's myself, / It shall be moon, or star, or what I list' (4.5.6–7). 'Petruchio's bedazzlement' is exactly that, and Kate here makes clear the playfulness of their linguistic games" (1987, 141).

6. Ranald comments that Benedick's list of characteristics seems to match Hero more closely than Beatrice (1987, 14, 25), but this view does not take into account the change Beatrice displays after the gulling sequences.

7. Edward Berry reminds modern readers that both Quarto and Folio assign the line "Peace, I will stop your mouth" to Leonato, although modern editors unanimously award the speech to Benedick (1984, 185). Berry proposes that Leonato precipitates the kiss between the two lovers in the same way that Beatrice supervises the embrace of Claudio and Hero after their betrothal: "Speak, cousin, or, if you cannot, stop his mouth with a kiss and let not him speak neither" (2.1.292–93). Even if Leonato speaks the line, however, Benedick still carries out the kiss that silences his bride. We may also note how this embrace parallels the public kiss that Kate is constrained to give to her husband as a sign of her obedience at the end of Shrew 5.1.

8. Critics who concur that Benedick's silencing of Beatrice with a kiss represents an act of subordination include Sales (1990, 116) and Straznicky (1994, 162).

9. Angelo's servant's recognition of Isabella as a religious votary at the beginning of this sequence—"One Isabel, a sister, desires access to you" (2.4.18)—indicates that she is most likely wearing the garments of her order.

10. Critics have already linked this passage to the law of the convent within the context of very different arguments; see Black (1973, 125) and Sundelson (1981, 86). Mariana's counterpart in Much Ado, Hero, also refuses to show her veiled face or speak during her reunion with Claudio until he, by taking her hand and swearing to marry her, accepts the authority of a husband (5.4.55–59).

11. Promptbooks for W. Bridges-Adams's and B. Iden Payne's productions at the Shakespeare Memorial Theatre record similar business, although in Bridges-Adams's case the embrace occurs before the line (1925, 86), while in Payne's it follows Valentine's acknowledgement of the Duke's gift (1938, 294).

12. Imagining such an ending to Measure, William Witherle Lawrence writes, "It has been noted that she does not formally assent to the Duke's proposal . . . . But I do not think that there is any doubt that Isabella turns to him with a heavenly and yielding smile. And I cannot see in the least why she should not" (1931, 106–7).

13. Since Beatrice's silence does not begin until she participates in the kiss that inaugurates her wedded life, there does not seem to be any basis to assume that her silence implies an unwillingness to marry. No stage production, to my knowledge, has ever suggested such resistance.

14. Similarly, Carolyn Asp claims that Isabella's silence "must not be taken as assent, but perhaps as just the opposite, a move of power and indepen-

dence, a stepping out of the circuit of desire" (1984, 40). Jerald W. Spotswood also sees Isabella's voicelessness as "an attempt to assert her independence" in her "battle against patriarchy" (1994, 111).

15. I have detailed such a staging in "'To Be Slow in Words is a Woman's Only Virtue': Silence and Satire in *The Two Gentlemen of Verona*" (1994, 6–8).

16. For a full treatment of this possible enactment, see Friedman (1990, 359–63).

17. I provide a description of Isabella's veiling as an affirmative response to the Duke's proposal in "'Wishing a More Strict Restraint': Feminist Performance and the Silence of Isabella" (1996, 7–9).

18. An optional addition to this staging involves a minor character who appears in the finale as well as the first scene in the fifth act, where the First Folio stage direction reads "*Enter a gentle Astringer*" (TLN 2601). This is often emended to "*Enter a Gentleman, a Stranger*" (5.1.6), but "astringer" is listed in the OED as an alternative spelling of "austringer," meaning a "keeper of goshawks." The Folio reading has some theatrical precedent: Alan C. Dessen records that Sir Peter Hall's 1992–93 RSC production employed "actor Griffith Jones (as the astringer) and two others [who] carried in three hooded falcons in 5.1" (1995, 45). If the astringer still carries his falcon when he enters in 5.3 and delivers Diana's petition to the King, he may retire to the rear of the stage near the spot where Diana will eventually kneel. This embodiment of the central metaphor of the taming pattern may then be visually associated with Diana's gesture of obedience to color the significance of her capitulation.

19. Chroniclers of the stage history of *The Winter's Tale* record theatrical intervention to solve a variety of perceived problems with the text, especially the sudden jealousy of Leontes, the geographical anomaly of Bohemia's seacoast, and various difficulties associated with time (the sixteen-year gap in the middle of the play, the anachronistic coexistence of the oracle at Delphi and the artist Julio Romano, and the appearance of the allegorical figure of Time himself). Certain scenes, particularly 1.1 (the conversation between Camillo and Archidamus) and 3.1 (the dialogue of Cleomenes and Dion on their way back from Delphi), along with the marriage of Paulina and Camillo at the end of the play, have often been cut from stage performances. However, none of these alterations seem designed to recuperate the Forgiven Comic Hero, whose pardon has not been perceived as an obstacle by most critics and performers. See Bartholomeusz (1982) and Draper (1985).

20. As Janet Adelman writes,

> The pattern of male bonding interrupted by women is given its most explicit statement in Shakespeare's plays in Polixenes' "twinned lambs" speech; there women, more precisely the temptations that women present . . . are identified as the agents not only of sin but also of the fall into individuation, the "vast" (1.1.28) now separating Leontes and Polixenes. The separation imaged by Polixenes is reiterated and actualized in the action of the first part of the play as Hermione's presence turns the twinning into attempted fratricide. (1985, 91–92).

21. The Shepherd who discovers Perdita enters musing on the misconduct of young men, including their reckless promiscuity: "I would there were no age between ten and three-and-twenty, or that youth would sleep out the rest, for there is nothing in the between but getting wenches with child, wronging the ancientry, stealing, fighting—" (3.3.58–62). When he happens upon the foundling, he assumes that the baby stems from a clandestine encounter and

has therefore been abandoned by its parents: "Sure some scape. Though I am not bookish, yet I can read waiting-gentlewoman in the scape. This has been some stair-work, some trunk-work, some behind-door-work. They were warmer that got this than the poor thing is here. I'll take it up for pity" (3.3.70–74). Only the Shepherd's generosity, like the kindness of Mistress Overdone (who houses Kate Keep-down's bastard child), saves the rejected infant from death.

22. According to Dolan, one of the characteristics of married but untamed shrews is that "they beat and humiliate their husbands" (1996, 10).

23. As Isabella displays, after her piercing tongue, the Shrew's favorite weapon is her fingernails. Benedick comments that, because Beatrice hates to hear a suitor swear he loves her, "some gentleman or other shall scape a predestinate scratched face" (1.1.124–25). Similarly, Paulina cautions any man who would impede her purpose to present Leontes with Hermione's child, "Let him that makes but trifles of his eyes / First hand me" (2.3.63–64).

24. Spotswood writes, "Paulina is uncharacteristically silent after Leontes hurriedly places her under the care of Camillo, neutralizing the power that she had acquired through her 'counsel' (5.1.52) over a sixteen-year period. Learning the ruse of Hermione's death . . . Leontes attempts to check Paulina's power by returning her to the status of wife" (1994, 110).

Works Cited

Adams, John F. 1961. "*All's Well that Ends Well*: The Paradox of Procreation." *Shakespeare Quarterly* 12: 261–70.

Adelman, Janet. 1985. "Male Bonding in Shakespeare's Comedies." In *Shakespeare's "Rough Magic": Essays in Honor of C. L. Barber*, ed. Peter Erickson and Coppélia Kahn, 73–103. Newark: University of Delaware Press.

———. 1989. "Bed Tricks: On Marriage as the End of Comedy in *All's Well that Ends Well* and *Measure for Measure*." In *Shakespeare's Personality*, ed. Norman N. Holland, Sidney Homan, and Bernard J. Paris, 151–74. Berkeley: University of California Press.

Allam, Roger. 1993. "The Duke in *Measure for Measure*." In *Players of Shakespeare 3: Further Essays in Shakespearean Performance by Players with the Royal Shakespeare Company*, ed. Russell Jackson and Robert Smallwood, 21–41. Cambridge: Cambridge University Press.

Althusser, Louis. 1970. *For Marx*. New York: Vintage.

Anderson, Linda. 1987. *A Kind of Wild Justice: Revenge in Shakespeare's Comedies*. Newark: University of Delaware Press.

Ansorge, Peter. 1967. "Contemporary Shakespeare." *Plays and Players*, August, 36–37.

Armstrong, Alan. 1992. "Oregon Shakespeare Festival." *Shakespeare Bulletin* 10, no. 4: 22–27.

———. 1995. "Shakespeare in Ashland: 1994." *Shakespeare Bulletin* 13, no. 2: 22–27.

Asp, Carolyn. 1984. "Desire, the Gaze and the Woman in *Measure for Measure*." *Shakespeare Newsletter* 34: 40.

———. 1986. "Subjectivity, Desire, and Female Friendship in *All's Well that Ends Well*." *Literature and Psychology* 32: 48–63.

Baines, Barbara J. 1990. "Assaying the Power of Chastity in *Measure for Measure*." *Studies in English Literature* 30: 283–301.

Barber, Lester E. 1979. "Great Lakes Shakespeare." *Shakespeare Quarterly* 30: 212–15.

Barnet, Sylvan. 1988. "*All's Well that Ends Well* on the Stage." In *All's Well that Ends Well*, ed. Sylvan Barnet, Signet Classics, 203–13. New York: New American Library.

Bartholomeusz, Dennis. 1982. The Winter's Tale *in Performance in England and America, 1611–1976*. Cambridge: Cambridge University Press.

Barton, Anne. 1974. Introduction to *Much Ado about Nothing*. In *The Riverside Shakespeare*, ed. G. Blakemore Evans, 327–31. Boston: Houghton.

————. 1993. "Shakespeare in the Sun." *New York Review of Books,* 27 May, 11–13.

Bawcutt, N. W., ed. 1991. *Measure for Measure.* Oxford Shakespeare. Oxford: Oxford University Press.

Beck, Dennis. 1993. *"All's Well that Ends Well*: Past Problems as Modern Proposition." *On-Stage Studies* 16: 104–25.

Becks, George. 1890s. Folger Promptbook: Two Gent, 1.

Bennetts, Leslie. 1988. "Romance Blooms in the Park." *New York Times,* 10 July, sec. 2, pp. 1, 5.

Berger, Harry, Jr. 1982. "Against the Sink-a-Pace: Sexual and Family Politics in *Much Ado about Nothing.*" *Shakespeare Quarterly* 33: 302–13.

Berry, Edward. 1984. *Shakespeare's Comic Rites.* Cambridge: Cambridge University Press.

Berry, Ralph. 1977. *"Measure for Measure* on the Contemporary Stage." *Humanities Association Review* 28: 241–47.

Betterton, Thomas. 1704. Folger Promptbook: Measure, 2. London, Lincoln's Inn Fields.

Bevington, David. 1995. "All's Well that Plays Well." In *Subjects on the World's Stage: Essays on British Literature of the Middle Ages and the Renaissance,* ed. David G. Allen and Robert A. White, 162–80. Newark: University of Delaware Press.

————, ed. 1997. *The Complete Works of Shakespeare.* Updated 4th ed. New York: Longman.

Birje-Patil, J. 1970. "Marraige Contracts in *Measure for Measure.*" *Shakespeare Studies* 5: 106–111.

Black, James. 1973. "The Unfolding of *Measure for Measure.*" *Shakespeare Survey* 26: 119–28.

Blatchley, John. 1962. Shakespeare Centre Promptbook: Meas. 9. Stratford-upon-Avon, Royal Shakespeare Theatre.

Boose, Lynda E. 1987. "The Family in Shakespeare Studies; or—Studies in the Family of Shakespeareans; or—The Politics of Politics." *Renaissance Quarterly* 40: 707–42.

Booth, Junius Brutus, Jr. c.1875. Folger Promptbook: Much Ado, 1.

Bowman, James. 1993. "All Shook Up." *American Spectator,* July, 56–57.

Brahms, Caryl. 1962. Review of *Measure for Measure.* Director John Blatchley. Royal Shakespeare Company, Stratford-upon-Avon. *Plays and Players,* June, 14–15, 46.

Branagh, Kenneth. 1993. Much Ado about Nothing *by William Shakespeare: Screenplay, Introduction, and Notes on the Making of the Movie.* New York: Norton.

Braunmuller, A. R. 1989. "Editing the Staging / Staging the Editing." In *Shakespeare and the Sense of Performance: Essays in the Tradition of Performance Criticism in Honor of Bernard Beckerman,* ed. Marvin and Ruth Thompson, 139–49. Newark: University of Delaware Press.

Bridges-Adams, W. 1925. Shakespeare Centre Promptbook: 2 Gent. 1. Stratford-upon-Avon, Stratford Memorial Theatre.

Brook, Peter. 1950. Shakespeare Centre Promptbook: Meas. 7. Stratford-upon-Avon, Shakespeare Memorial Theatre.

Brown, Carolyn E. 1986. "Erotic Religious Flagellation and Shakespeare's *Measure for Measure.*" *English Literary Renaissance* 16: 139–65.

Brown, John Russell. 1961. "Three Directors: A Review of Recent Productions." *Shakespeare Survey* 14: 129–37.

———. 1996. *William Shakespeare: Writing for Performance.* New York: St. Martin's.

Brown, Pamela. 1993. Review of *Much Ado about Nothing.* Director Robert Hupp. Jean Cocteau Repertory, New York. *Shakespeare Bulletin* 11, no. 3: 15–16.

Bulman, James C. 1996. "Introduction: Shakespeare and Performance Theory." In *Shakespeare, Theory, and Performance,* ed. James C. Bulman, 1–11. London: Routledge.

Byrne, Muriel St. Clare. 1957. "The Shakespeare Season at the Old Vic, 1956–57 and Stratford-Upon-Avon, 1957." *Shakespeare Quarterly* 8: 461–92.

———. 1959. "The Shakespeare Season at the Old Vic, 1958–59 and Stratford-upon-Avon, 1959." *Shakespeare Quarterly* 10: 545–67.

Cacicedo, Alberto. 1995. " 'She is fast my wife': Sex, Marriage, and Ducal Authority in *Measure for Measure.*" *Shakespeare Studies* 23: 187–209.

Calderwood, James L. 1963. "The Mingled Yarn of *All's Well.*" *Journal of English and Germanic Philology* 62: 61–76.

Campbell, Kathleen. 1997. "Reviewing Performance Editions." Paper presented to the Shakespeare Association of America. Washington, D.C., 28 March.

Caputi, Anthony. 1961. "Scenic Design in *Measure for Measure.*" *Journal of English and Germanic Philology* 60: 423–34.

Carlson, Susan. 1989. " 'Fond Fathers' and Sweet Sisters: Alternative Sexualities in *Measure for Measure.*" *Essays in Literature* 16: 13–31.

Chambers, E. K. 1925. *Shakespeare: A Survey.* London: Sidgwick.

Collins, Jane. 1998. Review of *Much Ado about Nothing.* Director Declan Donnellan. Cheek by Jowl, Brooklyn Academy of Music. *Shakespeare Bulletin* 16, no. 3: 10–11.

Collins, Michael J. 1994. Review of *Much Ado about Nothing.* Director Matthew Warchus. Infinite Space Ltd., Queen's Theatre, 1993. *Shakespeare Bulletin* 12, no. 1: 16–17.

———. 1998. Review of *Much Ado about Nothing.* Director Michael Boyd. Royal Shakespeare Company, Stratford-upon-Avon, 1996. *Shakespeare Bulletin* 16, no. 1: 21–22.

Cook, David. 1981. " 'The Very Temple of Delight': The Twin Plots of *Much Ado about Nothing.*" In *Poetry and Drama, 1570–1700,* ed. Antony Coleman and Antony Hammond, 32–46. London: Methuen.

Cook, Judith. 1983. *Shakespeare's Players.* London: Harrap.

Coursen, H. R. 1993. "The Director and the Critics: Stratford-upon-Avon, 1992." *Shakespeare Bulletin* 11, no. 2: 10–14.

———. 1997. "The 1994 BBC *Measure for Measure.*" *Shakespeare Bulletin* 15, no. 3: 41–42.

Coveney, Michael. 1994. Review of *Measure for Measure*. Director Steven Pimlott. Royal Shakespeare Company, Stratford-upon-Avon. *Observer*, 23 October, 13.

Cox, John D. 1989. *Shakespeare and the Dramaturgy of Power*. Princeton: Princeton University Press.

Cox, John F. 1979. "The Stage Representation of the 'Kill Claudio' Sequence in *Much Ado about Nothing*." *Shakespeare Survey* 32: 27–36.

———, ed. 1997. *Much Ado about Nothing*. Shakespeare in Performance. Cambridge: Cambridge University Press.

Craik, T. W. 1953. "*Much Ado about Nothing*." *Scrutiny* 19: 297–316.

Crosman, Robert. 1990. "Making Love out of Nothing at All: The Issue of Story in Shakespeare's Procreation Sonnets." *Shakespeare Quarterly* 41: 470–88.

Cushman, Robert. 1970. "Gentlemen and Players." *Spectator*, 1 August, 107–8.

Cutts, John P. 1968. *The Shattered Glass: A Dramatic Pattern in Shakespeare's Early Plays*. Detroit: Wayne State University Press.

Dash, Irene. 1980. "A Penchant for Perdita on the Eighteenth-Century English Stage." In *The Woman's Part: Feminist Criticism of Shakespeare*, ed. Carolyn Ruth Swift Lenz, Gayle Green, and Carol Thomas Neely, 271–84. Urbana: University of Illinois Press.

Davenant, William. 1874. *The Law against Lovers*. In *The Dramatic Works of William D'Avenant*. Vol. 5, 109–211. Edinburgh: Patterson.

David, Richard. 1951. "Shakespeare's Comedies and the Modern Stage." *Shakespeare Survey* 4: 129–38.

———. 1955. "Plays Pleasant and Plays Unpleasant." *Shakespeare Survey* 8: 132–38.

Dawson, Anthony B. 1978. *Indirections: Shakespeare and the Art of Illusion*. Toronto: University of Toronto Press.

———. 1988. *Watching Shakespeare: A Playgoer's Guide*. New York: St. Martin's.

Deese, Helen. 1994. Review of *All's Well that Ends Well*. Director Sheldon Epps. Old Globe Theatre, San Diego, 1993. *Shakespeare Bulletin* 12, no. 2: 38–39.

Denby, David. 1993. "Avon Calling." *New York Magazine*, 10 May, 62–63.

Desmet, Christy. 1986. "Speaking Sensibly: Feminine Rhetoric in *Measure for Measure* and *All's Well that Ends Well*." *Renaissance Papers* n.v.: 43–51.

Dessen, Alan C. 1971. *Jonson's Moral Comedy*. Evanston, IL: Northwestern University Press.

———. 1976. "The Oregon Shakespeare Festival, 1975." *Shakespeare Quarterly* 27: 83–93.

———. 1986. *Shakespeare and the Late Moral Plays*. Lincoln: University of Nebraska Press.

———. 1990. "Adjusting Shakespeare in 1989." *Shakespeare Quarterly* 41: 352–65.

———. 1993. "Taming the Script: *Henry VI, Shrew*, and *All's Well* in Ashland and Stratford." *Shakespeare Bulletin* 11, no. 2: 34–37.

———. 1995. *Recovering Shakespeare's Theatrical Vocabulary*. Cambridge: Cambridge University Press.

————. 1997a. "Solving (and Creating) Problems: Shakespeare on Stage in 1996." *Shakespeare Bulletin* 15, no. 1: 5–7.

————. 1997b. "Writing and Using Reviews of Shakespeare Productions: Problems and a Few Suggestions." Paper presented to the Shakespeare Association of America. Washington, D.C., March 28.

————. 1999. "Choices and Changes: Shakespeare on Stage in 1998." *Shakespeare Bulletin* 17, no. 1: 5–7.

Dodds, W. M. T. 1946. "The Character of Angelo in *Measure for Measure.*" *Modern Language Review* 41: 245–55.

Dolan, Frances E., ed. 1996. The Taming of the Shrew: *Texts and Contexts*. Boston: St. Martin's, Bedford.

Dow, T. Agnew. 1854. Folger Promptbook: Much Ado, 2. Philadelphia, Arch Street.

Dowden, Edward. 1877. *Shakspere*. New York: Macmillan.

Draper, R. P. 1985. *The Winter's Tale*. Text & Performance. London: Macmillan.

Dusinberre, Juliet. 1975. *Shakespeare and the Nature of Women*. New York: Barnes.

Eccles, Mark, ed. 1980. *Measure for Measure*. New Variorum Shakespeare. New York: MLA.

Edwards, Philip. 1968. *Shakespeare and the Confines of Art*. London: Methuen.

Ellis, David. 1989. "Finding a Part for Parolles." *Essays in Criticism* 39: 289–304.

Elze, Karl. [1874] 1970. *Essays on Shakespeare*. Trans. L. Dora Schmitz. Port Washington, NY: Kennikat.

Erickson, Peter. 1985. *Patriarchal Structures in Shakespeare's Drama*. Berkeley: University of California Press.

Evans, G. Blakemore, ed. 1997. *The Riverside Shakespeare*. 2nd ed. Boston: Houghton.

Findlay, Alison. 1994. *Illegitimate Power: Bastards in Renaissance Drama*. Manchester: Manchester University Press.

Flower, C. E., ed. 1889? *Measure for Measure: A Comedy, by William Shakespeare*. London, Samuel French.

Fraser, Russell, ed. 1985. *All's Well that Ends Well*. New Cambridge Shakespeare. Cambridge: Cambridge University Press.

Freud, Sigmund. 1961. *Civilization and its Discontents*. Trans. James Strachey. New York: Norton.

Frey, Charles. 1982. "Shakespeare in the Northwest." *Shakespeare Quarterly* 33: 400–409.

Friedman, Michael D. 1990. " 'Hush'd on Purpose to Grace Harmony': Wives and Silence in *Much Ado about Nothing.*" *Theatre Journal* 42: 350–63.

————. 1994. " 'To Be Slow in Words is a Woman's Only Virtue': Silence and Satire in *The Two Gentlemen of Verona.*" *Selected Papers from the West Virginia Shakespeare and Renaissance Association* 17: 1–9. Reprinted in Two Gentlemen of Verona: *Critical Essays*, ed. June Schlueter, 213–22. New York: Garland, 1996.

————. 1996. " 'Wishing a More Strict Restraint': Feminist Performance and the Silence of Isabella." *Selected Papers from the West Virginia Shakespeare and Renaissance Association* 19: 1–11.

———. 1997. "Prostitution and the Feminist Appropriation of *Measure for Measure* on the Stage." *Shakespeare Bulletin* 15, no. 2: 14–17.

Furness, Horace Howard, ed. [1899] 1964. *Much Adoe About Nothing*. New Variorum. 5th ed. New York: Dover.

Gay, Penny. 1994. *As She Likes It: Shakespeare's Unruly Women*. London: Routledge.

Geckle, George L. 1995. Review of *Measure for Measure*. Director Steven Pimlott. Royal Shakespeare Company, Stratford-upon-Avon, 1994. *Shakespeare Bulletin* 13, no. 1: 12–14.

Gelb, Hal. 1971. "Duke Vincentio and the Illusion of Comedy or All's Not Well that Ends Well." *Shakespeare Quarterly* 22: 25–34.

Gervinus, G. G. 1903. *Shakespeare Commentaries*. Trans. F. E. Bunnètt. 6th ed. London: Smith.

Gibbons, Brian, ed. 1991. *Measure for Measure*. New Cambridge Shakespeare. Cambridge: Cambridge University Press.

Gildon, Charles. 1987. *Charles Gildon's* Measure for Measure, or Beauty the Best Advocate: *A Critical Edition*. Ed. Edward A. Cairns. New York: Garland.

Girard, René. 1988. "Love Delights in Praises: A Reading of *The Two Gentlemen of Verona*." *Philosophy and Literature* 13: 231–47.

Goldberg, Jonathan. 1986. *Voice Terminal Echo: Postmodernism and English Renaissance Texts*. London: Methuen.

Greenblatt, Stephen, Walter Cohen, Jean E. Howard, and Katharine Eisaman Maus, eds. 1997. *The Norton Shakespeare: Based on the Oxford Edition*. New York: Norton.

Greer, Germaine. 1971. *The Female Eunuch*. New York: McGraw-Hill.

Guthrie, Tyrone. 1959. Shakespeare Centre Promptbook: All's Well 6. Stratford-upon-Avon, Stratford Memorial Theatre.

Haley, David. 1993. *Shakespeare's Courtly Mirror: Reflexivity and Prudence in* All's Well that Ends Well. Newark: University of Delaware Press.

Halio, Jay L. 1964. "*All's Well that Ends Well*." *Shakespeare Quarterly* 15: 33–43.

Hall, Jonathan. 1995. *Anxious Pleasures: Shakespearean Comedy and the Nation-State*. Madison, NJ: Associated University Presses.

Harbage, Alfred. 1947. *As They Liked It*. New York: Macmillan.

Harding, Davis P. 1950. "Elizabethan Betrothals and *Measure for Measure*." *Journal of English and Germanic Philology* 49: 139–158.

Harrawood, Michael. 1998. Review of *Measure for Measure*. Director Robert Cohen. Colorado Shakespeare Festival. *Shakespeare Bulletin* 16, no. 4: 34–35.

Hartley, Lodwick. 1965. "Claudio and the Unmerry War." *College English* 26: 609–14.

Hasler, Jörg. 1974. *Shakespeare's Theatrical Notation: The Comedies*. Bern: Francke.

Hawkes, Terence. 1994. "Shakespeare's Spooks, or Someone to Watch over

Me." In *Shakespeare in the New Europe*, ed. Michael Hattaway, Boika Soko-lova, and Derek Roper, 194–206. Sheffield: Sheffield Academic Press.

Hawkins, Harriet. 1974. "What Kind of Pre-Contract Had Angelo? A Note on Some Non-problems in English Drama." *College English* 36: 173–79.

Hillman, Richard. 1993. *William Shakespeare: The Problem Plays*. New York: Twayne.

Hodgdon, Barbara. 1996. " 'Here Apparent': Photography, History, and the Theatrical Unconscious." In *Textual and Theatrical Shakespeare: Questions of Evidence*, ed. Edward Pechter, 181–209. Iowa City: University of Iowa Press.

Holderness, Graham. 1989. "*Much Ado about Nothing*: Men without Women." In *Critical Essays on* Much Ado about Nothing, ed. Linda Cookson and Bryan Loughrey, 74–86. Harlow: Longman.

Holland, Peter. 1991. "Shakespeare Performances in England, 1989–90." *Shakespeare Survey* 44: 157–90.

———. 1992. "Shakespeare Performances in England, 1990–91." *Shakespeare Survey* 45: 115–44.

———. 1993. "Shakespeare Performances in England, 1992." *Shakespeare Survey* 46: 159–89.

———. 1997. *English Shakespeares: Shakespeare on the English Stage in the 1990s*. Cambridge: Cambridge University Press.

Howard, Jean E. 1987. "Renaissance Antitheatricality and the Politics of Gender and Rank in *Much Ado about Nothing*." In *Shakespeare Reproduced: The Text in History and Ideology*, ed. Jean E. Howard and Marion F. O'Connor, 163–87. London: Methuen.

Howard, Jean E., and Marion F. O'Connor. 1987. Introduction to *Shakespeare Reproduced: The Text in History and Ideology*, ed. Jean E. Howard and Mar-ion F. O'Connor, 1–17. London: Methuen.

Humphreys, A. R., ed. 1981. *Much Ado about Nothing*. Arden Shakespeare. London: Methuen.

Hunter, G. K., ed. 1959. *All's Well that Ends Well*. Arden Shakespeare. London: Methuen.

———. 1988. "The BBC *All's Well that Ends Well*." In *Shakespeare on Televi-sion: An Anthology of Essays and Reviews*, ed. J. C. Bulman and H. R. Coursen, 185–87. Hanover: University Press of New England.

Hunter, Robert Grams. 1965. *Shakespeare and the Comedy of Forgiveness*. New York: Columbia University Press.

Jackson, Berners W. 1971. "Shakespeare at Stratford, Ont., 1971." *Shake-speare Quarterly* 22: 365–70.

Jackson, Russell. 1979. " 'Perfect Types of Womanhood': Rosalind, Beatrice, and Viola in Victorian Criticism and Performance." *Shakespeare Survey* 32: 15–26.

———. 1995. "Shakespeare at Stratford-upon-Avon, 1994–95." *Shakespeare Quarterly* 46: 340–57.

Jacoby, Susan. 1983. *Wild Justice: The Evolution of Revenge*. New York: Harper.

Jaffa, Harry V. 1981. "Chastity as a Political Principle: An Interpretation of Shakespeare's *Measure for Measure*." In *Shakespeare as Political Thinker*, ed. John Alvis and Thomas G. West, 181–213. Durham: Carolina Academic Press.

Jardine, Lisa. 1989. *Still Harping on Daughters: Women and Drama in the Age of Shakespeare*. 2nd ed. New York: Columbia University Press.

Johnson, Samuel. 1968. *Johnson on Shakespeare*. Vol. 7 of *The Yale Edition of the Works of Samuel Johnson*, ed. Arthur Sherbo. New Haven: Yale University Press.

Johnson-Haddad, Miranda. 1992. "The Shakespeare Theatre, 1991–92." *Shakespeare Quarterly* 43: 455–72.

Kahn, Coppélia. 1981. *Man's Estate: Masculine Identity in Shakespeare*. Berkeley: University of California Press.

Kavanagh, James H. 1985. "Shakespeare in Ideology." In *Alternative Shakespeares*, ed. John Drakakis, 144–65. London: Methuen.

Kellet, E. E. 1923. *Suggestions: Literary Essays*. Cambridge: Cambridge University Press.

Kelso, Ruth. 1956. *Doctrine for the Lady of the Renaissance*. Urbana: University of Illinois Press.

Kemble, J. P. 1811–12. Folger Promptbook: Measure, 6. London, Covent Garden.

Kennedy, Dennis. 1993. *Looking at Shakespeare: A Visual History of Twentieth-Century Performance*. Cambridge: Cambridge University Press.

Keyishian, Harry. 1984. "The Shakespeare Plays on TV: *Two Gentlemen of Verona*." *Shakespeare on Film Newsletter* 9: 6.

———. 1984–85. Review of *The Two Gentlemen of Verona*. Director Janet Farrow. American Shakespeare Repertory, New York, 1984. *Shakespeare Bulletin* 2, no. 12–3, no. 1: 27.

Kilbourne, Frederick W. 1906. *Alterations and Adaptations of Shakespeare*. Boston: Poet Lore.

Kirsch, Arthur C. 1975. "The Integrity of *Measure for Measure*." *Shakespeare Survey* 28: 89–105.

———. 1981. *Shakespeare and the Experience of Love*. Cambridge: Cambridge University Press.

Kittredge, George Lyman. 1958. *The Complete Works of William Shakespeare*. New York: Grolier.

Knowles, Richard Paul. 1989. "Robin Phillips Measures Up: *Measure for Measure* at Stratford, Ontario, 1975–76." *Essays in Theatre* 8: 35–59.

Lang, Andrew. 1891. "The Comedies of Shakespeare: *Much Ado about Nothing*." *Harper's* 83: 489–502.

Laslett, Peter. 1980. "The Bastardy Prone Sub-society." In *Bastardy and Its Comparative History*, ed. Peter Laslett, Karla Oostererveen, and Richard M. Smith, 217–46. Cambridge: Harvard University Press.

Latham, Agnes, ed. 1975. *As You Like It*. Arden Shakespeare. London: Methuen.

Lawrence, William Witherle. 1931. *Shakespeare's Problem Comedies*. New York: Macmillan.

Leech, Clifford, ed. 1969. *The Two Gentlemen of Verona*. Arden Shakespeare. London: Methuen.

Leggatt, Alexander. 1988. *English Drama: Shakespeare to the Restoration, 1590–1660*. London: Longman.

Lever, J. W., ed. 1965. *Measure for Measure*. Arden Shakespeare. London: Methuen.

Levin, Richard. 1988. "Shakespearean Defects and Shakespeareans' Defenses." In *"Bad" Shakespeare: Revaluations of the Shakespeare Canon*, ed. Maurice Charney, 23–36. Rutherford, NJ: Fairleigh Dickinson University Press.

Levin, Richard A. 1982. "Duke Vincentio and Angelo: Would 'A Feather Turn the Scale'?" *Studies in English Literature* 22: 257–70.

―――. 1985. *Love and Society in Shakespearean Comedy: A Study of Dramatic Form and Content*. Newark: University of Delaware Press.

Lieblein, Leanore. 1996. "Theatre Archives at the Intersection of Production and Reception: The Example of Québécois Shakespeare." In *Textual and Theatrical Shakespeare: Questions of Evidence*, ed. Edward Pechter, 164–80. Iowa City: University of Iowa Press.

Love, John M. 1977. " 'Though many of the rich are damn'd': Dark Comedy and Social Class in *All's Well that Ends Well*." *Texas Studies in Literature and Language* 18: 517–27.

Low, John T. 1974. *Shakespeare's Folio Comedies*. Norwood, PA: Norwood.

Lowenthal, David. 1997. *Shakespeare and the Good Life: Ethics and Politics in Dramatic Form*. Lanham, MD: Rowman.

Lyons, Charles R. 1989. "Silent Women and Shrews: Eroticism and Convention in *Epicoene* and *Measure for Measure*." *Comparative Drama* 23: 123–40.

Macherey, Pierre, and Etienne Balibar. 1980. "Literature as an Ideological Form: Some Marxist Hypotheses." *Praxis* 5: 43–58.

Macready, William Charles. c.1840s? Folger Promptbook: Much Ado, 13. Transcribed for Charles Kean.

―――. 1841. Folger Promptbook: Two Gent, 11. London, Drury Lane.

Mares, F. H., ed. 1988. *Much Ado about Nothing*. New Cambridge Shakespeare. Cambridge: Cambridge University Press.

Marsh, D. R. C. 1963. "The Mood of *Measure for Measure*." *Shakespeare Quarterly* 14: 31–38.

Mason, Pamela. 1976. Much Ado at *Stratford-upon-Avon*. M. A. thesis, University of Birmingham, England.

McCandless, David. 1994. "Helena's Bed-Trick: Gender and Performance in *All's Well that Ends Well*." *Shakespeare Quarterly* 45: 449–68.

―――. 1997. *Gender and Performance in Shakespeare's Problem Comedies*. Bloomington: Indiana University Press.

McEachern, Claire. 1988. "Fathering Herself: A Source Study of Shakespeare's Feminism." *Shakespeare Quarterly* 39: 269–90.

McFeely, Maureen Connolly. 1995. " 'This day my sister should the cloister enter': The Convent as Refuge in *Measure for Measure*." In *Subjects on the World's Stage: Essays on British Literature of the Middle Ages and the Renaissance*, ed. David C. Allen and Robert A. White, 200–216. Newark: University of Delaware Press.

McGee, C. E. 1993. "Shakespeare in Canada: The Stratford Season 1992." *Shakespeare Quarterly* 44: 477–83.

McGuire, Philip C. 1985a. "Silence and Genre: The Example of *Measure for Measure*." *Iowa State Journal of Research* 59: 241–51.

———. 1985b. *Speechless Dialect: Shakespeare's Open Silences*. Berkeley: University of California Press.

McLuskie, Kathleen. 1985. "The Patriarchal Bard: Feminist Criticism and Shakespeare: *King Lear* and *Measure for Measure*." In *Political Shakespeare: New essays in cultural materialism*, ed. Jonathan Dollimore and Alan Sinfield, 88–108. Ithaca: Cornell University Press.

Mikkelsen, Robert S. 1958. "To Catch a Saint: Angelo in *Measure for Measure*." *Western Humanities Review* 13: 261–75.

Miles, Rosalind. 1976. *The Problem of* Measure for Measure: *A Historical Investigation*. New York: Barnes.

Miola, Robert S. 1993. "New Comedy in *All's Well that Ends Well*." *Renaissance Quarterly* 46: 23–43.

Morgan, Gareth. 1969. Shakespeare Centre Promptbook: 2 Gent. 4. Stratford-upon-Avon and Theatregoround Tour.

Much Adoe About Nothing. [1600] 1971. Shakespeare Quarto Facsimiles, no. 15. Oxford: Clarendon.

Mueschke, Paul, and Miriam Mueschke. 1967. "Illusion and Metamorphosis in *Much Ado about Nothing*." *Shakespeare Quarterly* 18: 53–65.

Mulryne, J. R. 1965. *Shakespeare*: Much Ado about Nothing. London: Arnold.

Nagarajan, S. 1962. "*Measure for Measure* and Elizabethan Betrothals." *Shakespeare Quarterly* 14: 115–19.

———. 1989. "Some Stage Versions of *Measure for Measure*." *Aligarh Critical Miscellany* 2: 26–59.

Neely, Carol Thomas. 1985. *Broken Nuptials in Shakespeare's Plays*. New Haven: Yale University Press.

Neill, Kerby. 1952. "More Ado About Claudio: An Acquittal for the Slandered Groom." *Shakespeare Quarterly* 3: 91–107.

Nelsen, Paul. 1991. Review of *The Two Gentlemen of Verona*. Director David Thacker. Swan Theatre, Stratford-upon-Avon. *Shakespeare Bulletin* 9, no. 4: 15–17.

———. 1997. "Prologue Season at the New Globe: Polemics and Performance." *Shakespeare Bulletin* 15, no. 2: 5–8.

Nevo, Ruth. 1987. "Motive and Meaning in *All's Well that Ends Well*." In *"Fanned and Winnowed Opinions": Shakespearean Essays Presented to Harold Jenkins*, ed. John W. Mahon and Thomas A. Pendleton, 26–51. London: Methuen.

Newman, Karen. 1987. "Renaissance Family Politics and Shakespeare's *The Taming of the Shrew*." In *Renaissance Historicism: Selections from* English Literary Renaissance, ed. Arthur F. Kinney and Dan S. Collins, 131–45. Amherst: University of Massachusetts Press.

Nicholls, Graham. 1986. Measure for Measure: *Text and Performance*. London: Macmillan Education.

Nightingale, Benedict. 1973. "Sylvia Excelling." *New Statesman*, May, 667.

———. 1994. "Bit of a Cheek." *Times* (London), 20 June, 37.

Nuttall, A. D. 1969. *"Measure for Measure*: Quid Pro Quo?" *Shakespeare Studies* 4: 231–51.

Odell, George C. D. [1920] 1963. *Shakespeare from Betterton to Irving*. 2 vols. New York: Blom.

Ornstein, Robert. 1986. *Shakespeare's Comedies: From Roman Farce to Romantic Mystery*. Newark: University of Delaware Press.

Orr, Paul A. 1985. "A Reinterpretation (and Restaging) of the Dull Scene in *Much Ado about Nothing.*" *Selected Papers from the West Virginia Shakespeare and Renaissance Association* 10: 68–70.

Osborne, Laurie E. 1996a. "Rethinking the Performance Editions: Theatrical and Textual Productions of Shakespeare." In *Shakespeare, Theory, and Performance*, ed. James C. Bulman, 168–86. London: Routledge.

———. 1996b. "The Rhetoric of Evidence: The Narration and Display of Viola and Olivia in the Nineteenth Century." In *Textual and Theatrical Shakespeare: Questions of Evidence*, ed. Edward Pechter, 124–43. Iowa City: University of Iowa Press.

Ostwald, David. 1982. *"The Two Gentlemen of Verona*: An Interpretation." *On-Stage Studies* 6: 123–33.

Ottenhoff, John. 1993. "Too much ado?" *Christian Century*, 25 August–1 September, 823–24.

Parker, Patricia. 1992. *"All's Well that Ends Well*: Increase and Multiply." *Creative Imitation: New Essays on Renaissance Literature In Honor of Thomas M. Greene*, ed. David Quint, Margaret W. Ferguson, G. W. Pigman III, and Wayne A. Rebhorn, 355–90. Binghamton: Medieval and Renaissance Texts and Studies.

Parker, R. B. 1984. "War and Sex in *All's Well that Ends Well.*" *Shakespeare Survey* 37: 99–113.

Payne, B. Iden. 1935. Shakespeare Centre Promptbook: All's Well 2. Stratford-upon-Avon, Stratford Memorial Theatre.

———. 1938. Shakespeare Centre Promptbook: 2 Gent. 2. Stratford-upon-Avon, Stratford Memorial Theatre.

Pearson, Harry. 1993. Review of *Much Ado about Nothing*. Director Kenneth Branagh. *Films in Review*, July, 260–61.

Pechter, Edward, ed. 1996. *Textual and Theatrical Shakespeare: Questions of Evidence*. Iowa City: University of Iowa Press.

Peterson, Jean. 1994. Review of *Measure for Measure*. Director Michael Rudman. New York Shakespeare Festival, 1993. *Shakespeare Bulletin* 12, no. 3: 10–11.

Pettigrew, John. 1970. "The Stratford Plays, 1969." *Journal of Canadian Studies* 4: 3–9.

Postlewait, Thomas. 1991. "Historiography and the Theatrical Event: A Primer with Twelve Cruxes." *Theatre Journal* 43: 157–78.

Powers, Alan W. 1988. " 'Meaner Parties': Spousal Conventions and Oral Culture in *Measure for Measure* and *All's Well that Ends Well.*" *Upstart Crow* 8: 28–41.

Price, Joseph G. 1968. *The Unfortunate Comedy: A Study of* All's Well that Ends Well *and Its Critics*. Toronto: University of Toronto Press.

Priest, Dale G. 1980. "Subjunctivity in *The Two Gentlemen of Verona.*" *Explorations in Renaissance Culture* 6: 28–46.

Prouty, Charles T. 1950. *The Sources of* Much Ado about Nothing: *A Critical Study.* Freeport, NY: Books for Libraries.

Quayle, Anthony. 1956. Shakespeare Centre Promptbook: Meas. 8. Stratford-upon-Avon, Stratford Memorial Theatre.

Quiller-Couch, Sir Arthur, and John Dover Wilson, eds. 1923. *Much Ado about Nothing.* New Shakespeare. Cambridge: Cambridge University Press.

———. 1929. *All's Well that Ends Well.* New Shakespeare. Cambridge: Cambridge University Press.

Ranald, Margaret Loftus. 1974. "The Manning of the Haggard; or *The Taming of the Shrew.*" *Essays in Literature* 1: 149–65.

———. 1987. *Shakespeare and His Social Context: Essays in Osmotic Knowledge and Literary Interpretation.* New York: AMS Press.

———. 1993. Review of *All's Well that Ends Well.* Director Richard Jones. Delacorte Theatre, New York. *Shakespeare Bulletin* 11, no. 4: 16–17.

Richman, David. 1990. *Laughter, Pain, and Wonder: Shakespeare's Comedies and the Audience in the Theater.* Newark: University of Delaware Press.

Ridley, M. R. 1938. *Shakespeare's Plays: A Commentary.* New York: Dutton.

Riefer, Marcia. 1984. " 'Instruments of Some More Mightier Member': The Constriction of Female Power in *Measure for Measure.*" *Shakespeare Quarterly* 35: 157–69.

Ringer, Dolores. 1990. "A Feminist Politics of Directing *The Two Gentlemen of Verona.*" Paper presented to the Mid-America Theater Conference.

Roark, Christopher. 1988. "Lavatch and Service in *All's Well that Ends Well.*" *Studies in English Literature* 28: 241–58.

Roberts, Peter. 1983. Review of *Much Ado about Nothing.* Director Terry Hands. Royal Shakespeare Company, Stratford-upon-Avon, 1982. *Plays and Players*, June, 33–34.

Ross, Lawrence J. 1997. *On* Measure for Measure: *An Essay in Criticism of Shakespeare's Drama.* Newark: University of Delaware Press.

Rothman, Jules. 1972. "A Vindication of Parolles." *Shakespeare Quarterly* 23: 183–96.

Rubin, Gayle. 1975. "The Traffic in Women: Notes on the 'Political Economy' of Sex." In *Towards an Anthropology of Women,* ed. Rayna R. Reiter, 157–210. New York: Monthly Review Press.

Rutter, Carol. 1991. "Helena's Choosing: Writing the Couplets in a Choreography of Discontinuity (*All's Well that Ends Well* 2.3)." *Essays in Theatre* 9: 121–39.

Ryan, Richard. 1993. "Much Ado about Branagh." *Commentary*, October, 52–55.

Sacks, Elizabeth. 1980. *Shakespeare's Images of Pregnancy.* New York: St. Martin's.

Sale, Roger. 1968. "The Comic Mode of *Measure for Measure.*" *Shakespeare Quarterly* 19: 55–61.

Sales, Roger. 1990. *William Shakespeare:* Much Ado about Nothing. London: Penguin.

Schanzer, Ernest. 1960. "The Marriage-Contracts in *Measure for Measure*." *Shakespeare Survey* 13: 81–89.

———. 1963. *The Problem Plays of Shakespeare*. London: Routledge.

Schleiner, Louise. 1982. "Providential Improvisation in *Measure for Measure*." *PMLA* 97: 227–36.

Schlueter, Kurt, ed. 1990. *The Two Gentlemen of Verona*. New Cambridge Shakespeare. Cambridge: Cambridge University Press.

Schoff, Francis G. 1959. "Claudio, Bertram, and a Note on Interpretation." *Shakespeare Quarterly* 10: 11–23.

Scott, Margaret. 1982. " 'Our City's Institutions': Some Further Reflections on the Marriage Contracts in *Measure for Measure*." *ELH* 49: 790–804.

Sedgwick, Eve Kosofsky. 1985. *Between Men: English Literature and Male Homosocial Desire*. New York: Columbia University Press.

Seiden, Melvin. 1990. Measure for Measure: *Casuistry and Artistry*. Washington, DC: Catholic University of America Press.

Seronsy, Cecil C. 1963. " 'Supposes' as the Unifying Theme in *The Taming of the Shrew*." *Shakespeare Quarterly* 14: 15–30.

Shaltz, Justin. 1994a. Review of *Measure for Measure*. Director Barbara Gaines. Shakespeare Repertory, Chicago. *Shakespeare Bulletin* 12, no. 2: 24–25.

———. 1994b. Review of *The Two Gentlemen of Verona*. Director Calvin MacLean. Westhoff Theatre, Normal, IL. *Shakespeare Bulletin* 12, no. 4: 34–35.

———. 1998. Review of *Much Ado about Nothing*. Director Robert E. Leonard. Illinois Shakespeare Festival, Bloomington, IL. *Shakespeare Bulletin* 16, no. 4: 25–26.

Shattuck, Charles H. 1965. *The Shakespeare Promptbooks: A Descriptive Catalogue*. Urbana: University of Illionis Press.

———, ed. 1974. *John Philip Kemble Promptbooks*. 11 vols. Charlottesville: University Press of Virginia.

Shell, Marc. 1988. *The End of Kinship*: Measure for Measure, *Incest, and the Ideal of Universal Siblinghood*. Stanford, CA: Stanford University Press.

Simon, John. 1985. "All Wet." *New York Magazine*, 15 July, 67–69.

Sinfield, Alan. 1992. *Faultlines: Cultural Materialism and the Politics of Dissident Reading*. Berkeley: University of California Press.

Slights, Camille Wells. 1983. "*The Two Gentlemen of Verona* and the Courtesy Book Tradition." *Shakespeare Studies* 16: 13–31.

Smallwood, Robert. 1972. "The Design of *All's Well that Ends Well*." *Shakespeare Survey* 25: 45–61.

———. 1982. "*All's Well that Ends Well* at the Royal Shakespeare Theatre." *Critical Quarterly* 24: 25–31.

———. 1989. "Shakespeare at Stratford-upon-Avon, 1988." *Shakespeare Quarterly* 40: 83–94.

———. 1990. "Shakespeare at Stratford-upon-Avon, 1989 (Part II)." *Shakespeare Quarterly* 41: 491–99.

———. 1991. "Shakespeare at Stratford-upon-Avon, 1990." *Shakespeare Quarterly* 42: 345–59.

————. 1992. "Shakespeare at Stratford-upon-Avon, 1991." *Shakespeare Quarterly* 43: 341–56.

————. 1993. "Shakespeare at Stratford-upon-Avon, 1992." *Shakespeare Quarterly* 44: 343–62.

Smith, Don. 1982. "Truth and Seeming Truth: The Language of *Measure for Measure* and *Troilus and Cressida*." In *Self and Society in Shakespeare's* Troilus and Cressida *and* Measure for Measure, ed. J. A. Jowett and R. K. S. Taylor, 45–60. Bradford: English University of Leeds Centre for Adult Education.

Smith, Robert M. 1950. "Interpretations of *Measure for Measure*." *Shakespeare Quarterly* 1: 208–18.

Snyder, Susan. 1992. " 'The King's not here': Displacement and Deferral in *All's Well that Ends Well*." *Shakespeare Quarterly* 43: 20–32.

————, ed. 1993. *All's Well that Ends Well*. Oxford Shakespeare. Oxford: Clarendon.

Spencer, Hazelton. 1927. *Shakespeare Improved: The Restoration Versions in Quarto and on the Stage*. Cambridge: Harvard University Press.

Spivack, Bernard. 1958. *Shakespeare and the Allegory of Evil*. New York: Columbia University Press.

Spotswood, Jerald W. 1994. "Isabella's 'Speechless Dialect': Subversive Silence in *Measure for Measure*." *Explorations in Renaissance Culture* 20: 107–25.

Sprague, Arthur Colby. 1944. *Shakespeare and the Actors: The Stage Business in His Plays (1660–1905)*. Cambridge: Harvard University Press.

Sprague, Arthur Colby, and J. C. Trewin. 1970. *Shakespeare's Plays Today*. Columbia: University of South Carolina Press.

Stauffer, Donald A. 1949. *Shakespeare's World of Images*. Bloomington: Indiana University Press.

Steele, Kenneth B. 1992. "The Stratford, Ontario, Festival 1992: A Canadian's Overview." *Shakespeare Bulletin* 10, no. 4: 13–17.

Stevenson, David Lloyd. 1966. *The Achievement of Shakespeare's* Measure for Measure. Ithaca: Cornell University Press.

Stokes, John. 1994. "Exposing What Men Lack." *Times Literary Supplement* 4 November, 21.

Straznicky, Marta. 1994. "Shakespeare and the Government of Comedy: *Much Ado about Nothing*." *Shakespeare Studies* 22: 141–71.

Stuart, Otis. 1993. "Mold of Fashion." *Village Voice* 25 May, 91–92.

Styan, J. L. 1984. *All's Well that Ends Well*. Shakespeare in Performance. Manchester: Manchester University Press.

Suhamy, Henri. 1979. "Some Textual Remarks on *Measure for Measure*." *Cahiers Elisabethains* 15: 57–64.

Summers, Joseph H. 1984. *Dreams of Love and Power: On Shakespeare's Plays*. Oxford: Clarendon.

Sundelson, David. 1981. "Misogyny and Rule in *Measure for Measure*." *Women's Studies* 9: 83–91.

Swinburne, Algernon Charles. 1880. *A Study of Shakespeare*. London: Chatto.

Taplin, Oliver. 1995. "Opening Performance: Closing Texts?" *Essays in Criticism* 45: 93–120.

Tatspaugh, Patricia. 1988. "Shakespeare Abroad: *Measure for Measure.*" *Shakespeare Bulletin* 6, no. 3: 10–11.

Taylor, Michael. 1985. "Persecuting Time with Hope: The Cynicism of Romance in *All's Well that Ends Well.*" *English Studies in Canada* 11: 282–94.

Tebbetts, Terrell L. 1985. "Talking Back to the King: *Measure for Measure* and the *Basilicon Doron.*" *College English* 12: 122–34.

Thaler, Alwin. 1927. "Shakespeare and the Unhappy Happy Ending." *PMLA* 42: 736–61.

Thatcher, David. 1995. "Questionable Purpose in *Measure for Measure*: A Test of Seeming or a Seeming Test?" *English Literary Renaissance* 25: 26–44.

Thomas, Vivian. 1987. *The Moral Universe of Shakespeare's Problem Plays.* Totowa, NJ: Barnes.

Thompson, Karl F. 1971. *Modesty and Cunning: Shakespeare's Use of Literary Tradition.* Ann Arbor: University of Michigan Press.

Thomson, Peter. 1971. "A Necessary Theatre: The Royal Shakespeare Season 1970 Reviewed." *Shakespeare Survey* 24: 117–26.

Timpane, John. 1994. Review of *Much Ado about Nothing.* Director Michael Kahn. Shakespeare Theatre, Princeton, NJ, 1993. *Shakespeare Bulletin* 12, no. 2: 9–10.

Trombetta, James. 1976. "Versions of Dying in *Measure for Measure.*" *English Literary Renaissance* 6: 60–76.

Turner, Robert Y. 1960. "Dramatic Conventions in *All's Well that Ends Well.*" *PMLA* 75: 497–502.

Victor, Benjamin. 1763. *The Two Gentlemen of Verona. A Comedy, Written by Shakespeare. With Alterations and Additions. As it is performed at the Theatre-Royal in Drury Lane.* London: n.p.

Waleson, Heidi. 1987. " 'Two Gentlemen' Act up Again in Central Park." *New York Times*, 26 July, sec. 2, pp. 5, 14.

Wall, Clare-Marie. 1997. " 'O these encounterers': Writing the Production and Performance Texts of the RSC *Troilus and Cressida*, 1996–1997." Paper presented to the Shakespeare Association of America. Washington, D.C., 28 March.

Wardle, Irving. 1970. "Stratford Integrity." *Times* (London), 2 April, 12a.

Warren, Roger. 1978. "Comedies and Histories at Two Stratfords, 1977." *Shakespeare Studies* 31: 141–53.

———. 1983. "Shakespeare in Stratford and London, 1982." *Shakespeare Quarterly* 34: 79–88.

———. 1984. "Spectacle and Speculation: The Canadian Shakespeare Festival." *Times Literary Supplement*, 21 September, 1056.

Watermeier, Daniel J. 1992. Review of *Measure for Measure.* Director Michael Langham. Stratford Festival, Stratford, Ontario. *Shakespeare Bulletin* 10, no. 4: 20–21.

Watson, Robert N. 1990. "False Immortality in *Measure for Measure*: Comic Means, Tragic Ends." *Shakespeare Quarterly* 41: 411–32.

Weil, Herbert S., Jr. 1978. "The Theater at Monmouth." *Shakespeare Quarterly* 29: 226–28.

———. 1986. "Stratford Festival Canada." *Shakespeare Quarterly* 37: 245–50.

Wells, Stanley. 1980. "Editorial Treatment of Foul-Paper Texts: *Much Ado about Nothing* as Test Case." *Review of English Studies* 31: 1–16.

Wells, Stanley, and Gary Taylor. 1987. *William Shakespeare: A Textual Companion*. Oxford: Clarendon.

———. 1988. General Introduction to *William Shakespeare: The Complete Works*, ed. Stanley Wells and Gary Taylor, xiii–xxxvii. Oxford: Clarendon.

Welsh, Alexander. 1978. "The Loss of Men and Getting of Children: *All's Well that Ends Well* and *Measure for Measure*." *Modern Language Review* 73: 17–28.

Wentersdorf, Karl P. 1979. "The Marriage Contracts in *Measure for Measure*: A Reconsideration." *Shakespeare Survey* 32: 129–144.

Westlund, Joseph. 1984. *Shakespeare's Reparative Comedies: A Psychoanalytic View of the Middle Plays*. Chicago: University of Chicago Press.

Wheeler, Richard P. 1981. *Shakespeare's Development and the Problem Comedies*. Berkeley: University of California Press.

Williamson, Jane. 1975. "The Duke and Isabella on the Modern Stage." *The Triple Bond: Plays, Mainly Shakespearean, in Performance*, ed. Joseph G. Price, 149–69. University Park: Penn State University Press.

Williamson, Marilyn L. 1986. *The Patriarchy of Shakespeare's Comedies*. Detroit: Wayne State University Press.

Willman, Noel. 1955. Shakespeare Centre Promptbook: All's Well 5. Stratford-upon-Avon, Stratford Memorial Theatre.

Winston, Mathew. 1981. " 'Craft Against Vice': Morality Play Elements in *Measure for Measure*." *Shakespeare Studies* 14: 229–48.

Wood, Roger, and Mary Clarke. 1954. *Shakespeare at the Old Vic*. London: Black.

Worthen, W. B. 1997. *Shakespeare and the Authority of Performance*. Cambridge: Cambridge University Press.

Zitner, Sheldon P. 1989. *All's Well that Ends Well*. New Critical Introductions to Shakespeare. Boston: Twayne.

———, ed. 1993. *Much Ado about Nothing*. Oxford Shakespeare. Oxford: Clarendon.

Index